Apple Pro Training Series
Logic Pro 8
Beyond the Basics

David Dvorin

Apple
Certified

Apple Pro Training Series:
Logic Pro 8: Beyond the Basics

David Dvorin
Copyright © 2008 by David Dvorin

Published by Peachpit Press. For information on Peachpit Press books, contact:

Peachpit Press
1249 Eighth Street
Berkeley, CA 94710
(510) 524-2178
Fax: (510) 524-2221
www.peachpit.com
To report errors, please send a note to errata@peachpit.com.
Peachpit Press is a division of Pearson Education.

Apple Series Editor: Nancy Peterson
Project Editors: Bob Lindstrom, Robyn G. Thomas
Contributing Writers, Cameos: Bob Lindstrom, Jim Akin
Production Coordinator: Laurie Stewart, Happenstance Type-O-Rama
Technical Editor: Robert Brock
Technical Reviewer: Raymond Barker
Copy Editor: Karen Seriguchi
Compositor: Happenstance Type-O-Rama
Media Producer: Eric Geoffroy
Indexer: Jack Lewis
Cover Illustration: Kent Oberheu
Cover Production: Happenstance Type-O-Rama

ISBN 13: 978-0-321-50288-9
ISBN 10: 0-321-50288-4
9 8 7 6 5 4 3 2 1
Printed and bound in the United States of America

Acknowledgments Sincere thanks to my wife Keri, son Jonah, and daughter Zinnia for enabling me to write the second edition of this book. Your understanding and moral support gave me the foundation to continue along this journey.

I could not have accomplished this task without the wise direction and knowledge of editor Bob Lindstrom and technical editor Robert Brock. You again have helped to make my life manageable during this arduous process.

Special thanks to my colleague Raymond Barker for providing valuable feedback, constructive scrutiny, and indefatigable enthusiasm.

Huge thanks to my dear friend Tom Langford for his generosity in providing the tracks from his wonderful song "I Was Raised." Look for Tom's music on GoDigital (http://www.godigitalartists.com/artists/tom_langford/).

Thank you to Grant Levin for furnishing his excellent composition "A Blues for Trane" and being so enthusiastic about its being mixed in surround sound.

"Thanks, mate!" to Phil Jackson for supplying his score to the Monterey Bay Sanctuary video.

Thank you to Mark Shelley, Sea Studios Foundation, and the Monterey Bay National Marine Sanctuary for the use of their beautiful video.

Thank you, Patty Montesion, for your unfaltering confidence and respect.

Enthusiastic appreciation to Nancy Peterson, Robyn Thomas, Karen Seriguchi, and the entire team at Peachpit for their valuable participation.

Thanks to Bob Hunt, friend and ex-Apple buddy who continues to tune me into all things Logic.

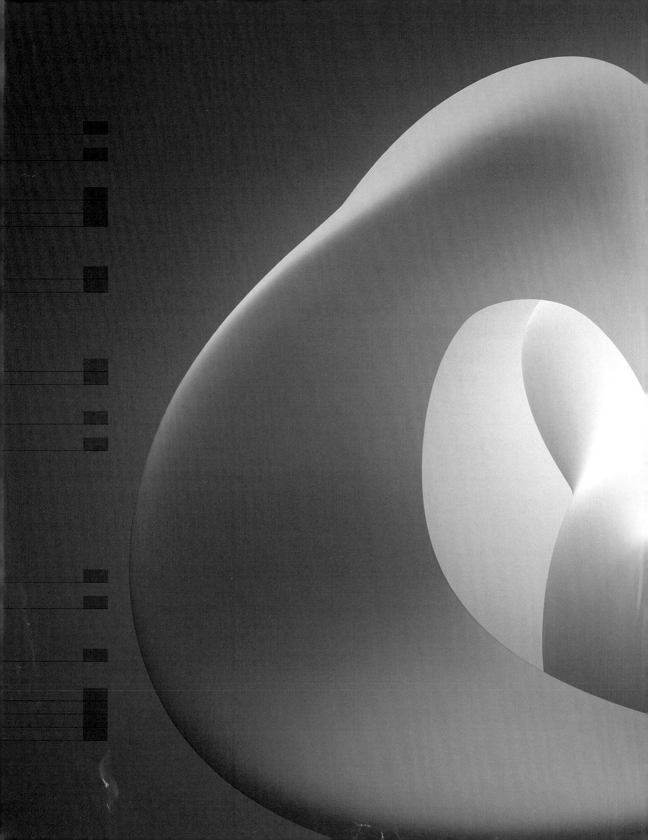

Contents at a Glance

Table of Contents

Getting Started

We are lucky to live during one of the most exciting periods in the music production industry. Just a few short years ago, you would need a studio filled with synthesizers, hardware effects processors, mixing consoles, and expensive multitrack tape machines to accomplish what you can now do in a small project-based environment with a computer, an audio interface, and the right software. It's a good time to be a musician.

Apple Pro Training Series: Logic Pro 8: Beyond the Basics is intended to show experienced composers, arrangers, and producers how to enhance their skills by working with real projects in real-world scenarios. You'll learn how to increase the efficiency of your production workflow, accelerate editing tasks, and create and manage multiple takes. You'll work on refining your mixing techniques, manipulating tempo and pitch, creating notated parts and scores, mixing for surround sound, and scoring for video and film. You'll discover powerful techniques for multitrack recording and explore the limitless potential of Logic's audio instruments.

Whether you're tweaking a song structure, applying effects processing, or editing audio and MIDI tracks, this book will give you the insider tips that will make your time with Logic Pro 8 more productive and more creative.

The Methodology

This book is written for those who already have a working knowledge of Logic Pro. (Beginning or less-experienced Logic users should read *Apple Pro Training Series: Logic Pro 8 and Logic Express 8* by David Nahmani.) Composers, audio engineers, and music producers currently working with Logic Pro will have the most to gain from reading this book.

The book is divided into five sections:

1   Lesson 1 lays the foundation by helping you customize your Logic workflow. You'll create an environment that will increase your efficiency on your own projects as well as on the exercises in the book.

2   Lessons 2 through 4 are designed to teach you how make the most of your production time. You'll start by creating and organizing audio and MIDI tracks for a multitrack song project. Then you'll use Logic's pitch and tempo correction to fix problems in the recordings, and you'll create Apple Loops for integration into your arrangement. Finally, you'll discover how audio instruments bring a wealth of musical resources to your sessions.

3   In Lessons 5 through 7 you'll shape your tracks into an arrangement. With Logic's MIDI and audio editing tools, you can refine the sound and structure of your composition, correcting production problems and making the most of your best takes.

4   A composition is only as good as it sounds, which makes mixing and mastering your arrangement an essential part of the creative process. Lessons 8 through 10 guide you in taking your composition to the final level, using Logic Pro's mixer, automation, and effects processing to bring the highest degree of production quality to your creative output.

5   For many projects, Logic Pro will be an all-inclusive working environment that takes composers and producers from musical idea to final recording. But there are times when you need to get your ideas on paper or when you're using your musical skills to serve a visual image. In Lesson 11, you'll create objects in the Environment to process MIDI data in all sorts of interesting ways. Lesson 12 shows you how to use Logic Pro's extensive notation capabilities to create musical parts and scores. Lesson 13 provides a foundation for developing your surround sound mixing skills by using Logic's extensive new surround support. In Lesson 14, you'll explore Logic Pro's power as a film and video scoring tool.

About the Apple Pro Training Series

Apple Pro Training Series: Logic Pro 8: Beyond the Basics is part of the official training series for Apple Pro applications developed by experts in the field. The lessons are designed to let you learn at your own pace. You'll find that this book explores many advanced features and offers tips and techniques for using the latest version of Logic.

Although each lesson provides step-by-step instructions for creating a specific project, there's room for exploration and experimentation. It is recommended that you follow the book from start to finish or at least complete the lessons in each part of the book in order. Each lesson concludes with a review section summarizing what you've covered.

System Requirements

Before beginning to use *Apple Pro Training Series: Logic Pro 8: Beyond the Basics*, you should have a working knowledge of your computer and its operating system. Make sure that you know how to use the mouse, navigate standard menus and commands, and also open, save, and close files. If you need to review these techniques, see the printed or online documentation included with your system.

These are the basic system requirements for Logic Pro 8:

▶ Macintosh computer with a 1.25 GHz or faster PowerPC G4 processor (PowerPC G5, Intel Core Duo, or Intel Xeon processors are highly recommended)

▶ Mac OS X v10.4.9 or later

▶ 1 GB of RAM (2 GB or more is highly recommended)

▶ QuickTime 7.2 or later

▶ DVD drive for software installation

▶ PCI Express, ExpressCard/34, USB, or FireWire-based multi-channel audio interface recommended

▶ Video display with 1024 x 768 pixel resolution (1280 x 800 or higher resolution is recommended)

▶ MIDI keyboard

▶ 5400 rpm hard drive (7200 rpm recommended) with at least 7 GB of available hard-disk space

NOTE ▸ If your display resolution is less than 1440 x 900, the included lesson files will display differently than shown in the book. Even so, you will be able to follow the lessons as described.

Copying the Logic Lesson Files

The DVD-ROM provided with this book includes folders that contain the lesson files used in this course. Each lesson has its own folder. You must have a standard installation of Logic Pro 8 on your hard disk to perform the exercises in this book.

To install the Logic project files:

1   Insert the *APTS_Logic Pro 8: Beyond the Basics* DVD into your DVD drive.

2   On your desktop, double-click the APTS_Logic 8_BTB icon to view the disk contents.

3   Drag the Logic 8_BTB_Files folder from the DVD to the Music folder on your hard disk.

About the Apple Pro Training Series

Apple Pro Training Series: Logic Pro 8: Beyond the Basics is both a self-paced learning tool and the official curriculum of the Apple Pro Training and Certification Program. Developed by experts in the field and certified by Apple, the series is used by Apple Authorized Training Centers worldwide and offers complete training in all Apple Pro products. The lessons are designed to let you learn at your own pace. Although each lesson provides step-by-step instructions for creating specific projects, there's room for exploration and experimentation. Each lesson concludes with review questions and answers summarizing what you've learned, which can be used to help you prepare for the Apple Pro Certification Exam.

For a complete list of Apple Pro Training Series books, visit www.peachpit.com/applebooklet.

Apple Pro Certification Program

The Apple Pro Training and Certification Program is designed to keep you at the forefront of Apple's digital media technology while giving you a competitive edge in today's ever-changing job market. Whether you're an editor, graphic designer, sound designer, special-effects artist, or teacher, these training tools are meant to help you expand your skills.

Upon completing the course material in this book, you can become a certified Apple Pro by taking the certification exam at an Apple Authorized Training Center. Successful certification as an Apple Pro gives you official recognition of your knowledge of Apple's professional applications while allowing you to market yourself to employers and clients as a skilled, pro-level user of Apple products.

For those who prefer to learn in an instructor-led setting, Apple offers training courses at Apple Authorized Training Centers worldwide. These courses, which use the Apple Pro Training Series books as their curriculum, are taught by Apple Certified Trainers who balance concepts and lectures with hands-on labs and exercises. Apple Authorized Training Centers have been carefully selected and have met Apple's highest standards in all areas, including facilities, instructors, course delivery, and infrastructure. The goal of the program is to offer Apple customers, from beginners to the most seasoned professionals, the highest-quality training experience.

To obtain more information or to find an Authorized Training Center near you, go to www.apple.com/software/pro/training.

Resources

Apple Pro Training Series: Logic Pro 8: Beyond the Basics is not intended as a comprehensive reference manual, nor does it replace the documentation that comes with the application. For more information about Apple Logic Pro 8, refer to these sources:

▶ *Logic Pro 8 User Manual.* Accessed through the Logic Pro 8 Help menu, the *User Manual* contains a complete description of all the features.

▶ Apple's website: www.apple.com

▶ Peachpit's website: As Logic Pro 8 is updated, Peachpit may choose to update lessons or post additional exercises as necessary on this book's companion webpage. Please check www.peachpit.com/apts.logic.btb for revised lessons.

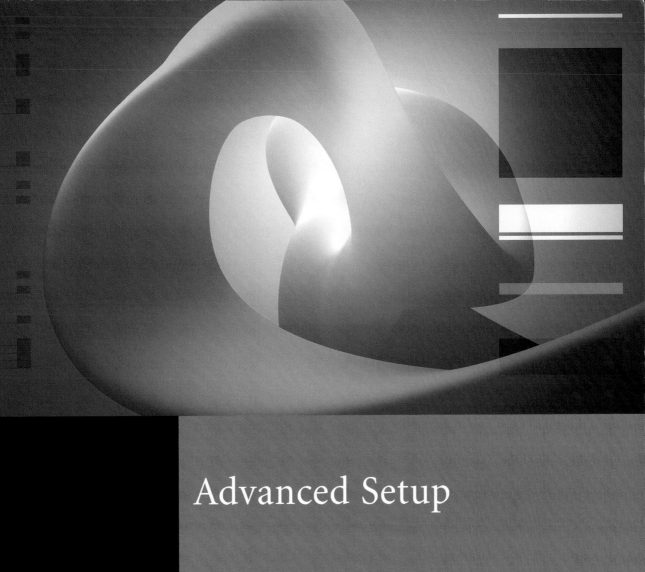

Advanced Setup

1

Time

Goals

This lesson takes approximately 90 minutes to complete.

Use project templates

Create and configure new tracks

Customize existing screensets for session needs

Learn the advantages and disadvantages of locking screensets

Assign key commands to speed up a workflow

Create and save your own custom template

Back up and share your settings

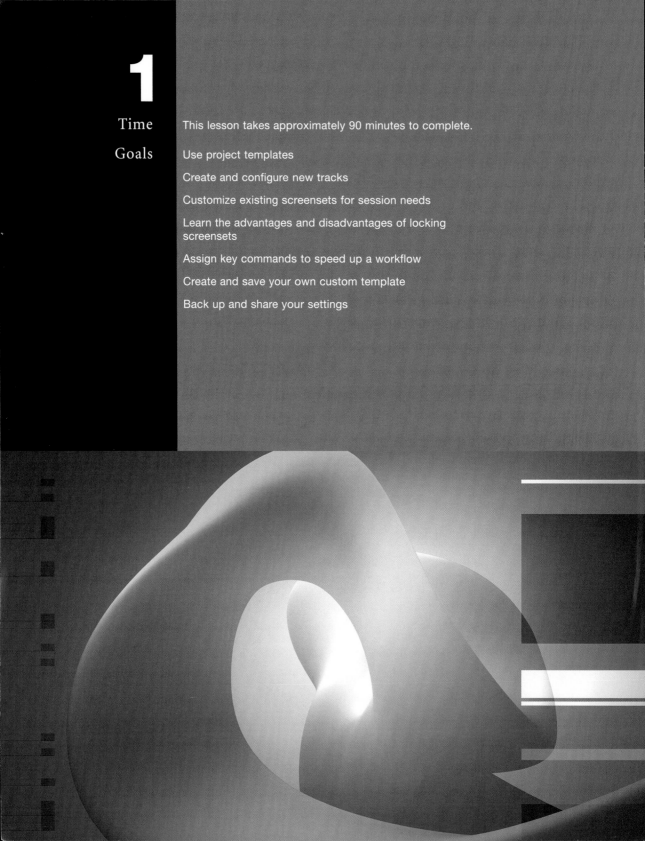

Lesson 1
Speeding Up
Your Workflow

Spending a little time up-front in preparation saves considerable production time when you are knee deep in a project. The quicker you can get your ideas into Logic, the more time you can spend creating and producing music and audio!

This lesson covers techniques to make your Logic sessions more efficient, going beyond the basics to speed up your workflow. Throughout, you will learn how to quickly access common functions and tools, as well as how to customize Logic to suit your individual needs.

Using Project Templates

Logic is a versatile application that can be configured in many ways. Usually you will want to display data, tracks, and windows according to the type of project you are working on. For example, songwriting calls for a vastly different work process than, say, stereo-mastering a CD.

To aid in this, Logic enables you to create and use multiple templates as the basis for a project. Having a catalog of blank project templates, tailored to a specific workflow, will let you get to work more quickly and easily.

You can start by opening up one of the many premade templates that come with Logic Pro 8.

1   Choose File > New.

The Templates dialog opens, labeled "New."

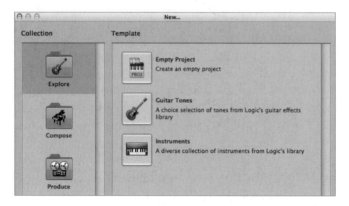

Logic Pro organizes its templates in four collections—Explore, Compose, Produce, and My Templates—each represented by a folder in the left pane. These collections contain individual templates suited to different workflows. Let's explore a few examples:

2   In the Collection pane, click the Compose folder.

3   In the Template pane, click the Songwriter button.

The Songwriter template opens and a Save As dialog appears. When loading templates, Logic automatically prompts you to name and save a project file so as not to overwrite the original template. Since you are simply exploring a few templates in this lesson, you do not need to save a new project file.

4   Click the Cancel button.

An untitled template file opens. The Arrange window displays multiple audio and software instrument tracks in the Arrange area, and the Inspector and the Library are open.

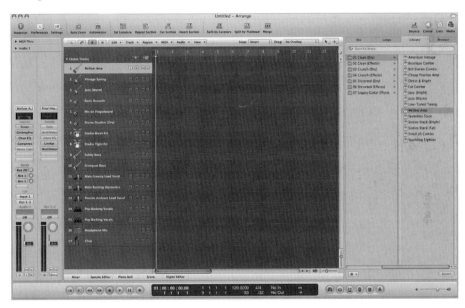

5   Select the tracks, one by one, by clicking in the track list.

As you can see in the Inspector's Arrange channel strip, each track is preconfigured for specific instruments (electric guitar, acoustic guitar, drums, bass, vocals, etc.), and has channel strips of effect and instrument plug-ins already instantiated.

6   At the bottom of the Arrange window, click the Mixer button.

The Mixer opens, displaying all the channels used in the track list.

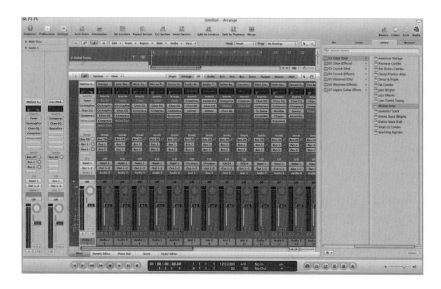

7   In the Mixer, try scrolling to the right to view all the channel strips.

In addition to the audio and instrument channels from the Arrange track list, a variety of preconfigured aux channels are also present, already set up for send effects, headphone mix, and submixes.

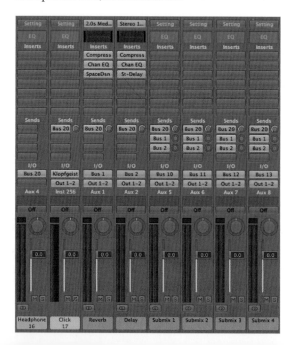

NOTE ▶ The green Send slots on each channel represent pre-fader (before the volume fader) sends to the Headphone channel (Aux 4). A pre-fader send enables you to have independence between the control room and headphone mix. This way, you can adjust the control mix normally (by adjusting the faders) and adjust the headphone mix via the send levels. All that's needed is to set the Headphone channel's output to any available stereo output on your audio interface.

8   In the Media area on the right, click a few of the channel strip presets listed in the far right column of the Library.

The channel strip setting changes for the selected track, reflecting different instrument settings and effects configurations in the Arrange channel strip. Having the Library accessible from the beginning makes it easy to create new channel configurations to suit your individual needs.

As you can see, this template's sole purpose is to help you start creating immediately, so you don't have to first create tracks and routings, instantiate instruments and effects, and open the Library.

9   Choose File > Close Project.

A message appears asking if you wish to save changes to the file.

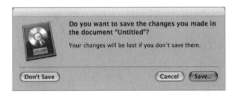

10 Click Don't Save.

The untitled file based on the Songwriter template closes.

Creating Your Own Template

Although an extensive collection of premade templates comes with Logic Pro, eventually you will want to create custom templates to suit your individual workflow. You can do this by modifying one of the premade templates or making an entirely new one. In the following exercises, you will create a custom template from scratch, then configure the interface for maximum workflow efficiency.

1 Choose File > New.

The Template dialog opens. You may have noticed that the Template pane always contains an Empty Project at the top, no matter which collection you select.

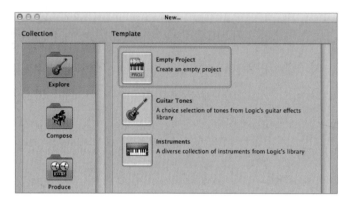

By clicking this button, you can create a project without any preconfigured tracks, routings, or display settings.

2 In the Templates pane, click the Empty Project button.

An empty project is created, and the New Tracks dialog opens awaiting input.

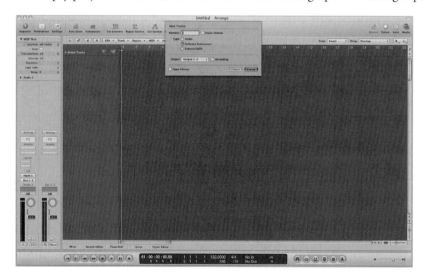

Creating New Tracks

The New Tracks dialog allows the quick creation and configuration of all types of tracks.

1   In the New Tracks dialog, click to select the Audio button, if necessary.

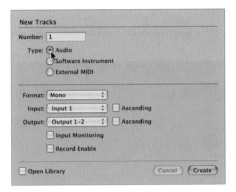

2   In the Number field, enter *8*.

3   In the Format menu, choose Stereo.

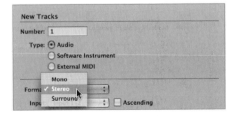

4   Click Create.

NOTE ▸ In the New Tracks dialog, you can assign inputs and outputs automatically (even assigning multiple tracks in ascending order), as well as set them to open with input monitoring turned on and recording enabled. This gets you ready for laying down new tracks immediately.

Eight new stereo audio tracks are created and appear in the Arrange area's track list.

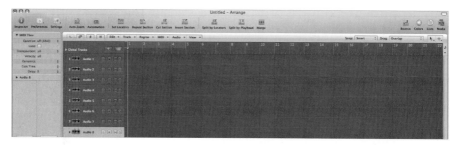

You can create additional groups of tracks at any time by opening the New Tracks dialog.

5   In the Arrange area's local menu bar, choose Track > New.

TIP ▸ You can also open the New Tracks dialog by clicking the Create Track (+) button at the top of the track list.

The New Tracks dialog opens.

6   In the Number field, enter *8*.

7   Click to select the Software Instruments button.

8   Select the Open Library checkbox.

By selecting the Open Library option, you can automatically create new tracks and display the Library in the Media area.

9   Click Create.

The Library opens, and eight software instrument tracks are created and displayed in the Arrange area's track list.

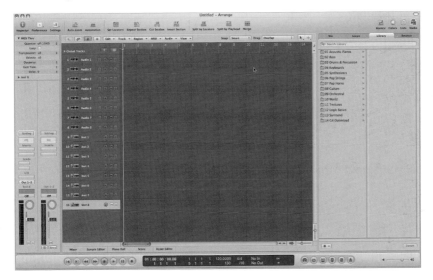

Customizing the Interface

Logic has the reputation of being a highly customizable software application for good reason. Not only can you conform the viewing area to a specific workflow, but you can also customize access to the functions you use the most, keeping them at your fingertips.

The Toolbar, new to Logic Pro 8, provides access to common editing functions and often-used areas. The Toolbar can also be customized.

1   Control-click the Toolbar area and choose Customize Toolbar from the shortcut menu.

The Customize Toolbar dialog appears.

Functions in the Customize Toolbar dialog can be added to the Toolbar by dragging their icons to the Toolbar.

2   Drag the Import Audio icon to the Toolbar, just to the right of the Merge button.

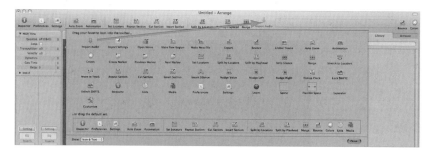

NOTE ▶ If you drag an icon to a location between two existing buttons, the buttons will move to make space for the new button.

3   Click Done.

The Import Audio button is added to the Toolbar.

NOTE ▶ Adding buttons to the Toolbar is a user preference and will be present in all project files.

In addition to customizing the Toolbar, you can also customize the Transport bar.

4   Control-click the Transport bar, and choose Customize Transport Bar from the shortcut menu.

The Customize Transport Bar dialog appears.

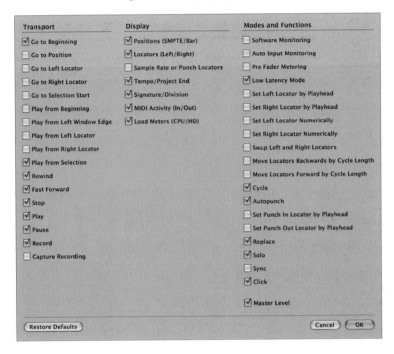

To customize the Transport bar, select the checkbox of each function you want to add.

5   In the Transport column of the dialog, select the Go to Position checkbox.

6   Click OK.

The button is added to the Transport section on the left side of the Transport bar.

NOTE ▶ Adding buttons to the Transport affects only the individual project file and
will not be present in all project files.

Creating Screensets

Logic Pro 8 has been redesigned to allow direct access to all editing and mixing functions from the Arrange area. This single window interface significantly speeds up workflow, but it can also get a little crowded when displaying many items at once.

Screensets enable you to assign area and window combinations (including all zoom settings and view options) to a number key on the computer's keyboard. In the following exercises, you will create a custom screenset for your template.

1   Click the various editor buttons at the bottom of the Arrange window.

It is especially apparent in the Mixer and Media area (Library) that screen real estate only goes so far! Even with a streamlined interface, a separate screenset dedicated to the Mixer could be advantageous.

NOTE ▶ Depending on your display size and resolution, you will have more or less visible screen area. Therefore, your view might differ from the screenshots presented throughout this book.

2   Click the button of the active editor to close the editing area.

By default, new project files have only one screenset. You can create a new screenset customized for mixing that still contains a small Arrange area to provide an overview of the project tracks.

3   Press the 2 key.

A new screenset is created, indicated by *Screenset 2* in Logic's menu bar.

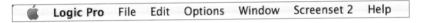

4   Click the Mixer button.

The Mixer appears at the bottom of the Arrange window.

You now have a screenset consisting of the Mixer area and a small Arrange area.

Maximizing Workspace

When you work with larger productions, it is helpful to have as much space as possible to view the musical data. You should set up Screenset 2 for maximum viewable space in both the Arrange area and the Mixer, while making sure that you're still able to access important project information.

Currently, the Arrange area may display only four tracks without your having to scroll. If this small Arrange area is to serve as an overview of the project's tracks, you must adjust the view to display as much of the arrangement as possible, both vertically and horizontally.

1   At the far right of the Arrange area, drag the vertical zoom control all the way up.

NOTE ▶ If you are using a smaller screen resolution than 1140 x 900, it is possible that the vertical zoom control will be hidden from view. If this is the case, use the Zoom Vertical Out key command (Control–Up Arrow) instead.

The Arrange area view shrinks vertically, but it still may not display all 16 tracks that you created earlier. To see all of the tracks, you need to gain screen space by closing infrequently accessed and redundant areas. Since you are devoting this screenset to mixing, access to the Toolbar's editing and viewing functions is not essential.

NOTE ▶ Even when the Toolbar is hidden, these commands are still accessible in the Arrange area's local Edit and View menus.

2   At the upper-right corner of the Arrange window, click the Toolbar button.

The window expands slightly, allowing a full display of all 16 tracks in the Arrange area.

Although the Inspector's channel strips and Parameter boxes are vital when you're working in the Arrange area, they are not needed when you're mixing a project.

3   In the Arrange area's local menu bar, choose View > Inspector to hide the Inspector.

The Inspector is hidden, allowing more channels to appear in the Mixer and more measures in the Arrange area.

In Logic (as in any other application), windows and areas must be in *key focus* for you to make any changes in them. That is, windows need to be active before you can interact with them. For your customized mixing screenset, it makes sense to have the Mixer area receive key focus.

4   Press the Tab key to shift key focus to the Mixer.

The Mixer's top bar will be highlighted to indicate that it has key focus.

NOTE ▸ Key focus can also be shifted to an area by clicking the area's top bar.

Locking Screensets

At present, your screenset is open to any additional changes, and it will always reflect the last state in which you left it. In Logic terms, the screenset is unlocked and can be continuously altered.

Considering that you just spent a fair amount of time configuring the screenset for mixing purposes, it makes sense to lock the screenset so you can always return to this state.

1   In the Screenset 2 menu, choose Lock.

A small bullet appears between *Screenset* and the number 2 in the menu bar, signifying that the screenset is locked.

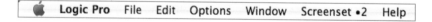

NOTE ▸ A screenset's menu displays the names of the areas or windows used in that screenset. These can be named anything you like by choosing Rename from the menu.

2   Press the 1 and 2 keys to switch screensets between the Arrange/Library screenset, and the Arrange/Mixer screenset you just locked.

Screenset 2 opens, configured as it was when locked.

Comparing Unlocked and Locked Screensets

When you are new to Logic, your tendency is to lock all screensets. However, the unlocked state has distinct advantages, because you can spontaneously tweak a screenset to suit each stage of your production (increasing or decreasing zoom levels, for example). An unlocked screenset is especially valuable during editing. Often you are bouncing between different editors and adjusting specific parts of the project. It is helpful, then, to return to a screenset that's in the same state that you left it when you continue work on a specific project area.

However, this takes some getting used to, and unintentional alterations can occur. If you are satisfied with the given configuration of a screenset, it is a good idea to lock it, protecting it from further changes until you unlock it again.

The next exercise will help you get a feel for using unlocked and locked screensets.

1 Press 1 to open the Arrange/Library screenset.

2 In the Tool menu, choose the Pencil tool.

3 On the Inst 1 track, click the grid line at bar 9 to create a blank region.

4 Hold down Control-Option while drawing a selection rectangle around the Inst 1 region that you just created.

The region will zoom in to a high degree.

5 Press 2 to open Screenset 2, then open Screenset 1 again.

Notice how recalling Screenset 1 restores the zoomed state in which you left it. Now repeat the same steps with Screenset 1 locked.

6 Control-Option-click the background of the Arrange area to return to the previous zoom state.

The Arrange area appears as it did when you started this exercise.

7 Choose Screenset 1 > Lock.

8   Hold down the Control-Option while dragging a selection rectangle around the Inst 1 region as you did previously.

9   Open Screenset 2, then open Screenset 1.

This time when you return to Screenset 1, the region is displayed exactly as it was when you locked the screenset. No matter what edits are performed within the screenset (zooming, in this case), it will return to a normalized state, almost like a template.

10   Delete the region you created by selecting it and pressing Delete.

Using Key Commands

As you become familiar with Logic's feature set, you'll notice that you perform some tasks more often than others. By assigning a command to a specific key on the computer's keyboard, you can execute common functions without reaching for the mouse and navigating a hierarchical menu system. Key command assignments are written to a location within the ~/Library/Application Support/Logic folder and are accessible to all Logic projects. This differs from the screensets that you created in the last exercise, which are saved within each project file.

Logic's Key Commands window is a powerful mapping tool that lets you assign a key (or key combination) to nearly every menu item within Logic, and also to some special functions that can be accessed only by using a key command.

If you've been working with Logic for some time, you are probably using default key commands and have assigned some custom commands of your own. Let's start by reviewing the basic procedure for key assignments and follow up with additional techniques to maximize the potential of this powerful feature.

Viewing Key Assignments

1   Open Logic's Key Commands window by choosing Logic Pro > Preferences > Key Commands.

The Key Commands window opens.

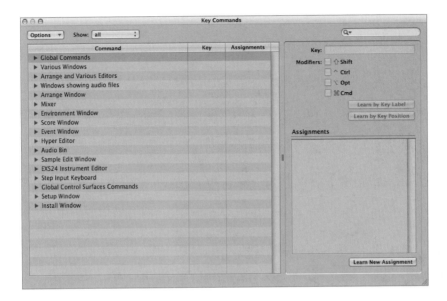

2 In the Key Commands window, from the Options menu, choose Expand All.

The list expands to show all possible key commands. Scroll down using the scroller to the right of the pane to get an idea of the breadth of the assignable functions within Logic. There are a vast number of choices, to be sure!

TIP It can be easy to get carried away and start assigning keys indiscriminately, but chances are that most of these assignments will be forgotten. Instead, assign key commands only to actions that you perform often. This way you will always have your most-used actions at your fingertips but avoid being overwhelmed.

3   In the Key Commands window, from the Options menu, choose Collapse All.

The Commands column now shows only those categories that represent the main application areas, instead of listing every available command. You can view key commands more methodically in this manner.

Topping the list is the Global Commands category, which contains actions that function regardless of the window or editor you are working in at a given time.

4   Click the disclosure triangle to the left of Global Commands.

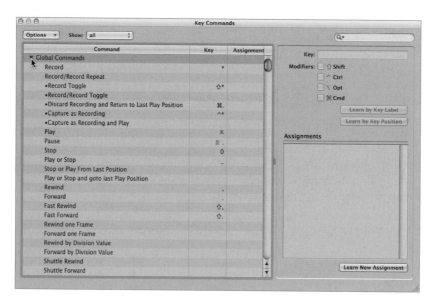

Clicking the disclosure triangle for a given window or category enables you to quickly view all the commands associated with it.

Assigning Keys to Commands

Let's assign a useful key command that doesn't already have a default assignment.

1   Click the Shuttle Rewind command, located near the bottom of the currently visible part of the list (use the scroller, if necessary).

2   Click the Learn by Key Label button, located at the right side of the window.

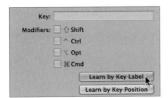

NOTE ▶ A key label is what is actually imprinted on the individual key. Since Logic has been localized for many languages, this becomes important, as computers sold internationally have different keyboard layouts. In this way, a function assigned to, say, the Y key will be activated regardless of where the key is on a given keyboard.

3 Press the comma key.

An alert message appears.

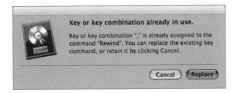

This message is Logic's fail-safe to keep you from assigning the same key to multiple commands. It also provides an option for quickly reassigning the key to a new command.

The Key column in the Key Commands window shows the key assignments in use. In the current example, you can clearly see that the comma key is assigned to the Rewind command. However, as you remember from scanning the list, not all functions are easily determined, which is why this alert message is beneficial.

4 Click Cancel.

5 With the Learn by Key Label button still active, press Control-comma.

The key combination you entered is displayed in the Key column next to the Shuttle Rewind command.

NOTE ▶ This combination of key (comma) plus modifier key (Control) is also represented in the area above the Learn by Key Label button.

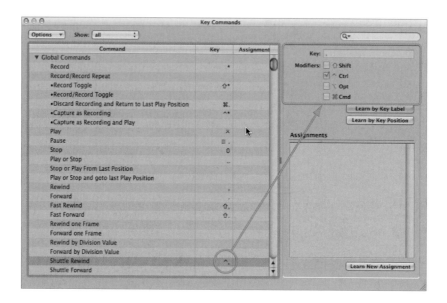

6   Click the Shuttle Forward command (located below Shuttle Rewind).

7   Press Control-period to assign that key combination.

8   Close the Key Commands window.

You have assigned two very useful key commands for getting around in the Arrange area. Try pressing these keys, observing their effect on the playhead. Note how you can increase the winding speed by repeatedly pressing the period or comma while holding down the Control key. Try initiating movement in a single direction, then "braking" by pressing the key in the opposite direction. This behavior is modeled after analog tape transports or video decks, where each press of the rewind or fast-forward button increases the direction speed.

> **TIP** ▶ For key commands to be useful, you must remember the key assignment. Therefore, choose assignments that provide a clue to their functions. The first letter of a function, or a graphic representation of it, represents a good place to start. (For example, the comma and period keys also have the less-than and greater-than symbols.) Also try to think about commands as parts of families of similar functionality, then assign related commands to keys with different modifiers. (For example, since comma is the command for Rewind, Control-comma is a logical choice for Shuttle Rewind.)

Using Key-Command-Only Functions

Some functions are accessible only via key commands and not available as menu items. These commands should not be overlooked, however, as they can be quite useful.

In the upper-right corner of the Key Commands window is a search field. This functions like the search in many other Apple software applications. If you are familiar with any of those, you will feel right at home. You can, for example, use it to search for Logic's many playback functions.

1   Open the Key Commands window, this time using its own key command, Option-K.

2   Click once in the search field and enter *play*.

> **NOTE** ▶ You do not need to press Return to initiate the search.

The left pane of the Key Commands window now lists every command that has the word *play* in it, regardless of the category. You'll notice that some of the commands have a bullet (•) in front of them.

The bullet indicates that this function is accessible only via key command, and it is not available as a menu choice.

3   Scroll down (if necessary), and click "•Set Rounded Locators and Cycle Play."

4   Assign "Set Rounded Locators and Cycle Play" to Shift-Spacebar.

5   Close the Key Commands window.

> **NOTE ▶** This useful key command packs multiple functions into a single keystroke. Used in the Arrange area or in any editor, it creates a cycle area (setting the locators first) around a selected region or event and then initiates playback. Use this command when you want to quickly audition the section around a given region or event.

Accessing the Tool Menu

Logic's Tool menus offer essential manipulation of data within a variety of windows. These tools are indispensable, changing the Pointer tool to act in a variety of helpful ways. It is therefore extremely important that you have easy access to these often-used objects. Let's take a moment to explore the ways you can gain quick access to the Tool menus.

There are many Tool menus in Logic. The available tools change depending on the functions of a window or editor.

Arrange area

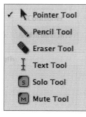

Event List

Score Editor

Hyper Editor

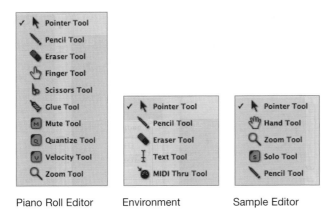

Piano Roll Editor   Environment   Sample Editor

As you can see in the previous figures, the Tool menus vary in number as well as types of tools. Even so, there is a great deal of overlap in frequently used tools (the Pointer tool, for instance).

In all cases, the Tool menus are located on the upper-right side of the screen, usually a distance away from where you wish to use the tool. This distance may seem small the first few times you move your mouse across the screen, but if you find yourself switching tools often while editing (and most of us do), then this movement can become tedious and ergonomically harmful. In the following exercises, you will use Logic's shortcuts to gain quick access to a Tool menu, enabling you to work in a more efficient manner.

Using the Alternate Tool

When working with objects in any window, you have two tools always available at the mouse position, represented by the two Tool menus. The left menu option is your default tool, and the right menu option is your alternate tool, made available by pressing the Command key. The ability to switch between these two tools at the place you are actually working (your current pointer position) enables you to more quickly toggle between often-used tools, which speeds workflow.

1   In the Arrange area, choose the Pointer tool within the left (default) Tool menu, if it is not already chosen.

2   In the right (alternate) Tool menu, choose the Pencil tool.

3   Move your pointer over the main part of the Arrange area and press the Command key while watching the pointer.

The pointer changes to the Pencil tool.

The Pencil tool in this case is referred to as the Command-click, or alternate, tool. You can think of the action as a momentary toggle to a tool that you've preset.

Tool assignments can be different for each area or window that has a Tool menu. These assignments are saved with the screenset, so let's add your Command-click assignment to the screenset that you created earlier in this chapter.

4   Unlock Screenset 1 by pressing Shift-L.

5   Lock Screenset 1 by pressing Shift-L again.

The Command-click tool designation is saved to the screenset.

TIP ▶ Take some time to think about which tools you use most often in each of the editors, and assign alternate tools in your screensets using the technique you just learned.

Quickly Accessing the Tool Menu

1   Move your pointer to the middle of the Arrange area.

2   Press the Esc key.

A floating Tool menu should appear at the pointer position.

3   Click the Eraser tool.

The Tool menu disappears, and the Pointer tool is now an Eraser tool.

This technique can save many a trip across the screen to select a new tool, because it opens the Tool menu when and where you need it for editing.

4   Press the Esc key again.

Instead of choosing the desired tool using the mouse, try an even quicker key command.

5   Press the 5 key on your computer keyboard.

The Tool menu disappears, and the Eraser tool changes to the Scissors tool.

NOTE ▶ When the floating Tool menu is open, the number keys that you usually use for screensets are overridden until a selection is made.

6   Press the Escape key twice to return to the Pointer tool.

TIP ▶ Many users assign key commands to their most-used tools. This lets you access common tools that are shared by separate editors (the Pointer tool, for instance). Try searching for the tool names in the Key Commands window to see your options.

Working with Hard-Wired Tool Menu Commands

Just as holding down the Command key lets you momentarily toggle to an alternate tool, so Logic can carry out common functions by using tools in conjunction with a modifier key. These "hard-wired" commands aren't listed within menus, so a list of the most useful ones is provided here:

Key	With Tool	Result
Control	Any tool	Opens a shortcut menu with associated functions when clicking
Control-Option	Any tool	Changes the tool to the Zoom tool
Option	Pointer tool	Creates copy when dragging a region or event
Shift	Pencil tool	Imports audio file at clicked location
Shift	Pointer tool	Selects nodes in automation track
Control-Option	Pointer tool	Adjusts curves in automation track
Control-Shift	Fade tool	Adjusts the crossfade curve

Key	With Tool	Result
Option	Fade tool	Deletes cross-fade
Option	Pointer tool	Time stretches/expands region when resizing

NOTE ▶ These commands are used throughout the lessons in this book.

Controlling the Tool Menu with a Two-Button Mouse

When using a two-button mouse with Logic, you gain another way to access the Tool menu. To do this, you must first designate the function of the right mouse button, choosing between two modes of operation.

These options are set within Logic's preferences.

1   Choose Logic Pro > Preferences > Global to view the Preferences window.

From here you can select different preference categories (Global, Audio, and so on) by clicking the buttons at the top. Once you select a category, you can access different aspects of preferences by clicking a tab.

2   Click the Editing tab.

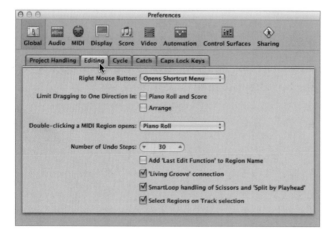

The screen shot shows Logic's Editing preferences, which include assignment of the second mouse button.

3   Click the pop-up menu next to the Right Mouse Button menu to view the options.

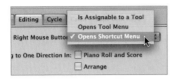

The first option, "Is Assignable to a Tool," enables you to assign a tool of your choice to the right mouse button. Once this option is chosen, a third Tool menu appears next to the default and alternate Tool menus, representing the right-click tool. Essentially, this assignment works similarly to the Command-click, or alternate, tool you looked at earlier. However, it functions independently of the Command-click tool, in effect providing three tool choices at your disposal at any given time.

The second option, Opens Tool Menu, works similarly to pressing the Esc key (see "Quickly Accessing the Tool Menu," earlier in this lesson), displaying a Tool menu at your current mouse position.

The third option, Opens Shortcut Menu, works similarly to pressing the Control key (see "Working with Hard-Wired Tool Menu Commands" in this lesson), displaying a shortcut menu with associated functions at the current mouse position.

4   Choose Opens Shortcut Menu, if it is not already chosen.

5   Close the Preferences window.

Saving a Project Template

You have spent quite a bit of time customizing this project. Now you'll need to save it as a template because you will be using this template in the upcoming lesson.

1   Choose File > Save as Template.

The "Save Template as" window opens, automatically pointing to a save location in the Project Templates folder that was created when you initially installed Logic Pro.

2   Enter the filename: *Advanced Logic.*

3   Click the Save button.

The template is now saved to your hard disk and will appear the next time you create a new project, in the My Templates collection.

Opening and Creating Projects Automatically

Having a selection of templates at your fingertips can be useful in any given situation. However, most of the time you'll want to start your sessions with the same basic configuration. You can configure Logic Pro to automatically launch a given template or empty project by setting a startup action preference.

1   Choose Logic Pro > Preferences > Global.

2   Click the Project Handling tab.

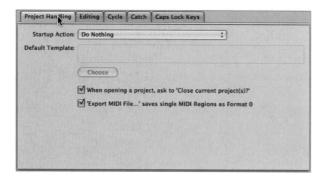

3   Click the Startup Action pop-up menu to view the menu items.

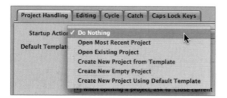

These commands dictate Logic's action on startup, ranging from Do Nothing (no project file is loaded) to Create New Project Using Default Template. Once you have created a general-purpose, or default, template (as you have been doing in this chapter), it is convenient to have Logic automatically base a new project file on it at startup. This will let you get to work as soon as Logic opens.

4   Choose Startup Action > Create New Project Using Default Template.

Now all that's needed is to specify which template Logic will use as the default.

5   Click the Choose button.

The Template dialog opens.

6   In the Collection pane, click My Templates.

7   In the Template pane, click Advanced Logic.

The file path pointing toward the Advanced Logic template is displayed in the Default Template field.

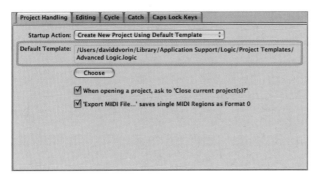

The next time you open Logic, it will automatically create a new project based on the template you created in this lesson.

8   Close the Preferences window.

Backing Up and Transporting Your Setup

After you've spent considerable time customizing your Logic setup, it is a good idea to back up your key commands and project templates for retrieval in the future.

If you work in multiple locations, it is advisable to take these with you when you work on another Logic setup in a different facility. USB flash drives are great for carting around your personal Logic settings. Use the table below to copy files from your main system.

Setting	File location
Key commands	~/Library/Application Support/Logic/Key Commands
Project templates	~/Library/Application Support/Logic/Project Templates

To benefit from the portability of your Logic settings, you must load them into the host system. The contents of both your Key Commands and Project Templates folders must be copied to the location listed above in the new system to make them available.

NOTE ▸ You can also export and import key commands from within the Key Commands window by choosing the item in the Options menu.

Importing Screensets

Sometimes when you're working on Logic song files from other people, you may wish to import your own screensets so that you can more comfortably navigate through their songs. You can do this as a settings import from one project file to another, and it only requires that you have a copy of one of your project files available.

1   Choose File > Project Settings > Import Settings.

The Import Settings file selector box opens.

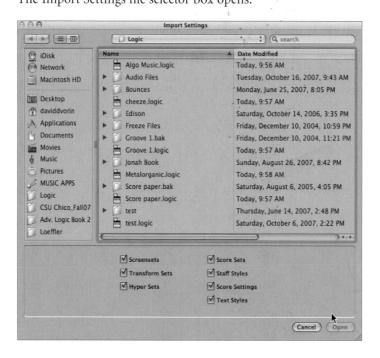

2   Select the Screensets checkbox if it isn't already selected.

3   In the file selector box, go to Music > Logic 8_BTB_Files > Lessons and select 03_The Only Light_Start.logic.

4   Click Open.

Logic copies the screensets to the current project.

5   Press the numbers 1–4 on your keyboard to view the imported screensets.

Accessing Your Settings over a Network

New to Logic Pro 8 is the ability to back up and share user-created plug-in settings, channel strip settings, and key commands over a network. This makes it convenient to transport your custom settings from machine to machine in a networked facility, or anywhere you have an Internet connection.

1   Choose Logic Pro > Preferences > Sharing.

The Preferences window opens, displaying Sharing preferences.

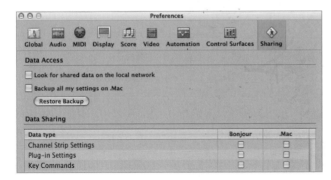

Data can be exchanged over a local network using Apple's Bonjour technology or over the Internet using a .Mac account.

NOTE ▶ Logic uses settings defined in your System Preferences to access your .Mac account, so make sure that these are configured prior to transfer.

To share your data over a network, first select the data type you are sharing (Channel Strip Settings, Plug-in Settings, or Key Commands), and how you would like to share it (Bonjour or .Mac).

2 Select the appropriate Channel Strip Settings, Plug-in Settings, and Key Commands checkboxes in the Bonjour and .Mac columns.

NOTE ▶ Depending on whether or not you've accessed your .Mac account with Logic before, you may receive a dialog asking permission to use the account information in your keychain. If this is the case, you need to click either Allow Once or Always Allow in order for Logic to gain access.

Backing Up Your Settings Using a .Mac Account

If you have access to a .Mac account, you are able to back up and restore Channel Strip settings, Plug-in Settings, and Key Commands to your iDisk. This enables you to efficiently back up precious custom settings without using external hard drives or optical media. It also provides a convenient way to retrieve your settings; all you need is Internet access.

To send data to a .Mac account, you need to select the "Backup all my settings on .Mac" checkbox within the Data Access area in the Sharing preferences.

1 In the Preferences window, select "Backup all my settings on .Mac."

The backup operation starts immediately, indicated by a status message at the bottom of the window.

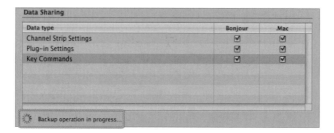

TIP ▶ You can find out the date and time of your last .Mac backup by placing your pointer over the "Backup all my settings on .Mac" checkbox.

After you've saved the settings to your .Mac account, you can retrieve them by clicking the Restore Backup button.

2 Click the Restore Backup button.

A message appears asking if you want to overwrite your local settings with the ones uploaded to the .Mac account.

3   Click the Restore button.

The data is restored to your computer.

NOTE ▶ You can access the settings backed up to a given .Mac account with any computer connected to the Internet by logging on to the iDisk Public folder for the .Mac account. The files are written to the Public/MusicAudioData directory. You can even access them via a web browser by using the following URL: http://idisk.mac.com/ *dotmacaccountname*/Public/MusicAudioData.

Sharing Settings on a Network

In addition to backing up and restoring your own settings, Logic can use an active network connection to gain access to the settings of others. This can be done by connecting to another's .Mac account (via the Internet) or using Bonjour (in a local network).

1   In the Sharing Preferences window, select "Look for shared data on the local network."

As long as a network connection is detected, you should be able to access any Mac running Logic with data sharing enabled. (See "Accessing Your Settings over a Network" in this lesson.)

NOTE ▶ To access settings via Bonjour, all machines must have Logic Pro open.

When connected, you can access shared key commands via the Options menu in the Key Commands window.

2   Close the Preferences window.

3   Open the Key Commands window by choosing Logic Pro > Preferences > Key Commands.

4   Click the Options menu and choose Presets.

The Presets menu displays a Bonjour menu containing the key command sets available from other machines on the local network.

5 Close the Key Commands window.

In addition to key commands, Bonjour also allows access to shared plug-in and channel strip settings wherever you normally use them (the Library, channel strips, and plug-in windows).

6 In the Library, click the Bonjour menu at the bottom of the list.

All available accounts are shown.

NOTE ▶ A target account must have user-created settings to display the Bonjour menu.

7 In the Bonjour menu, click an account to access the channel strip settings.

You can also use a .Mac account to share settings. To do this, you must have an active Internet connection and the appropriate account information to access the .Mac account.

8   At the bottom of the Library, click the Action pop-up menu at the bottom and choose "Connect to .Mac."

The Connect to .Mac dialog appears.

Here you can choose whether you want to connect to your own .Mac account or the public folder on another's (by entering the account name).

9   Click OK.

Once a connection is established, you can now access the .Mac account's settings by selecting within the Library.

NOTE ▸ The .Mac folder will list all user-created channel strip settings within account folders. If you haven't created any channel strip settings, the user account folder will be grayed out (unable to be selected). When new user channel strip settings are created, you need to disconnect then reconnect to the .Mac account before these display within the Library.

10 Close the project.

> **NOTE** ▸ You can disconnect from the .Mac account by choosing "Disconnect .Mac accounts" from the Library's Action menu.

Lesson Review

1. What are project templates?
2. What are some of the ways you can customize a project file?
3. What is the advantage to an unlocked screenset?
4. Identify two strategies for creating key commands that help you remember them.
5. Are all key commands accessible via menus?
6. In what ways can you quickly access the Tool menus?
7. In what ways can you back up and share your settings?

Answers

1. Project templates are premade project files containing various configurations specific to certain session tasks, such as composing and mixing.
2. Project files can be customized by adding buttons to the Toolbar and Transport bar and by maximizing various areas of the workspace.
3. An unlocked screenset can be advantageous during the editing stage because it allows a dynamic view of the current data.
4. Assign a key command only if you find yourself performing a menu command often. Assign keys that provide a clue to the function of a command, such as a key with a graphic representation or the first letter of the function.
5. No. Some useful functions are accessible only via key command, indicated by a bullet preceding the name in the Key Commands window.
6. You can access the Tool menus quickly by using alternate tools, using the Esc key to display the Tool menu at the pointer location, and using a two-button mouse.
7. Custom key commands, plug-in settings, and channel strip settings can be backed up to traditional storage media as well as to a Bonjour account on a local network or a .Mac account accessed via an Internet connection.

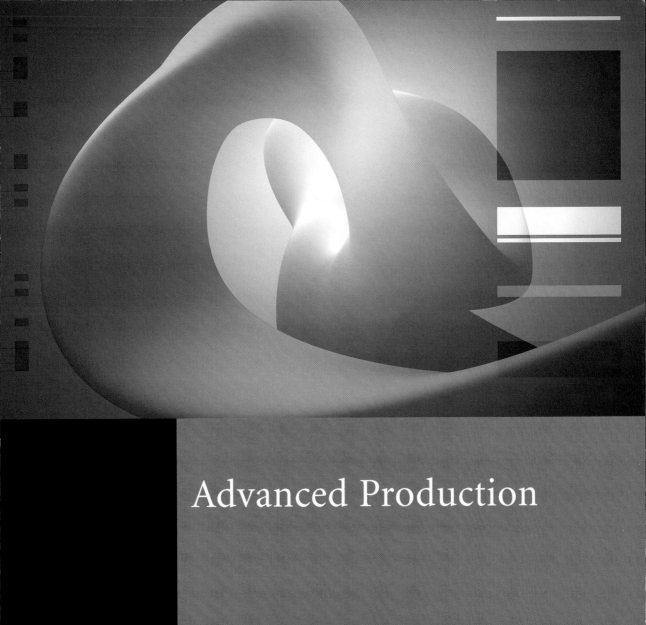

Advanced Production

2

Lesson Files	Logic 8_BTB_Files > Lessons > Templates > Advanced Logic.logic (template created in Lesson 1)
	Logic 8_BTB_Files > Lessons > 02_Creating and Managing Takes.logic
Media	Logic 8_BTB_Files > Media > Chimney
Time	This lesson takes approximately 90 minutes to complete.
Goals	Use project folders to organize your sessions
	Use dependent files in projects
	Create new tracks in a manner demanded by the workflow
	Capture multiple takes efficiently
	Record multiple audio and MIDI tracks simultaneously
	Record multiple MIDI tracks as layers and with simultaneous multiplayer input

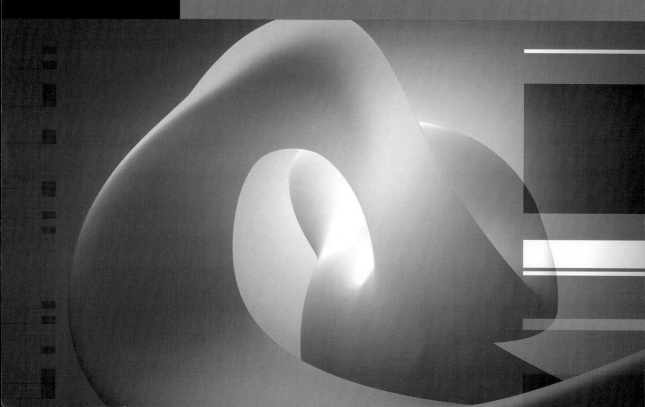

Managing Projects and Takes

In the previous lesson you learned that preparation goes a long way toward making a session fluid and effective. Templates can go only so far, however, as you will quickly exceed basic setups, especially with a large track count.

This section describes techniques you can use to make your tracking sessions more efficient and productive, which in turn will set you up for a more trouble-free editing stage.

Using Project Folders

Logic Pro organizes sessions by grouping related files in a project folder. At its most basic, a project folder contains two items:

▶ A project file

▶ An Audio Files folder containing related audio files

Often it also contains some or all of the following elements (depending on the project data, instrument choices, and plug-in choices):

▶ A Sampler Instruments folder, containing the sampler instruments used in the project

▶ A Samples folder, containing the audio files referenced by the sampler instruments used in the project

▶ An Ultrabeat Samples folder, containing the audio files referenced by any Ultrabeat instruments used in the project.

▶ An Impulse Responses folder, containing the impulse response files used by the project's instantiations of the Space Designer plug-in (convolution reverb)

▶ A Movie Files folder, containing video files referenced by the Logic project file

Creating a Project Folder

When dealing with multiple dependent files, it is absolutely necessary to keep everything in the right place for Logic's retrieval. Not to worry, however, as Logic automatically generates the appropriate folders in their correct locations when creating a new project. This helps to keep your sessions organized from start to finish.

> **NOTE** ▶ If you didn't complete Lesson 1, a version of the template used in this lesson is included with the Lesson 2 files in the following folder: Music > Logic 8_BTB_Files > Lessons > Templates. In order to do the exercises in this lesson, you must copy the file to the following location on your hard disk: ~/Library/Application Support/ Logic/Project Templates.

1 Choose File > New.

> **NOTE** ▶ If you chose to have Logic load the template you created in the last lesson at startup, all you need do is open Logic, then skip to step 3.

You should be looking at the Templates dialog that you explored in Lesson 1 (in the "Using Project Templates" section).

2   Click the My Templates folder in the Collection column, and select Advanced Logic from the Template column.

This is the project file you created in the last lesson. The Save As file window appears.

3   In the Save As field, enter *Lesson 2*.

4   Browse to Music > Logic 8_BTB_Files > Lessons > Completed.

> **NOTE ▶** By default, the file path for projects is set to a folder named Logic, which is created in your ~/Music directory. However, you might have a preferred location for your work (such as a separate location or an external drive); you can type in a path for a location where you want new work to be saved.

5   Select the Include Assets checkbox, if needed.

The window expands to show additional settings.

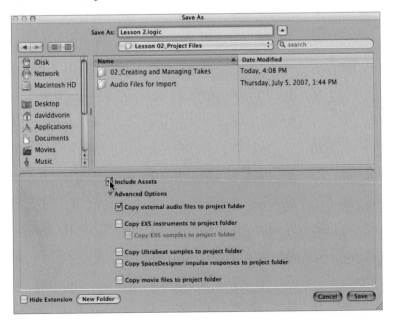

6 Select the "Copy external audio files to project folder" checkbox, if needed.

7 Select the "Copy EXS instruments to project folder" checkbox, if needed.

When you select this checkbox, the "Copy EXS samples to project folder" option becomes available.

8 Select the "Copy EXS samples to project folder" checkbox, if needed.

9 Select the "Copy SpaceDesigner impulse responses to project folder" checkbox, if needed.

10 Click Save to create a new project folder.

To better understand what you just did, look in Logic's Browser to locate the files and folders that you created.

11 In the open Media area (the Library is currently displayed), click the Browser tab.

In effect, the Browser is your direct portal to the media files on your hard disk(s) from within Logic. To find your files, the Browser provides bookmark and navigation buttons, a Path menu, and a search field.

12 Click the List button, if it is not already on.

NOTE ▶ You can display files in the Browser in List view or Browser view, which are similar to the Finder's list and column views, respectively.

13 Click the Project button, one of the bookmark buttons at the top of the Browser.

The Project button provides access to all media associated with the project. Notice that the project folder contains a new project file, also named Lesson 2, as well as an Audio Files folder.

In effect, you have created a new project, based upon your template, that organizes all the files related to that project. The Audio Files folder is created automatically to contain any audio tracks that will be associated with the project file, recorded or imported.

NOTE ▶ The next time you save the project, Logic will automatically create a safety copy of the project file within a Project File Backups folder located within the Project folder.

Working with Assets

The options you selected in the Include Assets section of the Save As window will determine how Logic handles dependent files (files that are referenced by the project) for the new project. When these options are enabled, Logic automatically creates copies of related elements (such as imported audio files, EXS24 instruments and samples, and impulse responses used by the Space Designer plug-in) and places them in organized folders in the project folder. As a result, the project folder will have all project-related files located in one convenient, transportable folder, maintaining their dependent relationships.

Importing Audio Files into a Project

To better understand the relationship and organization of dependent files, you'll load some audio files to use in creating a quick arrangement.

1   At the top of the Media area, click the Bin tab.

2   In the Audio Bin's local menu bar, choose Audio File > Add Audio File.

A file selector box opens. You can use the file selector to load a block of audio files that you will use for the project.

3   Navigate to Music > Logic 8_BTB_Files > Lessons > 02_Audio Files for Import.

4   Click the Add All button.

5   Click the Done button.

All the files located in the folder are added to the project's Audio Bin.

NOTE ▶ Audio files can be auditioned from this window by selecting them and then clicking the Play button in the Open file window.

Now let's bring them into the arrangement, all at once. To do this, you must select the first track to which you want to import.

6   In the track list, select the Audio 1 track (track 1).

Imported files are placed at the current playhead location. In this case, you want them to be placed at the beginning of the project, so you need to make sure that the playhead is at 1 1 1 1.

7 Click the Go To Beginning button in the Transport bar, if needed.

8 From the Audio Bin's local menu bar, choose Edit > Select All.

All the audio files are selected.

9 Choose Audio File > Add to Arrange.

The Add Selected Files to Arrange dialog appears.

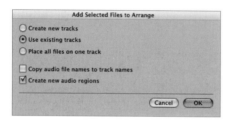

10 Select "Use existing tracks" and "Create new audio regions," if not already selected.

11 Click OK.

The selected audio files are placed in the first five audio tracks, starting at bar 1.

NOTE ▶ This command uses both the selected track and the playhead position to determine where to place the files.

12   At the top of the Region Parameter box, located on the left side of the Arrange window, select the Loop checkbox.

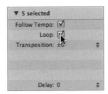

The selected regions are now displayed as looping in the Arrange area.

13   Click the background of the Arrange area to deselect the regions.

14   Drag the Folk Mandolin region on track 3 to the second beat of measure 7 (7 2 1 1).

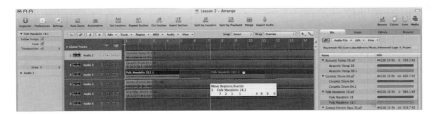

15   Drag the Groovy Electric Bass region on track 4 to measure 5 (5 1 1 1).

16   Drag the Live Edgy Drums region on track 5 to measure 5 (5 1 1 1).

Importing EXS Instruments and Samples into a Project

Now that you have a few audio files imported and situated within the Arrange area, you'll add a few more elements to work with in the project.

1   In the Media area, click the Library tab.

The Library is a database of all factory- and user-created settings, such as channel strip settings, software instrument programs, and plug-in presets. The database is unique in that it is context sensitive: the settings it displays depend on what element is highlighted in the channel strip.

2   Select the Inst(rument) 1 track.

Look at the Arrange channel strip in the Inspector. Notice that the Setting button has a faint white border, indicating that the channel strip settings are the focus of the Library. All the listings in the Library should now reflect only channel strip settings.

3   In the Library tab, choose 12 Logic Basics > EXS24 Sampler.

As soon as you click the entry in the list, a "blank" (no sampler instrument) EXS24 is instantiated, along with a bypassed suite of useful insert effects.

4   In the channel strip's I/O area, click EXS24.

The Library focus changes to EXS sampler instruments.

The Library also has a sophisticated search function that enables you to search for settings by text name.

5   Type *percussion* into the search field, and press Return.

The Library now displays all EXS sampler instruments with the word *percussion* in their names.

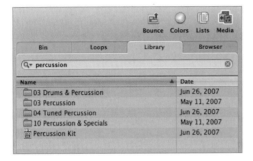

6   Select Percussion Kit.

The EXS24 mkII loads the Percussion Kit sampler instrument.

7   Play your MIDI keyboard to audition the Percussion Kit.

8   Clear the search field by clicking the cancel (X) button on the far right of the search field.

Importing Space Designer Impulse Responses

Logic's Space Designer also uses dependent files. Being a convolution reverb, it relies on a library of recorded audio files (impulse responses) to function. It is sometimes advisable to save these dependent files along with the project for transportability, especially when using nonfactory settings. A Space Designer reverb plug-in is already inserted on the EXS24 track, instantiated when you selected the EXS24 sampler channel strip in the Library.

1   Option-click the Space Designer Insert slot to turn the plug-in on. (It is currently bypassed.)

The plug-in becomes active, and the Library now displays Space Designer presets.

2   In the Library, choose 03 Small Spaces > 01 Rooms > 0.4s Live Chamber.

3   Play your MIDI keyboard to audition the Percussion Kit through the Space Designer reverb.

4   In the main menu bar, choose File > Save.

A Progress window appears, indicating that Logic is copying dependent audio files (Apple Loops, samples, impulse response files, and so on).

5   After Logic completes the copying, click the Browser tab in the Media area.

6   Click the Project button, if not already selected.

The project folder that previously contained only the project file, Audio Files folder, and Project Backups folder now includes other folders (Impulse Responses, Sampler Instruments, and Samples).

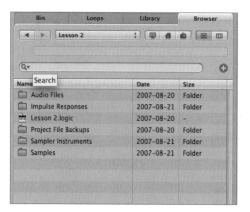

7   Double-click the Audio Files folder to view its contents.

All the audio files used in the project are listed.

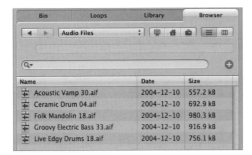

8 Click the Back button to return to the project contents.

TIP ▶ You can also use the Path menu to quickly navigate through the folder structure.

When creating a project, Logic keeps track of all dependent files by placing them in organized folders. In this example, the folders are:

▶ Audio Files folder—five audio files that you imported

▶ Impulse Responses folder—an impulse response audio file used by the drum reverb

▶ Project File Backups folder—an automatically created backup of the project

▶ Sampler Instruments folder—the Percussion Kit EXS instrument added to the Inst 1 track

▶ Samples folder—audio files used by the EXS Percussion Kit instrument

These files have been copied, not moved, to this new location. This way, you are able to bring all the elements related to a project from one system to another while still maintaining the locations of the original files that were installed with Logic.

Quickly Accessing Additional Tracks

No matter what the size of your computer display may be, only so much can fit onscreen. Because of this, it doesn't make sense to create templates with large track counts of every type (audio, software instrument, and MIDI) in the Arrange area. Displaying 128 audio and 64 software instrument tracks in the track list would be impractical, as scrolling up and down the huge list would take up valuable time.

Logic is an object-oriented application; all audio and MIDI channel strips (tracks, software instruments, auxiliaries, MIDI devices, and so on) are represented in the Environment. Beginning with Logic Pro 8, channel strip objects are automatically created and managed in the Environment when new tracks are created, eliminating the need to first create channel objects in the Environment, and then assign them in the track list. This new system is extremely flexible because it creates new channels as your project grows.

> **NOTE ▸** If you don't wish to have Logic manage channel strips in such a manner, you can choose File > Project Settings > Audio and deselect the Automatic Management of Channel Strip Objects checkbox. However, even if the new mode is active, you can create channels of any type in the Environment and freely assign tracks to them by Control-clicking in the track list and choosing Reassign Track Object from the shortcut menu.

In the previous lesson, you created multiple tracks using the New Tracks dialog. In this exercise, you will quickly create and assign tracks for takes and overdubs that are related to the channels already present in the project's track list.

> **NOTE ▸** The following exercises apply to both MIDI and audio recordings, unless otherwise specified.

Creating Tracks Automatically While Recording

Often, takes and overdubs are performed within an isolated section of a composition—an instrument solo or vocal chorus, for example. Logic's Cycle mode enables you to concentrate on these smaller sections, playing them over and over.

Cycle mode is also helpful for grabbing multiple takes, recording one pass after another in rapid succession. This is especially useful if you wear the hats of engineer, producer, and artist while working; often it is impractical to put down your instrument to get your hands on the computer keyboard.

In this exercise, you will set up Logic to automatically record multiple takes in succession to create a simple part.

NOTE ▸ For the sake of this exercise, you are encouraged to record with any audio input signal you choose, playing along with the project. If it is impractical to do so, follow the steps of the exercise by recording "blank" (no input) parts. Later, you can open a premade project with multiple takes of a simple guitar part for your examination. That project can be found in Music > Logic 8_BTB_Files > Lessons > 02_Creating and Managing Takes.

1 Close the Browser by clicking the Media button.

2 On the Audio 6 track, click the Record Enable button.

NOTE ▸ Depending on your Audio Record Path settings, a Save As window may appear when you're record-enabling the track. If a window appears, use the default name of Untitled Audio and write the file to the lesson's Audio Files folder in Music > Logic 8_BTB_Files > Lessons > Completed > Lesson 2.

3 Create an eight-bar cycle area from 7 1 1 1 to 15 1 1 1 by dragging in the Bar ruler.

The Cycle button on the Transport bar will turn green to indicate that Cycle mode is on.

4 Play the project.

NOTE ▸ Because you haven't done any mixing on the previously imported audio files, the output level is quite hot, peaking at 6.0 dB. If the output sounds distorted (or you need to lower the listening volume a bit), reduce the Master Level slider to −8.0 dB to compensate.

Observe how playback is looped within the eight-bar cycle you set.

5 Try playing along with the playback, creating a part that fits with the meter (4/4) and key (C major/A minor) of the tracks.

6 Stop the project when you're comfortable with a simple impromptu part.

7   Put Logic into record mode by clicking the Record button, and perform your part along with the tracks.

> **NOTE ►** Logic is set by default to provide one bar of count-in for recording. You can set as much pre-roll time as you like by choosing File > Project Settings > Recording to open the Recording project settings and choosing an option from the Count-in menu.

8   When the cycle reaches the end (bar 15), immediately try recording the part again, building takes in passes.

9   If you're feeling adventurous, record a third take.

10 Click the Stop button after you have finished.

11 Logic recorded each pass over the previous take. What results is a single take folder, containing all passes of the recording.

> **NOTE ►** MIDI recordings can also be recorded as take folders. Choose File > Project Settings > Recording to open the Recording project settings. In the MIDI section, choose "Create take folders" from the Overlapping recordings pop-up menu. If you want to record in an overdub fashion, adding a layer at a time to the same region, then choose "Merge only in Cycle record."

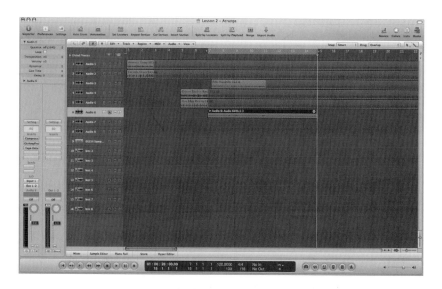

12 Open the take folder by clicking the disclosure triangle to the left of the name.

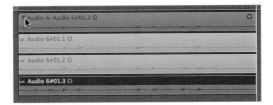

The take folder should contain each pass that you recorded. Each region is automatically labeled with numbers corresponding to the channel (Audio 6), take (#01) and pass (.1 to .3).

NOTE ▶ When recorded sequentially, all takes are simply regions within a single audio file recording.

The last take is highlighted, and the top lane displays its name and waveform information. The top lane simply provides an overview of what is selected in the take folder and, more important, what will be heard during playback.

13 Close the project.

14 Open the following premade file to continue with the lesson: Music > Logic 8_BTB_Files > Lessons > 02_Creating and Managing Takes.logic (mentioned earlier).

15 Play the project.

16 While it's playing, click each of the three take regions one at a time, listening to them in the context of the project.

17 Stop the project.

MORE INFO ▶ One of the best applications of take folders is an easy method for assembling composite tracks, described in depth in Lesson 6, "Advanced Audio Editing."

Creating Channels for Double-Tracking

Double-tracking (the doubling of a recorded track) is an often-used technique for creating a fuller sound by blending two or more overdubs of the same part. Each overdub channel needs to have an identical channel strip setting to maintain the same sonic signature as the original. This process differs from recording takes, as the tracks need to be on separate channels in order to hear them both upon playback.

1   Select the Audio 8 track (track 8).

2   Open the Library by clicking the Media button and clicking the Library tab.

3   With the channel strip setting field highlighted, in the Library, choose 06 Voice > 01 Choral > Pop Backing Vocals.

Several plug-ins are instantiated on the Audio 8 channel.

Let's pretend that you just recorded a pass of backing vocals for a session. The artist immediately wants to record another pass of the part to thicken the sound. You must quickly create a new track that is assigned to a new channel and has the same channel strip settings.

4   From the Arrange area's local menu bar, choose Track > New with Duplicate Setting.

A new audio track, Audio 9, is created below the selected track with a channel strip—complete with any plug-ins and input and channel settings—identical to the previous channel strip. The new channel strip is also adjacent to the previous one, which will help keep things organized.

Recording Multiple Tracks Simultaneously

In Logic, recording multiple tracks simultaneously closely parallels the recording of single tracks—with a few differences. In this exercise, you will record several audio and MIDI tracks at the same time.

NOTE ▶ This lesson is geared toward setups with audio interfaces that have four or more inputs. Don't worry If you are working with a stereo input device; you can easily substitute two inputs whenever four are mentioned in the exercise. By recording with both inputs as mono sources, you will still get a feel for multitrack audio recording in Logic.

Let's start by recording four audio tracks from separate inputs. To do this with existing tracks, you need to assign different inputs to each channel on which you want to record, then record-enable them one at a time. However, if your existing tracks are already filled, in the New Tracks dialog you can create new tracks that are already assigned to ascending inputs and are record-enabled.

1 In the Transport bar, turn off Cycle mode.

2 Click the Stop button to return to the beginning of the project.

3 In the Arrange area's local menu bar, choose Track > New.

The New Tracks dialog appears.

4 In the New Tracks dialog, enter *4* in the Number field.

5 Select the Audio button, if necessary.

6 From the Format menu, choose Mono.

7 From the Input menu, choose Input 1.

8 Select the Ascending checkbox next to the Input menu.

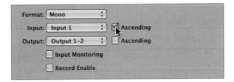

9   Select the Record Enable checkbox near the bottom of the dialog.

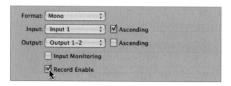

10 Click Create.

Four new mono audio tracks are created (Audio 10 through 13), assigned to Inputs 1 through 4, respectively, and record-enabled.

NOTE ▶ If a track does not have an assigned input, it will not be record-enabled. Likewise, if two tracks share the same input assignment, then only the track that was most recently record-enabled will be active.

11 In the Transport bar, click the Record button.

NOTE ▶ For the sake of this exercise, you will be recording "blank" tracks without input signal. However, you are encouraged to record with any input signal you choose, playing along with the project.

12 After about 30 seconds, click the Stop button. (You can, of course, record a full pass if you're playing along.)

In the Arrange area, you should see four audio regions recorded on the Audio 10 through Audio 13 tracks (tracks 10 through 14).

13 Disable record-enable for all tracks.

> **TIP** ▶ To disable record-enable for multiple tracks, Option-click any of the Record Enable buttons in the track header. This technique works in the track header, Mixer, and in the Arrange window's Inspector.

Recording MIDI and Audio at the Same Time

The process of recording MIDI and audio simultaneously works in a manner similar to that of multitrack audio recording. Logic directs the incoming signals to the appropriate track (MIDI input to MIDI track, and audio input to audio track).

> **NOTE** ▶ If you have another person in your studio to participate in the recording, feel free to have him or her supply the audio performance while you supply the MIDI input.

1 In the track list, first record-enable Audio 7 (track 7), and then the EXS24 Sampler track (track 14).

NOTE ▶ When recording MIDI and audio at the same time, you need to select the MIDI track in the track list to receive input.

2   Locate to the beginning of the project, and put Logic into record mode.

3   Play your MIDI controller to input some data (otherwise the EXS24 Sampler track will appear to not contain a recording).

4   Click the Stop button after about 30 seconds.

5   Turn off the Record Enable button on the audio track.

You just recorded an audio track (Audio 7) and a MIDI track (EXS24 Sampler) simultaneously.

Recording Layered MIDI Tracks

When you're recording multiple MIDI tracks simultaneously, you can build complex sounds by layering the output of different instruments. In effect, the MIDI input is routed to multiple tracks with separate channel objects, recording the same part to multiple tracks in a single pass.

NOTE ▶ All multitrack MIDI techniques discussed here work equally well with classic MIDI tracks and hardware, such as synthesizers and samplers.

Let's look at this process by creating a simple layer of sounds from two of Logic's software instruments.

1   In the track list, select Inst 2.

2   In the Arrange channel strip, click the Instrument slot and choose ES E (Ensemble Synth) > Stereo.

3   Click the Preset menu and choose Deep Space.

4   Close the ES E window.

5   Play your MIDI controller to familiarize yourself with the ES E patch.

6   In the track list, select Inst 3.

7   In the Arrange channel strip, click the Instrument slot and choose EFM1 (FM Synth) > Stereo.

8   Click the Setting menu and choose 07 Warped FM > Aqua Enchant.

9   Close the EFM1 window.

10   Play your MIDI controller to familiarize yourself with the EFM1 patch.

11   Click the Record Enable buttons for both the Inst 2 and Inst 3 tracks, one at a time.

The Record Enable buttons should be active on both tracks (shaded red).

NOTE ▶ Only the track list includes Record Enable buttons for software instrument and external MIDI tracks.

12   Play your MIDI controller.

You should hear the software instruments playing simultaneously.

13 Alternate selecting the enabled tracks while adjusting the volume level in the channel strips to achieve a good blend of the sounds. Try playing the C2 note on your MIDI controller as you adjust. (This is the note you will record in the next step.)

14 With either track selected, record a sustained C2 note at measure 3 for two bars.

Logic automatically creates both a MIDI region on the highlighted track and an alias for the other track.

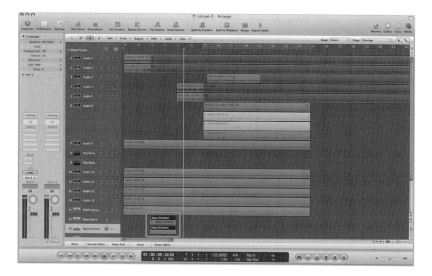

This alias mirrors the MIDI region in every way and reflects any change made to the original. When layering MIDI instruments, Logic creates an alias for every track except the one selected at the time of recording.

MORE INFO ▶ For more on aliases, see Lesson 7, "Advanced MIDI Editing."

Recording Multiplayer MIDI Tracks

In addition to layering instruments as described in the previous exercise, you can record multiple performers using separate software instruments on multiple tracks. In this case, MIDI channels are used to differentiate incoming data, routing each player's MIDI controller to the right track.

NOTE ▶ This exercise is geared toward setups with two MIDI controllers. If you don't have two controllers at your disposal, you can use one controller and change its MIDI channel output as you record.

1   Set one MIDI controller to output on MIDI channel 1.

   NOTE ▸ The sending MIDI channel is usually set in the global setup section of the MIDI controllers.

2   Set the other MIDI controller to output on MIDI channel 2.

3   Select the Deep Space track (Inst 2, or track 15).

4   In the Track Parameter box, click the disclosure triangle to display its contents.

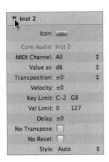

   By default, software instruments are set to receive on all MIDI channels. To separate the incoming MIDI data while you're recording, you need to set your tracks to receive on separate MIDI channels.

5   Click the MIDI Channel menu and choose 1.

6 Select the Aqua Enchant track (Inst 3, or track 16).

7 In the Track Parameter box, change the MIDI Channel menu option to 2.

One last step remains to set up recording in multiplayer mode. It determines Logic's behavior when recording multiple MIDI tracks and is set within the project settings.

8 Choose File > Project Settings > Recording.

9 In the MIDI section, select the "Auto demix by channel if multitrack recording" checkbox.

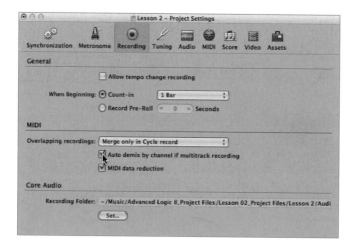

Both tracks should still be record-enabled from the previous exercise, which will ensure that the instruments are receiving MIDI data. You are now ready to test the setup.

10 Close the Project Settings window.

11 Play each MIDI controller one at a time, making sure that each is connected to the appropriate software instrument channel.

12 Try recording a short impromptu part from each MIDI controller (ideally you should record from them simultaneously) starting from measure 7.

Each track should have regions containing only the routed MIDI data from a single MIDI controller.

Deleting Unused Tracks

You now have a few too many empty tracks showing in the track list. Since you now know how to create tracks on demand, you can safely delete those extra tracks.

1   Select the Audio 8 track (track 8).

2   Press Delete.

This is Logic's most basic technique for deleting tracks. Let's look at a few others.

3   Position the pointer over the icon at the left of the Audio 9 track (which is now track 8 after you deleted the last track).

The pointer should change to a hand when it's in the right position.

4   Grab the track by clicking the track icon, and drag the track to the left so that it is positioned outside the track list.

The hand changes to an eraser.

5   Release the mouse button.

The track is removed from the track list.

Both of these techniques are useful for quickly deleting single tracks, but cleaning up a tracking session often requires the deletion of multiple blank tracks of different types (audio, software instruments, and so on). Logic's Delete Unused function comes in handy for these situations.

6   From the Arrange area's local menu bar, choose Track > Delete Unused.

Any track that does not have a region is deleted from the Arrange area's track list.

7   Choose File > Save to save the work you performed in this lesson.

Lesson Review

1.   What does a project folder contain?
2.   How are tracks and channels managed by Logic?
3.   What happens when Logic records multiple passes within a cycle area?
4.   What must you do first to record multiple audio tracks simultaneously?
5.   What must you do first to route MIDI and audio tracks when recording both simultaneously?
6.   What are the two ways that Logic can record multiple MIDI tracks simultaneously?
7.   How do you delete unused tracks?

Answers

1.   A project folder contains all dependent files associated with a given project, organized in folders of the same file type.
2.   Logic automatically creates and manages channels strips in the Environment when new tracks are created.
3.   When recording multiple passes within a cycle area, Logic automatically creates a take folder containing each overdub.
4.   Recording multiple audio tracks simultaneously requires that you set the tracks to separate inputs.

5.   Although Logic handles the routing of MIDI and audio when recording both types simultaneously, you have to select the MIDI track before initiating recording in order for it to receive input.

6.   MIDI tracks can be multitracked via layering sounds or by triggering separate sounds via multiple MIDI controller inputs (a multiplayer recording).

7.   Unused tracks can be deleted individually or all at once using the Delete Unused command.

3

Lesson Files	Logic 8_BTB_Files > Lessons > 03_Time and Pitch_Start.logic
	Logic 8_BTB_Files > Lessons > 03_The Only Light_Start.logic
Media	Logic 8_BTB_Files > Media > The Only Light That's On
	Logic 8_BTB_Files > Media > Chimney
Time	This lesson takes approximately 1 hour to complete.
Goals	Achieve better results when shifting time and pitch
	Use the Apple Loops Utility to create your own Apple Loops
	Use the Time and Pitch Machine to make exact time and pitch changes
	Use Harmonic Correction when pitch shifting to preserve the resonant characteristics of an audio file
	Match a project's time grid to a freely played recording for further editing and development

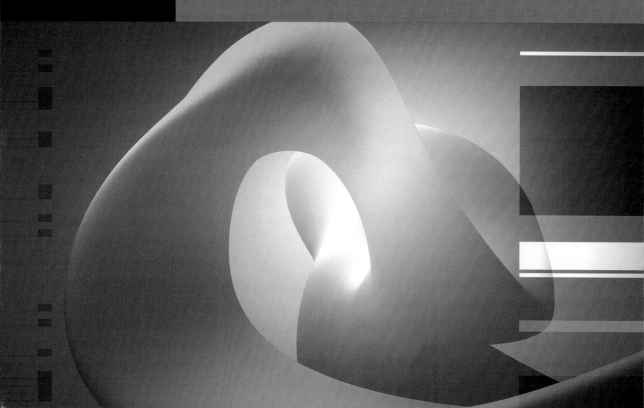

Lesson 3
Matching Tempo and Pitch

Working with music in the digital domain lends itself well to collage, the combining of material from multiple sources into a cohesive whole. Modern music productions increasingly incorporate audio material from disparate sources, whether it is material from sample libraries or excerpts from existing recordings. The major production stumbling block has been matching the tempos and keys of the sound sources.

When a tape is slowed down or a digital audio file's sample rate is increased, the pitch is altered as well. Not too long ago, you couldn't alter the timing and pitch of a recording independently. Recent trends in audio production technology have attempted to address this, incorporating features that specifically deal with matching the tempo and pitch of audio material.

Modern techniques use algorithms that transpose, extend, or compress audio material, giving you the ability to alter pitch or time (or both) without changing the character of the original file. These operations are quite complex, requiring an analysis of the audio data to determine what to leave or cut out, and where to insert material.

These decisions aren't always suitable for a specific piece of material, however, and unexpected results (desirable or not) can occur. To achieve a better outcome, you need to manipulate the available parameters and help the computer make more appropriate choices.

In this lesson, you will use Logic Pro's time-stretching and pitch-transposition features to match disparate elements within a project.

Working with Apple Loops

Apple Loops are essentially audio files with additional information written to the file's header. In software such as Logic and GarageBand, the information enables the time stretching and pitch shifting of the audio data to be done independently of each other in real time.

This file format is a boon for arranging, as Apple Loops have the distinct advantage of automatically conforming to Logic's time grid, and they provide a great deal of flexibility. Libraries of Apple Loops can be freely imported into any project file; and, in addition, all audio recorded, bounced within, and exported from Logic Pro will have the ability to follow the project's tempo. Standard audio files (such as .aif, .wav, and .sd2 files not formatted as Apple Loops) have time and pitch attributes that are not conformed when the files are imported. Even so, those formats are easily converted with specific tools to create Apple Loops that will seamlessly conform to a project's tempo and key.

In the upcoming exercises, you will use a project file containing basic elements from previous exercises (similar to the project file you created in Lesson 2), including audio files in the Apple Loops format.

1   Choose Music > Logic 8_BTB_Files > Lessons > **03_Time and Pitch_Start.logic**.

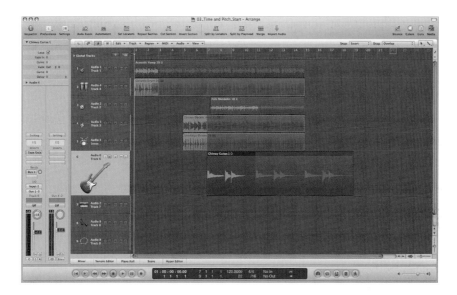

Look at the first five tracks containing audio regions. Note that each region has a small symbol (similar to a loop-the-loop) following its name. This symbol indicates that the audio file is an Apple Loops file.

2   Click each track in the track header, taking a look at the Region Parameter box on the far left.

Examine the Region Parameter box on the far left. Note that Follow Tempo is selected for all Apple Loops regions. This parameter ensures that the Apple Loops will conform to any tempo change.

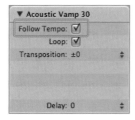

The Follow Tempo parameter is deselected by default for audio that is recorded into Logic. If you want the audio regions to conform to the project's tempo, this parameter needs to be selected.

In addition to the Apple Loops tracks, track 6 contains a guitar part, Chimey Guitar, that was imported into the project. Note that this region does not have Follow Tempo parameter within the Region Parameter box, nor does it have an Apple Loops symbol because it is a standard mono audio file.

3 Play the project to familiarize yourself with the arrangement.

The project moves along at a pretty fast clip and feels a little rushed. Let's slow the tempo to achieve a better feel for the groove.

4 In the Transport bar (at the bottom of the Arrange window), double-click the numerical field of the Tempo display, type *110*, and press Enter.

5 Play the project.

The groove feels significantly better at this slower tempo, but a major problem has occurred. The Chimey Guitar track, which matched the original tempo of 120 bpm (beats per minute), is now out of tempo.

Using the Apple Loops Utility

One of the easiest ways to make the Chimey Guitar region's tempo match the other tracks is to convert it into an Apple Loops file. That way you can make tempo adjustments in the arrangement and have all audio regions follow along. Logic Pro ships with an application, the Apple Loops Utility, that enables you to create Apple Loops from any standard audio file.

1 If necessary, in track 6 select the Chimey Guitar region.

2 In the Arrange area's local menu bar, choose Audio > Open in Apple Loops Utility.

A dialog appears asking you to identify the length of the audio file.

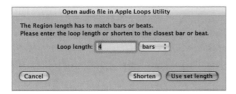

For the Apple Loops Utility to analyze the data, it must discern how the file length relates to music beats and bars. The Apple Loops Utility makes an educated guess based on the region length compared to Logic's own bar/beat ruler. This region originally lasted four bars (at 120 bpm), so the program "guessed" correctly in this case.

3   Click "Use set length."

The Apple Loops Utility opens, displaying the filename in the Assets drawer (at the far right), with the Tags tab open.

Tagging Files

Tags are pieces of information used by many applications, including those that support the Apple Loops file format. Adding tags will not directly affect the tempo or pitch properties of a file, but tags are essential if you plan on adding a file to the Apple Loops library (accessed by Logic's Loop Browser). These bits of information constitute a database, enabling you to search for material based on specific criteria. Let's look at these properties by creating tags for the Chimey Guitar file that you imported.

The upper-left portion of the Tags tab contains property tags related to the file's musical content.

The Apple Loops Utility supplies default values for the time signature, number of beats, key, and tonality. The Chimey Guitar region you are working with will be looped within the arrangement, so it is necessary to indicate this within the property tags.

Move down to the Search Tags pane, where you can define the music genre and instrument type for the file.

1   If not already selected, click the Looping radial button next to the File Type option

2   From the Genre pop-up menu, choose Rock/Blues.

3   In the Instrument pane, choose Guitars > Electric Guitar.

4   Move to the right to the Descriptors pane and look at the list that describes the musical content.

5   Matching the next figure, click to select the radio buttons for the options that best describe the musical characteristics of the Chimey Guitar part.

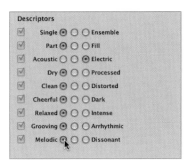

Working with Transients

Now that you've defined the search tags of the audio file, it is time to work with properties that directly relate to time stretching and pitch transposition.

1 At the upper left of the window, click the Transients tab.

The Transients tab opens, displaying the audio file waveform.

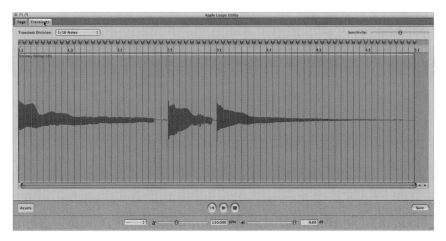

NOTE ▶ You may need to enlarge the window and zoom in to better view the information within this window.

Transients are good indicators of where beats occur in an audio file, and they typically show up as sharp attacks with the highest amplitude (widest areas of a waveform). The Apple Loops Utility automatically detects transients and applies markers based on their characteristics in conjunction with the bar and beat information that you supplied when opening the utility. These transient markers are used as a map, enabling Logic to make decisions about where best to apply time stretching and pitch transposition.

By default, the Apple Loops Utility uses sixteenth-note divisions, but this might not always be appropriate for the given material. It is best to check results by listening to the file played from within the utility, which will immediately apply time stretching and pitch transposition based on the settings.

2   If it is not already done, make sure that the Tempo slider (marked with a metronome symbol) is set to the recording's original tempo (120 bpm, in this case).

3   At the bottom of the window, click the Play button.

The file plays, looping over and over. Depending on the settings that were in use the last time the Apple Loops Utility was opened, the file could play back in the wrong key.

4   If necessary, click the Key pop-up menu in the lower part of the window and choose "–" to indicate the original key of the part.

The file now plays in its original key (C major).

5 While playing the file, try selecting different keys from the Key pop-up menu, listening to them one at a time.

The loop transposes up smoothly via semitones and sounds as expected until it reaches the F♯/G♭ setting (the augmented fourth/diminished fifth from C). The pitch immediately drops down 11 semitones (an octave below what is expected). This still reflects the key accurately but achieves better-sounding results.

NOTE ▶ This octave transposition is mirrored when Apple Loops are played back in the Arrange area. While an octave transposition accurately represents the key, it might create surprises when moving from the root to the fifth or in similar progressions.

6 Return to the original key, by choosing "–" in the Key pop-up menu.

7 While playing, drag the Tempo slider to a value of 110.000 bpm.

The loop plays at a slower tempo.

Listen to the sound that is produced when you adjust the tempo to your target (110 bpm). The sound has a slight tremor that falls at the sixteenth-note divisions. This was not present in the original file, so you should use the Transient Division menu to home in on a more acceptable sound.

8 Click the Stop button.

Look at the numbers displayed above the waveform (1.1, 1.3, 2.1, 2.3, and so on). These correspond to bars and beats, separated by a period. Thus, 1.1 represents the first bar, first beat; 1.3 represents the first bar, third beat. You can use this reference to compare the transients of the audio file with the bar/beat ruler.

The Transient Division setting should reflect the smallest significant note division for the loop. In this exercise, you can look at the waveform and discern that the notes aren't struck any faster than at half-note intervals (2.3 to 3.1), so setting the Transient Division to match is a good place to start.

9   From the Transient Division pop-up menu, choose 1/2 Notes. Click Play to listen to the results.

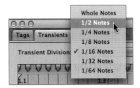

This sounds significantly better, and considerably less jittery.

10   Stop the playback, and at the upper right of the window, drag the Sensitivity slider all the way to the right.

As you do this, notice that more transients are detected, matching up to smaller peaks in the audio waveform and occurring at closer intervals than the half-note value you defined in the Transient Division menu.

Increasing the sensitivity achieves a better result for the glissando between 2.3 and 3.1, but it also brings back the jittery sound, especially for the sustained vibrato between 1.1 and 2.3. Instead of using these results, you can drag the Sensitivity slider back to the middle and add only the transient markers that you need.

11   Drag the Sensitivity slider to the halfway point.

12   Click the dark gray area above the ruler in the middle of the 2.3–3.1 range.

A transient marker is created at approximately bar 2, beat 4.

TIP ▶ You can adjust transients by dragging them to a new location, or delete them by selecting them and pressing Delete.

13 Click in the dark gray area to create another transient marker between the one you just created and the one at 3.1.

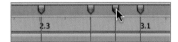

A transient marker is created at approximately the upbeat of bar 2, beat 4.

The playback is pretty smooth now, with acceptable results.

14 If the playback is still looping, click the Stop button.

Creating Apple Loops

To take advantage of the adjustments and the information that you defined, you have to save the file. When you save the file, the new data is added to the file and made accessible to any application that reads Apple Loops.

1 In the lower-right corner of the interface, click the Save button.

The information you provided, both tags and transients, is saved to the file.

2 Choose Apple Loops Utility > Quit Apple Loops Utility.

3 If necessary, bring forward Logic Pro, which should still be in the background.

Look at the Chimey Guitar audio region in the Arrange area. The Apple Loops symbol is now next to the filename and the region has a length of exactly four measures.

4 Play the project.

The Chimey Guitar region now plays in time.

Using the Time and Pitch Machine

Before Apple Loops were integrated within Logic, all tempo and pitch adjustments to audio files were done with the Time and Pitch Machine, which functions differently from Apple Loops. The most obvious difference is that Apple Loops work in real time, dynamically changing pitch and tempo in relation to the project, while using the Time and Pitch Machine is an offline, file-based process that permanently alters a file's pitch and tempo.

Even so, the Time and Pitch Machine has its advantages, especially with regard to control. Apple Loops offer automatic adaptability, but they are locked to a given project's tempo or key and are not very useful when you want to shift audio material independently of a project's tempo or make pitch adjustments of less than a semitone.

Let's open another piece of material and use the Time and Pitch Machine to conform it to the arrangement.

1   On the Toolbar, click the Media button to open the Audio Bin.

2   Drag the **Synth Layer.aif** file to the Audio 7 track at the beginning of measure 2.

    The nine-bar Synth Layer region is imported to measure 2.

3   Close the Media area.

4   Double-click the Synth Layer region, opening the Sample Editor.

5   Resize the window to display the file in its entirety, zooming out horizontally if necessary.

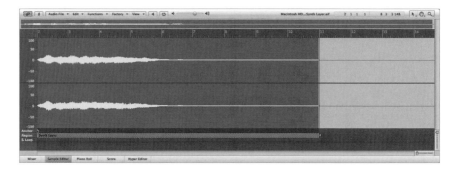

6   At the top of the sample editor, click the Play button to hear the Synth Layer audio file.

NOTE ▶ The Sample Editor (as well as the Bin Audio, Apple Loops Browser, and Browser) uses a special Prelisten audio channel strip to play the displayed content. This channel strip is automatically created within the project's Mixer and can be found in the Environment.

7 Adjust the Volume slider to the right of the Play button to change the playback for the Sample Editor.

The audio file consists of a synth pad that slowly grows to a climax, then tapers off.

For this exercise, you will shorten the long synth pad to work better in the project. In this instance, the Apple Loops Utility is not suitable for a variety of reasons. The swelling sound of the synth pad has no beat-related transients on which to base the pitch and time shifting.

In addition, Apple Loops are geared toward repeated, rhythmically based material that always relates to the project's tempo. For this exercise, you only need to shorten the file's length, without accounting for tempo. Creating an Apple Loops file from the selection would have no effect unless you later changed the project's master tempo.

8 In the sample editor's local menu, choose Factory > Time and Pitch Machine.

The Time and Pitch Machine window opens.

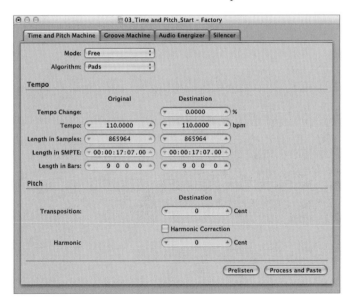

9 In the Tempo Change parameter, click the Destination field and type *50*.

After you enter the value, note that the information displayed in the Destination column now reflects this change.

The Time and Pitch Machine offers nine algorithms designed to work with different types of audio material, prioritizing certain musical aspects to better make decisions that affect the time and pitch shifting.

10 In the Algorithm menu, choose Pads.

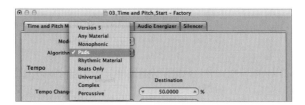

By choosing the Pads setting, you are indicating that the material has a minimum of transients and that it is a sustained sound.

TIP ▶ Although operations in the Sample Editor are usually destructive (and thus permanently change the file), algorithms can be tried on material without destructive results. Logic Pro will cache changes to disk depending on the number of undo steps set within the Sample Editor preferences (Preferences > Audio > Sample Editor). After an operation is completed, you can always undo by choosing Edit > Undo in the Sample Editor or by pressing Command-Z.

11 Click the Process and Paste button.

An alert dialog appears asking if you are sure you want to go ahead with the operation.

12 Click Process.

The operation is performed while Logic Pro displays the progress. This may take a few moments, depending on the speed of your computer.

13 Close the Time and Pitch Machine window.

14 Click the Play button to listen to the results.

The file plays true to its original sound quality, but with a shorter length.

15 Click the Sample Editor button to close the Sample Editor.

16 Play the project file to hear the Synth Layer region within the context of the project.

This fits much better with the arrangement, building up until the drums and bass enter, then tapering off.

TIP ▶ Better results are usually achieved in contracting audio files than in expanding them. When the operation increases the speed of the audio, the computer must cut out material deemed nonessential, potentially removing important elements such as transients. But things get considerably trickier when you need to decrease the speed, because the computer must invent entirely new material based on the existing waveform and insert it at appropriate places to fill the desired length.

Using Harmonic Correction with Pitch Transposition

Pitch transposition usually involves shifting the complete frequency spectrum up or down by a constant value. In effect, everything within the sound source is shifted, including natural resonances (called *formants*). This works well for some material, but it can create unnatural results in material (such as instruments or voices) containing a harmonic structure that is integral to the sound.

A good example is the pitch shifting of a cello note. When all the material is shifted upward (including formants), the pitch changes, and the "body," or timbre, of the instrument changes as well. What results is a higher pitch that sounds as if it were emanating from a smaller instrument (a viola or violin in this case), rather than the original instrument.

If your aim is to change the pitch of a given file while maintaining its resonances, then the formants must be left unaltered. The Time and Pitch Machine can be set to use such a process, called *Harmonic Correction*, to achieve natural results when pitch shifting.

Try this out by changing the pitch of the Synth Layer region using Harmonic Correction.

1   Option-drag the Synth Layer region to measure 13.

    The region is copied to the new location.

    Since you will be transposing this copy of the region, it must be saved as a unique audio file rather than another reference of the original. This will allow you to make changes to the copied file without altering the regions you worked with previously.

2   Select the newly copied region and, from the Arrange area's local menu bar, choose Audio > Convert Regions to New Audio Files.

    A dialog appears, prompting for a location to which to save the converted file.

3   Click Save to save the file to the location of the original file.

The region is saved as an independent audio file.

NOTE ▶ When copying regions, Logic appends a "." (period) followed by a number in order to avoid creating duplicate names.

4   Double-click the newly saved region to open it in the Sample Editor.

5   In the Sample Editor's local menu, choose Factory > Time and Pitch Machine to open the Time and Pitch Machine.

The Time and Pitch Machine window opens.

NOTE ▶ The Time and Pitch Machine opens with the last setting you input, so it is important to clear out the tempo change that you performed in the previous exercise *before* you perform an unrelated operation (unless you want to affect the file in similar ways).

6   In the Tempo Change parameter, click the Destination field and type *0*. Press Enter.

The goal is to transpose the pitch of the file up a fifth from C to G while retaining the inherent resonances of the sound.

7   In the Transposition parameter, click the Destination field and type *700*. Press Enter.

This will transpose the sound up 700 cents, or seven semitones (there are 100 cents in a semitone). Note that the Harmonic parameter value also changes to 700. With Harmonic Correction deselected, Logic will adjust the pitch and the formants together.

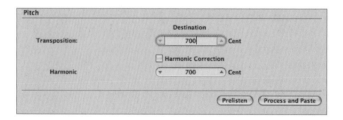

8   Just below the Transposition parameter's Destination field, select the Harmonic Correction checkbox.

9   In the Harmonic parameter, click the field and type *0*, then press Enter.

This tells the Time and Pitch Machine that you wish to retain the original formants of the file, altering the pitch independently.

10 Click the Process and Paste button.

An alert dialog appears asking if you are sure you want to go ahead with the operation.

11 Click Process.

The operation is performed while Logic Pro displays the progress. This process takes a bit longer than the tempo shifting that you performed earlier, because the computations for Harmonic Correction are more extensive.

NOTE ▶ Tempo, pitch, and harmonic (formant) changes can be applied simultaneously or independently of each other.

12 Close the Time and Pitch Machine window, and play the file from within the Sample Editor.

The synth pad retains all of its original character but sounds a fifth higher.

13 Close the Sample Editor by clicking the Sample Editor button.

14 Play the project to hear the new region within the context of the composition.

Performing Time Stretching and Compression in the Arrange Area

You can also time stretch and compress audio regions directly within the Arrange area. This can be an extremely convenient way to make adjustments to audio regions while visually referencing the project's tempo grid.

Accessing the Time and Pitch Machine in the Arrange Area

Sometimes a small adjustment is needed to conform slightly slower or faster regions to the project's tempo. Fortunately, you can simply stretch the region to the next bar using the power of the Time and Pitch Machine, entirely within the Arrange area.

1   Click the Media button, opening the Audio Bin tab.

2   Drag the **Bells.aif** file to the Audio 8 track at the beginning of measure 7.

The Bells region is imported to measure 7.

3   Play the project to listen to the newly imported region.

Notice that the Bells region sounds out of sync and doesn't quite reach all the way to the next bar.

4   In the Arrange area's local menu bar, choose Audio > Time Machine Algorithm > Percussive.

As you probably noticed, the available choices reflect the algorithms presented within the Time and Pitch Machine when accessed in the Sample Editor.

5   From the Arrange area's Audio menu, choose "Adjust Region Length to Nearest Bar."

An alert dialog appears asking if you are sure you want to go ahead with the operation.

6   Click Process.

The region conforms to exactly one bar. You can now loop the region and have it play back in perfect time with the other material.

TIP ▶ The "Adjust Region Length to Locators" command works in an almost identical fashion, using the Time and Pitch Machine's engine to time stretch or compress the audio region to the region defined via the left and right locators.

Time Stretching and Compression by Dragging

The time of an audio region can also be manipulated by graphically dragging out its border to line up with a given bar or beat. This can be especially handy for creating a half-time or double-time feel for a given region.

1   Drag the **Tambourine.aif** file to the Audio 9 track at the beginning of measure 7.

The Tambourine region is imported to measure 7.

2   Play the project to listen to the newly imported region.

The Tambourine part sounds a little jerky and would sound considerably better at double the speed.

3   Option-drag the lower-right corner of the Tambourine region to the left, making the region one measure long, half of its original length.

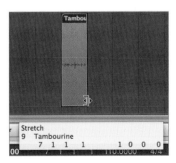

The following dialog appears:

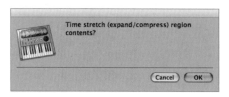

4 Click OK.

NOTE ▶ If Cancel is clicked, only the audio region's borders will be adjusted, without affecting the audio file.

Another dialog appears, asking if you want to proceed and indicating the number of undo steps remaining.

5 Click Process.

The region is time compressed to half its previous value.

6 Play the project to hear the tambourine play twice as fast.

You can now loop the region and have it play back in perfect time with the other material.

TIP ▶ This process also works with MIDI regions.

7 Choose File > Save As to save the project, naming it *03_Time and Pitch_End*.

8 Close the project by choosing File > Close.

Working with Rubato Passages

In Logic, you will generally be working with music based on a constant tempo or recorded to a metronome click. In this common situation, Logic's tempo and time-signature settings create a time grid in which you plot events. This enables data to be displayed musically, in relation to bars and beats.

However, sometimes you will want to record without a click, gaining the freedom to vary the tempo and play with rhythmic flexibility (to play with *rubato*, in music parlance). In this situation, the trick is not only to maintain a performer's interpretation, with its deviations in tempo, but also to display the musical data in correct time (bars and beats). You can use beat mapping to align Logic's time grid with these tempo variations.

Once the time grid matches the performance, you can use Logic's compositional and arranging features (quantization, time-based effects, notation, Apple Loops, and so on) to work with data as if it had been recorded to a metronome click.

For this exercise, you will use Logic's Beat Mapping track to create tempo changes for each event that deviates from a constant tempo.

Using the Beat Mapping Track

The Beat Mapping track, one of Logic's global tracks, works hand in hand with related tracks such as the Signature and Tempo tracks. Think of it as working like an adaptive ruler, letting you graphically tie events to particular bars and beats (all derived from the Signature track). When events are defined according to their bar positions in the Beat Mapping track, tempo changes are created in the Tempo track to align the grid.

Both MIDI and audio tracks can form a basis on which to generate a beat map. Let's start by opening the project file used in this exercise, which contains both MIDI and audio versions of a rubato piano piece.

1   Choose Music > Logic 8_BTB_Files > Lessons > **03_The Only Light_Start.logic**.

   The project contains a single MIDI track being output through the EXS24 mkII instrument (a piano sample), along with a muted audio track of the same material.

2   Play the project to familiarize yourself with the material.

3   In the Transport bar, click the Metronome button to turn on Logic's click.

4   Play the project again, this time listening to the tempo deviations of the piece against the click.

Things start off without too much deviation, but the click is really out of sync by measure 4.

5   At the upper-left corner of the Arrange area, click the Global Tracks disclosure triangle.

The global tracks appear, displaying only the tracks used for this exercise: Signature, Tempo, and Beat Mapping.

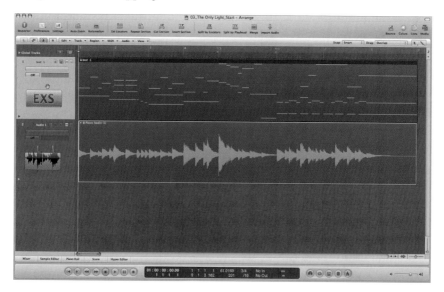

TIP   You can display any or all of the global tracks by choosing View > Configure Global Tracks and choosing whatever you wish to view. This setting will be saved with the screenset and can be hidden or exposed at any time using a key command or menu selection.

As you can see in the Signature track, the piece starts in 3/4 but also contains bars of 5/4 and 4/4. The time signatures are reflected in the Beat Mapping track, with bars and beats displayed graphically by lines representing the time grid (not unlike the Bar ruler).

If this grid is to be used as a reference, Logic's division value (a freely definable part of a beat) must reflect the smallest rhythmic value within the piece of music. The music you are using is based on a triplet feel, so it is necessary to select a division of 12 instead of 16 (the default).

6   In the Transport bar, double-click the Division field in the Time Signature display and type *12*.

The ruler and grid now display triplet divisions instead of sixteenth notes.

Beat Mapping a MIDI Region
To start aligning the grid to the music, you need to select the material you want to work with.

> **NOTE ▶** The Beat Mapping track works with regions, not tracks (which contain multiple regions).

1   If it is not already selected, select the MIDI region on the Inst 1 track.

Colored lines appear in the Beat Mapping track, indicating each MIDI event (with velocities) in the selected region. You will use both these lines and the bar/beat lines above, "tying" them together to realign the grid.

2   Zoom in horizontally until about four bars are visible in the Arrange area.

This enables you to see greater detail when working in the Beat Mapping track.

3   In the top portion of the Beat Mapping track, drag the line representing measure 1, beat 2 (1 2 1 1) downward, connecting it to the light green event (1 1 3 305) in the bottom portion of the track.

The line turns yellow as you are connecting it and a help tag (Set Beat To) displays the event's position before alignment.

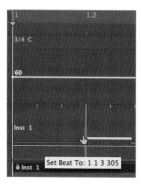

When you release the mouse button, the points are aligned, and a new tempo event is created (61.0169) in the Tempo track.

NOTE ▶ Logic uses very fine tempo increments (as small as 1/10,000 of a beat!) for accurate alignment.

4   Using the same technique, connect the line representing measure 1, beat 2, division 3 (1 2 3 1) to the light green line located below and slightly to the left (1 2 2 294).

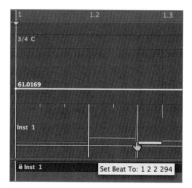

Another tempo event is created in the Tempo track (63.7053).

5   Connect the line representing measure 1, beat 3 (1 3 1 1) to the light blue line located below and slightly to the right (1 3 1 34).

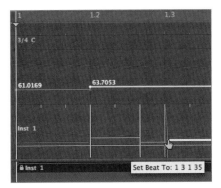

Another tempo event is created in the Tempo track (57.5868).

6   Connect the line representing measure 1, beat 3, division 3 (1 3 3 1) to the light blue line located below and slightly to the left (1 3 2 294).

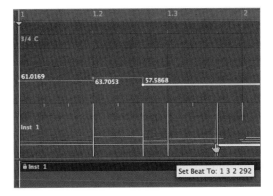

For every note event connected, a new tempo is indicated, creating an accurate depiction of the region's timing. Therefore, the more events that are beat mapped, the closer Logic's time grid will conform to the music.

For the rest of this exercise, you will finish beat mapping the entire piano part, creating an accurate time map of the piece.

Here are two areas to watch out for:

Position	Situation	Recommendation
2 1 1 1	The slur and slightly staggered chord entries create multiple possibilities to draw connections.	Try experimenting with what works best in representing the downbeat.
3 1 2 1	Deviates from triplet feel to eighth notes for one beat	Change the division to /8 (eighth notes) to work with the grid above the two eighth notes.

7   Continue connecting related lines in the Beat Mapping track, moving from left to right for the entire region.

TIP ▶ If you make a mistake, you can erase any beat allocation by double-clicking it or using the Eraser tool.

8   When you are finished, check your work by listening to the EXS24 mkII piano part along with the metronome click.

For comparison, a beat-mapped Tempo track has been created for you as a reference. You can access this in the Tempo Alternative menu in the Tempo track.

NOTE ▶ The Tempo Alternative menu allows you to save and recall up to nine tempo "maps" created in the Tempo track.

9   From the Tempo Alternative pop-up menu, choose 2.

The Tempo track now displays the premade tempo events created from beat mapping.

10 Play the project with the click to compare the premade Tempo track with your results, toggling back and forth between Tempo tracks using the Tempo Alternative menu choices (1 and 2).

Checking Your Results in the Piano Roll Editor

You can check how well you performed beat mapping by viewing the events graphically within the Piano Roll Editor. Here you can clearly see the individual events lined up on the time grid and compare the results achieved with beat mapping to the original, non-beat-mapped track.

1 With the MIDI region selected, click the Piano Roll button to display the MIDI events in detail.

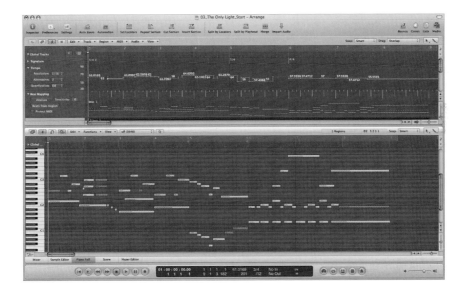

2 In the Tempo Alternative menu, switch among 1 (your beat map), 2 (the premade beat map), and 5 (not beat-mapped) options, comparing how the note events align to the grid.

You can see major discrepancies between the beat-mapped (1 and 2) and non-beat-mapped (5) versions, especially from measure 4 onward.

Beat Mapping an Audio Region

Using an audio region as the source for beat mapping involves a technique similar to using a MIDI region. Instead of using MIDI note events, however, the Beat Mapping track uses audio transients for alignment points. To do this, Logic needs to analyze the source to detect the transients (somewhat like the Apple Loops Utility).

Let's mute the MIDI track and unmute the audio track before we start working with the audio track version.

1   Close the Piano Roll Editor to display the regions in the Arrange area.

2   Mute the Inst 1 track by clicking the Mute button on the track.

The EXS24 mkII piano track is muted.

3   Unmute the Audio 1 track by clicking the Mute button on the track.

4   From the Tempo Alternative pop-up menu, choose 3.

5   Click in the track header of the Beat Mapping track (but do not click the buttons or menus) to select everything in the track, and press Delete.

All beat events are erased, allowing you to continue with a fresh slate.

NOTE ▶ Neither the work you performed with beat mapping nor the premade Tempo track is deleted when you do this, because they were saved to the first two Tempo Alternative slots.

6   Select the Piano Audio region in the Audio 1 track.

The audio waveform is displayed in the Beat Mapping track.

7   Click the Analyze button in the Beat Mapping track.

A progress bar appears for the transient-detection process. After the analysis of the selected audio is performed, the detected transients are displayed in the Beat Mapping track as vertical white lines.

NOTE ▶ Depending on your settings, Logic may prompt you asking to confirm if you want to overwrite all previous transients. For the sake of the exercise, click OK.

8   Zoom out horizontally so that you can see the entire track.

Take a close look at the results displayed in the Beat Mapping track. Most of the softer notes were not detected as transients. Fortunately, the detection sensitivity can be adjusted to pick up these softer transients.

9   Drag in the Sensitivity field, scrolling upward, increasing the value.

New transients are detected, providing a better picture of the relevant timing events in the audio file.

TIP ▶ It is advisable to start with a lower Sensitivity setting and switch to a higher setting only if important rhythmic events are not detected.

Now that you have timing events in the Beat Mapping track, you are ready to begin the process of aligning the time grid.

10 Connect related lines in the Beat Mapping track as you did in the previous exercise, moving from left to right for the entire region.

11 When you're finished, play the track with the metronome click to check your results.

> **NOTE** ▸ A premade Tempo track using the audio region as a guide has been provided for comparison in Tempo Alternative slot number 4.

Lesson Review

1. True or false: The timing, pitch, and formants of an audio file can be manipulated independently of the others.

2. Which important aspect of an audio file determines how the Apple Loops Utility manipulates timing?

3. Which two attributes of a Logic project determine how Apple Loops are conformed?

4. Which Logic feature is used to exercise detailed control over an audio file's timing and pitch, irrespective of the project's tempo and key?

5. Which feature of the Time and Pitch Machine lets you adjust the natural resonances (formants) of a given sound?

6. Which global track lets you graphically align Logic's time grid to a rubato part?

7. True or false: Both audio and MIDI regions can be beat mapped.

8. Which menu allows you to toggle between multiple tempo "maps"?

Answers

1. True. The timing, pitch, and formants of an audio file can be changed independently or in combination.

2. Transients. They must be defined accurately through automatic and manual means to achieve the best results when creating Apple Loops.

3. The project's key and tempo determine how Apple Loops are conformed.

4. The Time and Pitch Machine provides detailed control and functions independent of the project's tempo or key.

5. Harmonic Correction is used during pitch shifting to preserve the natural resonances of a given sound.

6. The Beat Mapping track allows the accurate rescaling of the time grid to a rubato part.

7. True. Both audio and MIDI regions can be used as the basis for beat mapping.

8. The Tempo Alternatives menu enables you to toggle among multiple tempo tracks per project.

4

Lesson Files Logic 8_BTB_Files > Lessons > Templates > Advanced Logic.logic
(template created in Lesson 1)

Logic 8_BTB_Files > Lessons > 04_Software Inst_Start.logic

Logic 8_BTB_Files > Lessons > 04_Sculpture_Start.logic

Media Logic 8_BTB_Files > Media > Working with Software Instruments

Logic 8_BTB_Files > Media > Sculpture Tutorial

Time This lesson takes approximately 90 minutes to complete.

Goals Use Logic Pro's suite of software instruments

Program Ultrabeat, Logic Pro's drum synthesizer

Use channel strip settings to recall combinations of instruments and
effects

Use global tracks to create quick arrangements

Incorporate external MIDI hardware into your production

Program Sculpture, Logic Pro's component-modeling synthesizer

Lesson 4
Working with Software Instruments

Logic's palette of software instruments provides a wide array of sound generators for use in professional production. As this list increases, understanding the functions of Logic instruments becomes more and more important in making choices that are suitable to the needs of a project.

In this lesson, you will explore selected instruments that represent each type of sound generator that Logic offers, and you'll learn how best to integrate your external MIDI hardware. In addition, you will try your hand at programming two powerful instruments: Ultrabeat and Sculpture.

Getting Familiar with the Instruments

Logic Pro 8 comes with 13 powerful software instruments (not including the 20 GarageBand instruments) ranging from emulations of vintage instruments to tools that provide revolutionary ways to create and shape sounds. To better understand the unique characteristics of each instrument and its application, it is helpful to group the instruments according to the way they generate sound.

Synthesizers

Instrument	Description	Application suggestions
ES M	Analog-style mono synthesizer	Bass lines, synth leads
ES P	Analog-style polyphonic synthesizer	Brass sounds, pads (eight voices)
ES E	Analog-style polyphonic synthesizer with chorus and ensemble effects	Stringlike pads, ensemble sounds
ES1	Analog-style synthesizer with two oscillators	Basses, leads, percussion
ES2	Versatile analog-style synthesizer offering three oscillators and two filters along with a comprehensive FX modulation section	Evolving pads, leads, basses, rhythmically synchronized sounds
EFM1	Polyphonic (16 voices) FM synthesizer	Bells, digital sounds
EVOC 20 PS	Vocoder with built-in polyphonic synthesizer	Classic vocoder effects
Ultrabeat	Rhythm synthesizer with built-in step sequencer	Analog and sampled percussion
Sculpture	Component-modeling synthesizer	Sound design, organically rich pads and leads

Vintage keyboards

Instrument	Description	Application suggestions
EVP88	Physically modeled electric pianos with built-in effects	Electric pianos (Rhodes, Wurlitzer, Hohner)
EVD6	Physically modeled electric clavinet with built-in effects	Electric clavinets and other physically modeled strings
EVB3	Physically modeled electro-mechanical tonewheel organ with rotating cabinet simulation	Hammond organs

Sampler

Instrument	Description	Application suggestions
EXS24 mkII	24-bit sampler with advanced modulation capabilities, as well as virtual memory for streaming large samples from hard disk	Multipurpose

Understanding the User Interface

Most of Logic's software instruments share interface features that represent how sound is generated and shaped. With synthesizers, it is especially important to trace the signal flow through controls that affect a particular aspect of the sound. Let's look at two instruments in Logic's synthesizer family and compare their interfaces.

1 Choose File > New.

2 The Templates dialog appears. In the left (Collection) pane, click the My Templates button.

3 In the right (Template) pane, click the Advanced Logic Template.

   The template opens, followed by a Save As dialog.

NOTE ▶ If you didn't complete Lesson 1, a version of the template used in this lesson is included in the following folder: Logic 8_BTB_Files > Lessons > Templates > Advanced Logic.logic. In order to do the exercises in this lesson, you must copy the file to the following location on your hard drive: ~/Library/Application Support/Logic/Project Templates.

4 Click the Cancel button.

A new project file opens based on the template. For this exercise, it is not necessary to build a project folder and include assets. By clicking Cancel, you can open up a project file without any links to assets.

5 Select the Inst 1 track.

6 In the Arrange channel strip, click the Instrument slot to open the Instrument Plug-in menu, and choose ES2 (Synthesizer 2) > Stereo.

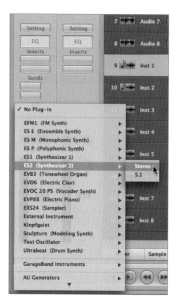

NOTE ▶ Logic's software instruments come in a variety of formats to accommodate mono, stereo, multi output, or even 5.1 projects. The formats available to you depend on the specific instrument.

Look at the ES2's interface and follow the signal flow in this instrument. On the upper-left side, you can see the three oscillators that are an integral part of its sound generation.

Oscillator section   Filter section   Output section

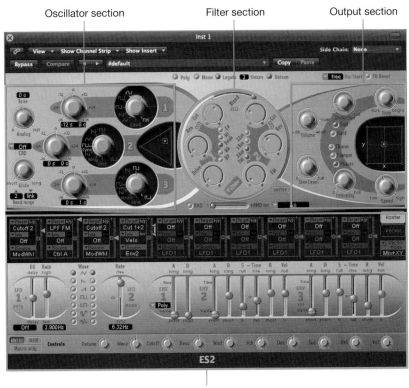

ES2

Modulation section

Surrounding each oscillator are controls for tuning and mixing.

Moving to the right, you find the filter section, where the frequency spectrum of the raw sound is shaped.

At the far right is the output section for the ES2, with controls for volume and effects (distortion, chorus, flanger, and phaser).

Below the main part of the graphical interface is the modulation section, where you can manipulate any of the ES2's controls via any other parameter and real-time input.

7   If needed, click the Link button on the upper left of the ES2 window.

NOTE ▶ Having Link turned on allows you to use a single plug-in window to display selected plug-ins one at a time.

8 Click the Inst 2 track, and from the Instrument Plug-in menu, choose ES1 > Stereo.

NOTE ▶ You might need to move the ES2 plug-in window in order to see the track list.

Now look at the ES1's interface. On the far left are the oscillators, along with controls that directly affect them (octave selection and the mix between the primary oscillator and the sub-oscillator).

Oscillator section   Filter section   Output section

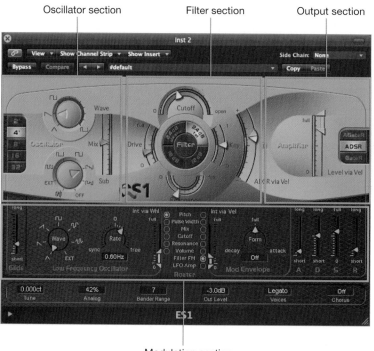

Modulation section

To the right of the oscillator section is the filter section, including the Key slider for controlling the cutoff frequency that is modulated by the keyboard pitch.

Farther to the right is the output section.

At the bottom of the synthesizer is the modulation section.

The interfaces you just looked at are nearly identical; the differences in controls pertain to their unique sound-generation processes. In general, a signal flows from left to right in all of the Logic synthesizers, with sections that closely parallel those in ES1 and ES2.

9 Click the Inst 3 track, and from the Instrument Plug-in menu, choose EXS24 mkII (Sampler) > Stereo.

Note that even though EXS24 mkII is a sampler, it shares many interface characteristics with the ES2 and ES1 synthesizers. It has filter, output, and modulation sections in similar places (the modulation matrix is identical to the ES2's).

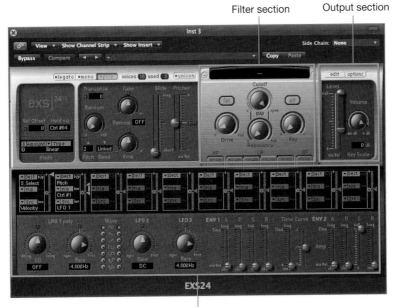

Filter section   Output section

Modulation section

10 Choose File > Close Project.

An alert message appears asking if you want to save the project before closing.

As this project doesn't contain any project data, it is not necessary to save it.

11 Click Don't Save.

Using Ultrabeat

Ultrabeat's inspiration stems from the drum machines of the 1980s as well as the currently popular sample-based hardware groove boxes. Ultrabeat is similar to them in functionality, offering both sound generation and integrated step sequencing.

What truly sets Ultrabeat apart, however, are its multiple sound sources (analog synthesis, FM, audio sample, physical modeling), built-in signal processing (bit crushing, distortion, ring modulation, EQ, and stereo effects), sophisticated step sequencing, and highly flexible sound architecture.

> **NOTE** ▶ Middle C may be designated as either C4 or C3, depending on the manufacturer of your MIDI keyboard. You will need to set the "Display Middle C as" preference to C3 (Yamaha) to accurately follow the directions within this exercise (and others throughout the book). This command can be found in the Preferences > Display > General tab.

1 Choose File > Open.

2 In the file selector box, navigate to Music > Logic 8_BTB_Files > Lessons and open **04_Software Inst_Start.logic**.

3 Select the Inst 1 track if not already selected.

4 Double-click Ultrabeat in the Instrument slot to display the Ultrabeat interface.

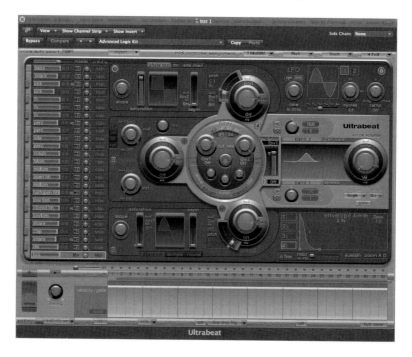

NOTE ▸ The Ultrabeat interface follows the common signal-flow arrangement you looked at in the previous exercise. Oscillators are on the left, feeding into the filter section, and then into the processing/output section on the right.

5   In the upper-left corner of the Ultrabeat window, click the Link button.

6   Play your MIDI controller's keys in the C1 to B2 range to hear the various sounds within the kit.

TIP ▸ When you select a software instrument in the track list for the first time, there might be a slight delay (around 100 milliseconds) at first. This is because Logic does not engage live mode until it receives its first MIDI message. The delay doesn't affect the playback of sequenced material, but it can interfere with live performance and tracking. If you require perfect timing for the first played note, you need to send silent MIDI events in advance (for example, sustain pedal, pitch bend, or modulation wheel).

In addition to two octaves of individually mapped percussion sounds, a kit contains a slot for a sound that is automatically pitch-mapped over three octaves.

7   Play keys C3 and above on your MIDI controller.

You should hear an analog synthesizer bass sound that changes pitch as you move up and down the keyboard.

Working with Drum Sounds

The left side of Ultrabeat's interface contains the Assignment section, which contains the 25 drum sounds of a drum kit and a mixer. Each drum sound has independent parameters that can be adjusted for volume, soloing, muting, pan position, and audio output.

1 Click a few of the drum names (kick, snare, and so on).

The main section of the interface changes with each selected sound. This is because every drum sound has its own independent sound-generation, filter, modulation, processing, and volume settings, which are viewed by clicking its name.

NOTE ▶ The active drum sound has a gray frame surrounding it and its mixer parameters.

2 At the upper left of the interface, click the Voice Auto Select On/Off button so that voice auto select is turned on.

3 Play a few notes in the C1 to B2 range, as you did earlier.

The interface changes with each new note played. When voice auto select is on, the most current note triggered is displayed.

4   Select the kick drum by clicking the name or playing the appropriate MIDI note (C1) on your MIDI controller.

TIP ▶ If you do not have a MIDI controller, try clicking the onscreen musical keyboard to the left of the drum name to audition the sound in the Ultrabeat window.

5   In the main part of the interface, look at the top oscillator (Osc1).

It is the only oscillator currently active (the power button at the left is lit), so it is responsible for generating the raw sound that makes up the kick drum.

The oscillator is set to Phase Osc, which uses the Slope, Saturation, and Asymmetry controls to shape the waveform into almost any basic synthesizer waveform.

6   Drag the Saturation control all the way down to 0.00.

The waveform changes slowly from a square wave to a slightly rounded triangle.

7   Repeatedly press the C1 key on your MIDI controller while you drag the Saturation control slowly upward until it reaches the top (1.00).

You can hear the sound change as you transition toward the square wave.

This kick drum needs less "beater" (midrange click) to suit the project you will be working with. You can move to the EQ controls in the processing section of Ultrabeat to see how you can change the sound.

8   Look to the right side of the instrument (immediately to the right of the filter section) to find the EQ controls.

Note that the kick drum sound has a slight parametric dip at 170 Hz and a rather large boost centered at 1600 Hz.

9   Position the Pointer tool over the large peak (band 2).

The peak is highlighted, and a dot appears at the apex.

If you are familiar with Logic's Channel EQ, you'll recognize the same graphical controls for adjusting the EQ band.

10 Drag the peak to the right.

The peak moves along with the mouse movement.

11 Drag the dot at the apex of the peak up and down.

The bandwidth narrows and expands accordingly.

12 Click the Band 2 button to bypass band 2 of the EQ.

The large peak disappears.

13 Audition the kick by clicking the musical keyboard to the left of the Assignment section or playing your MIDI controller (C1).

The kick now has less midrange attack.

14 Select the crash cymbal by clicking the name or playing C♯2 on your MIDI controller.

15 In the main part of the interface, look at the bottom oscillator (Osc2).

The power button is on, and Oscillator 2 is set to Sample. In the Oscillator 2 section, you'll also see an audio waveform display.

The crash cymbal in this kit is generated from an audio sample. Oscillator 2 can be configured for all three types of sound generation offered by Ultrabeat: phase oscillator, sample playback, and even component modeling.

16 To try out the other sound-generation modes offered, click the Phase Osc and Model buttons.

17 Switch back to Sample mode.

The waveform returns.

The crash sample (**Crash 19.ubs**, displayed above the waveform) doesn't work for the project you will be building for this lesson. Let's load a new sample waveform.

18 Click the disclosure triangle next to the sample's name and choose Load Sample from the pop-up menu.

A file selector box appears, displaying the contents of the Ultrabeat Samples folder.

NOTE ▶ The Load Sample command automatically brings you to the location where Logic Pro installed the default Ultrabeat samples (Library/Application Support/Logic/Ultrabeat Samples). This makes it easy to browse samples specially designed for use in Ultrabeat.

19 Double-click the Crash Cymbals folder and choose **Special Crash.ubs**.

NOTE ▶ The .ubs extension signifies a proprietary sample format that has multiple velocity layers built into the file. Although no user-accessible way exists to create files in the .ubs format, you can import velocity-mapped EXS instruments by clicking the Import button at the top of the Ultrabeat window.

20 Click the Open button.

21 Play the C♯2 key on your MIDI controller, or click the musical keyboard to the left of the Assignment section to audition the crash.

You should hear a higher-sounding cymbal.

TIP ▶ You can import your own samples (.aif, .wav, etc.) by dragging them directly to the waveform display in Oscillator 2.

22 Drag the blue volume slider (around the name of the crash sound) to the right until the help tag reads *3.0dB*.

This is the volume control for the sound.

23 Hold down the pan knob in the mini crash mixer, and drag the Pointer tool down until the help tag reads *–0.45*.

The sound is panned further to the left side of the stereo field.

24 Audition the sound to hear the results.

Working with the Step Sequencer

At the bottom of Ultrabeat's interface is an integrated 32-step sequencer that greatly aids in the production of drum loops and beat patterns. These patterns, including any user-created patterns, are saved within each of the Ultrabeat settings.

1 Turn on the sequencer by clicking the power button at the upper left of the sequencer.

2 Click the Play/Stop button located immediately to the right of the power button.

The sequencer starts and Ultrabeat plays a sequenced pattern.

NOTE ▶ Ultrabeat's sequencer has independent playback in relation to the project. As long as Ultrabeat's sequencer is powered on, it will automatically start when the project is played. Ultrabeat will read the project's tempo, ensuring tight synchronization.

3 At the lower-left corner of the Ultrabeat window, click to open the Pattern pop-up menu and choose various patterns, listening to the results.

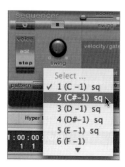

You'll notice that slots with sequence data recorded are marked with *sq* (for *sequence*). Looking at the list for this drum kit (Advanced Logic Kit), we see that there are patterns contained only within the first 5 of a possible 24 slots; the rest are available for user-programmed patterns.

NOTE ▸ Each slot is assigned an associated note value (pitch and octave) that is displayed in parentheses. You will be using these MIDI note values to trigger sequence playback later in this lesson.

4 From the Pattern menu, choose "1 (C–1) sq."

5 In the Ultrabeat interface, click the Play/Stop button to stop pattern playback.

Sequencing Sounds

The actual sequencing of a given sound takes place in an area called the step grid. Here, events can be graphically inserted and edited to create each element of the pattern.

1 Select the snare drum sound (D1).

The snare sound's sequence is displayed in the step grid.

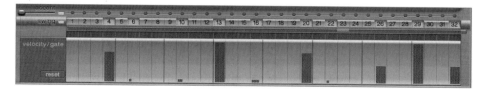

2   To the right of the drum name, click the Solo (S) button to solo the snare drum.

NOTE ▶ The *sq* next to the name indicates that this sound has a step sequence within the current pattern.

3   Click the step sequencer's Play/Stop button to play the pattern.

The snare sound is triggered whenever an event is displayed in the step grid.

4   Click the 2 button above the step grid.

This array of buttons is called the trigger row.

The next time the pattern cycles, you should hear a soft snare attack on step 2.

5   Drag up the event at step 2 in the step grid until the event stretches to the top.

The next time the pattern reaches this step, the event will be louder.

6   Click the Solo button for the snare drum to hear the entire pattern (with all drum sounds).

NOTE ▶ Step width indicates the length (gate time) of the notes in the trigger row. In this case, the sound being triggered has an extremely short release, so this parameter does not audibly affect the sound.

Applying Swing to the Pattern

The Swing knob, located to the left of the step grid, lets you adjust the rhythmic feel of the pattern by increasing the distance between notes. Notes on odd-numbered steps remain unchanged, while even-numbered notes are slightly shifted. This control affects all drum sounds that have swing enabled in the pattern (different swing amounts cannot be assigned to sounds individually).

1   While the sequencer is playing, drag the Swing knob up and down to adjust the value.

Listen to the results.

2   To the left of the trigger row, click the Swing button to turn off swing for the snare part.

The snare drum sequence's "feel" changes in relation to the rest of the drum sounds in the pattern.

3   Click the Swing button to turn on swing again for the snare drum.

4   Drag the Swing knob, setting the swing value back to about 58%.

5   Stop playback of the pattern.

Copying a Sequence Part from One Sound to Another

The pattern you are working with uses a different kick drum sound (A$\sharp$2) from the one you edited in an earlier exercise (C1). In this exercise, you want to use the same sequence part but have it trigger the kick you edited. You can do this by copying and pasting the sequence data from one sound to another.

When creating or editing step sequences for multiple sounds, it is advisable to use the full-view function, which displays all sounds at once within the Ultrabeat window.

1   In the lower-right corner of the Ultrabeat interface, click the Full View button.

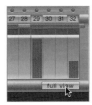

The interface switches to a graphical view of each drum sound's trigger row.

2   Near the top of the interface (A♯2), click the kick drum sound.

In essence, each row of triggers represents the data created in the step grid, and vice versa.

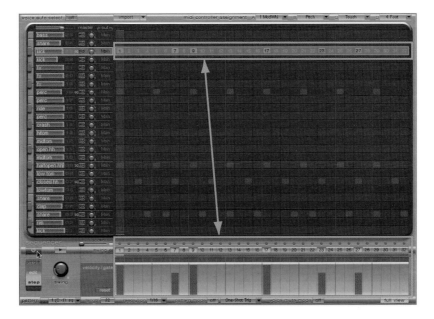

NOTE ▶ Although full view works great for creating triggers while referencing other sounds, you can adjust only velocity and gate time within the step grid.

3   Control-click the kick drum trigger row within the step grid.

A menu appears containing sound-trigger editing commands.

4   Choose Copy.

5   At the bottom of the track list (C1), Control-click the kick drum trigger row in the step grid and choose Paste.

TIP▶   This menu contains many handy tools for quickly generating and editing step sequences for individual sounds.

6   Click the Mute (M) button next to the kick drum that you just copied from (A♯2) to mute the original kick drum sequence.

7   Play the pattern.

The kick drum sequence now triggers the kick you want in addition to the original sound (which is muted).

Automating Parameters in Step Mode

Ultrabeat not only lets you program sound triggers via step sequencing but also lets you do the same for each sound's parameters. This mode, called Step mode, provides step-by-step automation of any sound-shaping control within the synthesizer.

1   Click the Full View button to return to the sound-editing controls.

    NOTE ▶ You cannot work within Step mode if full view is turned on.

2   Click Step on the bottom part of the Edit Mode switch located in the lower left of the interface.

The sound-editing area darkens, and, in the synthesizer, yellow frames appear around all of the parameters that are available for automation. In addition, the step grid changes to display parameter offset instead of velocity/gate.

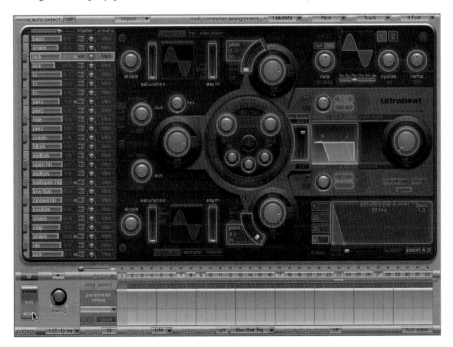

When in Step mode, the step grid is used to effect changes to the yellow highlighted parameters by offsetting the current sound settings.

3 Click the percussion (perc) sound (or play F2 on your MIDI controller) to display the parameters for the tambourine part.

For this exercise, you will be offsetting the pitch of the active oscillator (Osc 2) by changing the speed of the tambourine sample.

NOTE ▶ When you click on a control, you define the target parameter for Step mode.

4 Click the pitch control for Oscillator 2.

5 Click within the step select row for step 5, right below the trigger row.

6 Drag the Pitch control for Oscillator 2 down to B0.

Notice that the step grid displays your adjustment as a negative offset (below center line) to the original pitch (C3). This offset is expressed as a percentage.

NOTE ▶ The parameter offset now displays *Osc2 Pitch* in the Offset menu, which is the parameter you are changing. This menu enables you to toggle between sequenced parameters for a single sound while in Step mode.

7   Click in the step grid for step 9, and drag the value bar down until you reach a value of –32% (the pitch D0 appears in Oscillator 2).

8   Using either of the techniques you just explored, change Oscillator 2's pitch for steps 17 and 25, to F0 and B–1, respectively.

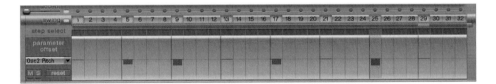

9   Play the sequence, and stop when you've heard the results.

The pitch of the tambourine sample changes for the altered steps.

10   Click the Mute button located at the lower left of the step grid.

This control enables you to mute the currently displayed parameter offsets, returning the part back to its unaltered state.

TIP ▶ When creating offsets in Step mode, you may decide that you want to make a quick change in the original drum sound. To quickly do this without losing your momentum, press Option-Command to temporarily toggle Ultrabeat back into Voice mode.

11   Click the Edit Mode switch to return to Voice mode.

Triggering Patterns Using MIDI

Now that you have done some work on an existing pattern, you can incorporate it into the project. Each pattern in Ultrabeat can be triggered via an incoming or recorded MIDI note; this allows the starting and stopping of patterns on the fly (especially advantageous for live performances).

1   At the bottom of the window, click the Pattern Mode Off button.

The button now displays the On state.

This enables Ultrabeat to receive incoming MIDI data as pattern triggers.

2   To the immediate right, click the triangle button to open the Playback Mode menu, and choose Sustain.

This menu lets you choose how the pattern will be triggered with incoming MIDI notes. Since you have selected Sustain, the pattern will repeat as long as you have the key depressed.

3   Play the C–1 through E–1 keys on your MIDI controller, holding down each for a short period of time.

NOTE ▶ The specific trigger notes were chosen because they are located far below the most commonly used range on a MIDI keyboard. You may have to transpose your MIDI controller (using its octave buttons) to activate the pattern triggers. You can double-check your octave range in the the Transport's MIDI Activity display at the bottom of the screen.

A different pattern is triggered for each key depressed.

Look at the Pattern menu you accessed earlier. Each pattern has a number designating the slot, as well as a MIDI note number (in parentheses) next to it. The MIDI note number indicates which incoming MIDI note will trigger which pattern.

Recording with Ultrabeat

Now you can create a drum track by using pattern triggers in conjunction with individual sound triggers.

1   Close the Ultrabeat interface.

The Inst 1 track that has Ultrabeat instantiated has a blank MIDI region that you will use for your part.

2   Select the blank MIDI region on track 1, and at the bottom of the Arrange window, click the Piano Roll button.

The Piano Roll Editor opens.

TIP ▶ You can set a preference that allows you to open the Piano Roll Editor (or any other editor) by double-clicking a MIDI region; then choose Preferences > Global > Editing, and go to the "Double-clicking a MIDI region opens" menu.

3   Zoom out horizontally so that you can see about 16 bars in the timeline, and approximately C–1 to C3 on the piano keyboard at the left of the editor.

4   Select the Pencil tool and draw in a C♯–1 note that starts on measure 1 and lasts for eight bars.

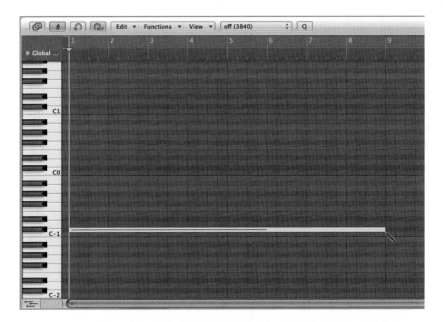

This triggers pattern number 2.

NOTE ▶ When the MIDI Out button is turned on (by default), Logic will send data to the track instrument.

5 Draw a C–1 note at measure 9 lasting four bars.

This triggers pattern number 1, the one you edited.

NOTE ▶ Logic automatically inserts a note with a length based on the last note entered. However, you can create a new note of any duration by selecting the Pencil tool and dragging the note horizontally until the correct length is reached.

6 Draw a C♯2 note at measure 13 for four bars.

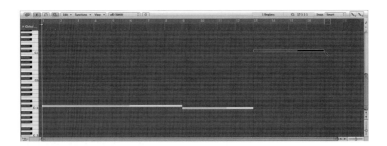

This is the crash cymbal you edited earlier.

TIP ▶ Logic should create another note with a length equal to the previous one (four bars). Logic always inserts events by using the last created event as the length and velocity default.

7 Close the Piano Roll Editor.

8 Play the project.

You just created a drum part stringing together two patterns (C♯–1 and C-1) and a triggered sound (crash cymbal).

TIP ▶ If you would like to edit Ultrabeat's patterns within Logic's many MIDI editors, you can drag the button immediately to the left of the Pattern menu and drop it anywhere in the Arrange area. The pattern will then be copied as an individual region, ready for editing, processing, or looping.

Routing Individual Sounds for Processing

There are times when you might want to process individual aspects of the kit separately, applying different compression and reverb to individual sounds. For instance, the kick oftentimes needs dynamic and ambient treatment different from what the snare drum, cymbals, or toms need. To handle this, you need to isolate the kick drum on its own channel for individual processing. Fortunately, Ultrabeat allows you to route individual sounds through separate virtual "outputs" to accomplish just that.

To use this special function, you need to instantiate Ultrabeat as a multi output instrument. So far you've been working with Ultrabeat as a stereo instrument and have done quite a bit of work modifying sounds and patterns. Luckily, Logic allows you to keep all of the current settings when changing from stereo to multi output instantiations.

> **NOTE** ▶ This holds true for any software instrument: all settings and content contained in a software instrument will be transferred when switching modes (mono, stereo, multi output, and 5.1).

1 Open the Mixer by clicking the button at the bottom of the Arrange window.

2 On the Inst 1 channel strip, click-hold the Instrument slot to open the Instrument Plug-in menu and choose Ultrabeat (Drum Synth) > Multi Output (8xStereo, 8xMono).

The Ultrabeat interface opens after reloading the associated samples and current settings.

3 To the right of the kick drum (C1) Panorama knob, click to open the Output Selection menu and choose 17.

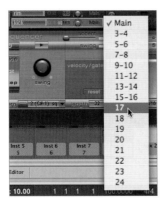

NOTE ▸ The first eight selections represent stereo routings, and the last eight selections represent mono. You are choosing the first mono routing (17) to send a mono sound (the kick drum).

If necessary, move the Ultrabeat window so you can see the Inst 1 channel strip.

4   Just under the Solo button, click the small plus button (+) on the Inst 1 channel strip.

A new Aux 3 channel strip is created immediately to the right of the Inst 1 channel strip. This will be the receiving channel for our kick drum. Notice that the new Aux 3 channel strip that Logic creates is a stereo one. You will need to make it mono in order to receive a mono send from the multi output instrument.

NOTE ▸ By default, Logic creates an aux channel with the default stereo input of 3-4 for the associated multi output instrument.

5   At the bottom of the Aux 3 channel strip, click the Format button.

6   Click-hold to open the Input slot menu for the Aux 3 channel strip and choose Inst 1 >
UB 17.

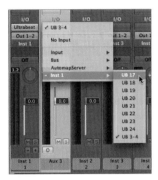

7   Play the project.

The kick drum now plays through the Aux 3 channel. Already the kick sounds better,
as the new routing allows a dry signal to be sent without being affected by the send
on the original Ultrabeat channel. With this routing in place, you can easily continue
refining the kick drum sound by inserting separate compression and EQ on the Aux 3
channel.

8   Close the Mixer.

9   Close the Ultrabeat window.

TIP ▶ The EXS24 mkII sampler also has multi output capability and can output
separate zones and groups through stereo or mono routings.

Using the EXS24 mkII Software Sampler

Hands down, the EXS24 mkII is Logic Pro's most versatile tool. With 24-bit audio resolution,
virtual memory for streaming samples from disk, and an advanced modulation matrix, the
EXS24 mkII is a full-featured sampler that can serve as a workhorse for your productions.

To best utilize the EXS24 mkII, you must understand how it functions. Sound generation
in this sampler consists of three main components: samples, sampler instruments, and
playback parameters. Samples are basically standard digital audio files that are organized
into sampler instruments, which are then triggered and processed.

In the following exercises, you will examine each of the main components that create and play back EXS24 mkII sounds.

Opening the EXS24 mkII Instrument Editor

1   Select the Inst 2 track.

2   In the Arrange channel strip, click the Instrument slot to open the Instrument Plug-in menu and choose EXS24 mkII (Sampler) > Mono.

The EXS24 mkII interface opens.

3   Click to open the Sampler Instruments menu, and choose 02 Bass > 02 Electric Bass > Fretless Electric Bass.

The EXS24 mkII takes a moment to load the samples into RAM.

NOTE ▶   While the EXS24 mkII needs to load a sampler instrument in order to use its playback functions, it can output a simple sine wave without an instrument being loaded. This allows you to determine if the EXS24 mkII is functioning correctly without having to load an instrument.

4   Play your MIDI keyboard to audition the Fretless Electric Bass instrument.

NOTE ▶   If you used the octave transposition buttons of your MIDI controller to play the Ultrabeat patterns earlier in this lesson, you will need to transpose up to play in the Fretless Electric Bass range. Use the MIDI display in the Transport bar to check your range.

5   To the right of the Sampler Instruments menu, click the Edit button.

The EXS24 mkII Instrument Editor opens.

NOTE ▸ Depending on the size of your display, you might need to resize the EXS24 Instrument Editor to see all of the available information.

The EXS24 Instrument Editor allows you to peek into the construction of the Fretless Electric Bass sampler instrument. Let's get familiar with the areas within the editor. The Instrument Editor has two views: Zones and Groups. The following screen shot shows the Zones view.

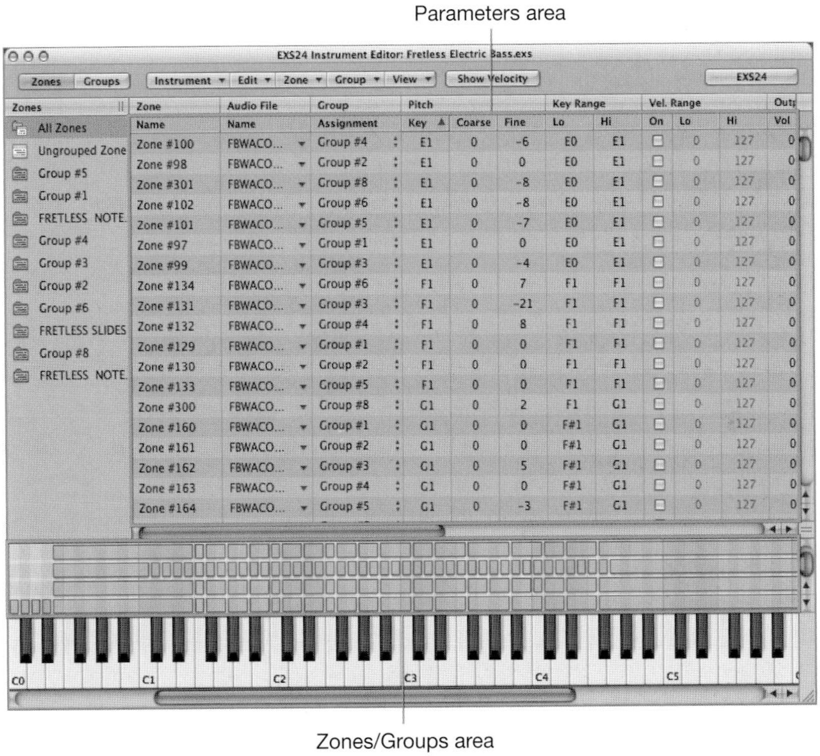

Parameters area

Zones/Groups area

The bottom portion of the window (in the Zones view it is the Zones area) contains the key mapping for each sample. Each gray bar, called a zone, represents a single audio file that is mapped across a range of keys (represented graphically by the piano keyboard at the bottom). These zones can then be assigned into groups, which offer additional control over multiple zones via their own parameters.

NOTE ▶ Groups that you create are displayed in the Zones column on the far left. You can display the zones associated with a group by selecting the group in this column. This functionality mirrors iTunes' playlists, down to the ability of dragging and dropping zones into groups.

For each zone, the EXS24 mkII automatically pitch-shifts the audio in relation to the pitch of the keyboard. Zones with the same key range are stacked vertically and can be triggered simultaneously (in layers) or separately, depending on MIDI velocity. Generally, the zones at the bottom are triggered at lower velocities, and the upper zones at higher velocities.

Take a detailed look at one of the zones.

6 In the lower left of the Zones area, click the zone that starts on E0 and ends on E1 (see the following figure).

The top portion of the Instrument Editor contains the parameters for each of the zones depicted below. The zone you select in the Zones area will be highlighted in the list of zones in the Parameters area.

TIP ▶ To use your MIDI controller to select zones, choose Zone > Select Zone of Last Played Key. This is similar to Ultrabeat's Voice Auto Select function that you used earlier in the lesson.

Each zone is listed with a set of parameters (pitch, key range, velocity range, volume, pan, and so on) that control how the audio file will be played. You can also view the audio file referenced by the zone for further editing and for setting loop points.

7 In the Audio File column for Zone #101, click the disclosure triangle (this is the zone that you selected by clicking in the Zones area), and choose Open in Sample Editor.

The Sample Editor opens, displaying the audio file used in the zone (**FBWACO1E1X05.aif**).

NOTE ▶ You might get an alert message stating that the audio file does not have suffi-cient access privileges to save an overview. Go ahead and click OK, as this won't keep you from looking at the file.

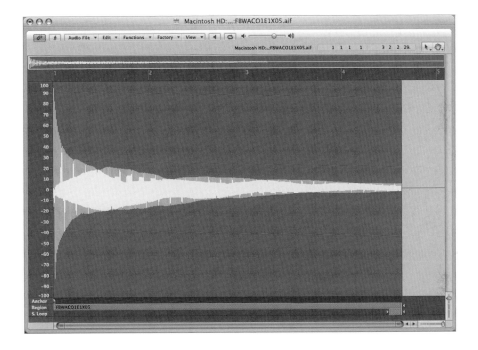

8 Close the EXS24 and EXS Instrument Editor window (which might be obstructing the view).

NOTE ▶ You may need to resize the Sample Editor window or drag the zoom sliders to see the entire sound wave.

You now can see a detailed depiction of the audio file used by the selected zone. This illustrates the total integration of the EXS24 mkII with Logic Pro; you can edit samples without ever leaving Logic.

9 Click the Play button located at the top of the window.

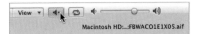

A single bass note sounds.

10 Close the Sample Editor.

> **TIP** ▶ Double-clicking an audio file within a zone also opens the audio file in the Sample Editor.

Processing a Sampler Instrument

Now that you've seen how a sampler instrument is constructed, look at how the EXS24 mkII's controls can shape and process the sampler instrument.

1 Reopen the EXS24 mkII interface by double-clicking EXS24 mkII in the Arrange channel strip's Instrument slot.

2 While playing your MIDI controller, drag the Cutoff knob in the filter section, listening to the results.

By default, the Filter mode is set for a low pass (12 dB), so you get a gradual roll-off of some of the high frequencies by reducing the cutoff value.

You could easily continue to sculpt the sound using the instrument's controls, adjusting the volume envelope, adding distortion, applying low-frequency oscillators to modulate parameters, and so on. This is similar to the way you would work with a subtractive synthesizer, but here you would use the sampler instrument as the sound-generation source instead of a generated raw waveform.

3 In the Transport bar, click the Solo button.

This will enable you to hear one part at a time while you work with the various instruments.

4 Play the project, listening to how the part plays through the EXS24 mkII.

Using the EVP88 Vintage Electric Piano

The EVP88 (like the other instruments in the vintage keyboards line, the EVD6 and EVB3) is a physically modeled instrument dedicated to simulating the sounds of classic electric pianos such as the Fender Rhodes, Wurlitzer 200A, and Hohner Electra. The instrument generates its sound not by triggering samples, but by using complex algorithms that recreate a physical event occurring in the real world. Basically, the EVP88 simulates the physical movement of the various electric piano reeds, tines, and tone bars in the electric and magnetic fields of the pickups found in the original instruments. The result is an extremely accurate and playable instrument that synthesizes the ringing, smacking, and bell-like transients of the attack phase, as well as the hammer action and damper noises.

In this exercise you will load, audition, and then modify a stock sound, listening to the results.

1   Select the Inst 3 track.

2   In the Arrange channel strip, click the Instrument slot to open the Instrument Plug-in menu and choose EVP88 (Electric Piano) > Stereo.

The EVP88 interface opens.

3   Play your MIDI keyboard to audition the instrument.

4   To the left side of the instrument, click the Open disclosure triangle.

Additional controls are revealed, including the Model dial, which enables you to select an electric piano model.

When instantiated, the EVP88 defaults to the SuitcaseMkI model (based on the Fender Rhodes Suitcase MkI), with somewhat generic settings. You can add character to the sound via the EVP88's built-in effects section, which contains processing that has become closely associated with classic recordings of electric piano sounds.

5   Drag the EQ parameter's Bass knob, and lower the Bass EQ a few decibels.

6   Drag the Drive parameter's Gain knob, and raise its level to about 16.

This should add some bite to the sound.

7   Drag the Phaser parameter's Rate and Color knobs, bringing them up a few notches to activate the stereo phaser to your liking.

8   Play the project, listening to the electric piano part (and effects) through the EVP88.

Using the EVD6 Vintage Clavinet

The EVD6 is also a physically modeled instrument, accurately recreating the sound of the classic Hohner D6 electric clavinet, from the buzzing of the strings and key clicks right down to the pickup configuration.

For this exercise, you will load a setting and modify it by using the EVD6's built-in effects to customize the sound.

1   Select the Inst 4 track.

2   In the Arrange channel strip, click the Instrument slot to open the Instrument Plug-in menu and choose EVD6 (Electric Clav) > Stereo.

    The EVD6 interface opens.

3   Click to open the Settings menu and choose 01 Clean Clav > Low Stiff Clav.

4   Play your MIDI keyboard to audition the instrument.

    The EVD6 also has a complementary effects section, complete with distortion, modulation effects (phaser, flanger, chorus), and wah.

5 At the top of the wah section (upper-right side), click to open the Wah Mode pop-up menu (it currently reads Off) and choose ResoLP.

This activates a resonant low-pass wah.

6 Drag the Envelope knob up to a value of 2.600.

7 Play the project to hear the part (and effects) through the EVD6.

TIP You can rearrange the order of the EVD6 effects signal chain using the FX Order buttons below the effects section (D = Distortion, M = Modulation, and W = Wah).

Using the EFM 1 FM Synthesizer

The EFM 1 is a digital synthesizer that uses frequency modulation to generate sound (that is, one oscillator's audible frequency modulates another, creating new harmonics). The EFM 1, like its famous FM predecessor, the Yamaha DX7, excels at producing metallic timbres such as bells.

1 Select the Inst 5 track.

2 In the Arrange channel strip, click the Instrument slot to open the Instrument Plug-in menu and choose EFM1 (FM Synth) > Stereo.

The EFM 1 interface opens.

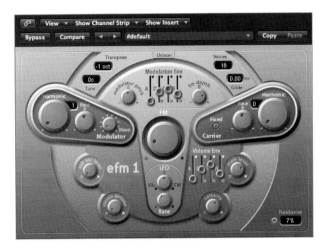

3   Click to open the Settings menu and choose 06 FM Bells > Bell Swarm.

4   Play your MIDI keyboard to audition the instrument.

NOTE ▶ The track is panned to the far left side of the stereo field.

5   In the center of the interface, drag the FM (Intensity) knob up to increase the amount of frequency modulation between the modulator oscillator and the carrier oscillator.

The amount of harmonics increases.

6   Return the FM (Intensity) knob to about the 8 o'clock position to return it back to its previous setting.

7   Play the project to hear the part through the EFM 1.

Using the ES1 Virtual Analog Synthesizer

The ES1 was the first software instrument developed exclusively for Logic, kicking off a development surge that led to the multitude of instruments currently available in Logic Pro. It was specifically designed to emulate the subtractive synthesis of vintage analog synthesizers.

1   Select the Inst 6 track.

2   In the Arrange channel strip, click the Instrument slot to open the Instrument Plug-in menu and choose ES1 (Synthesizer 1) > Mono.

The ES1 interface opens.

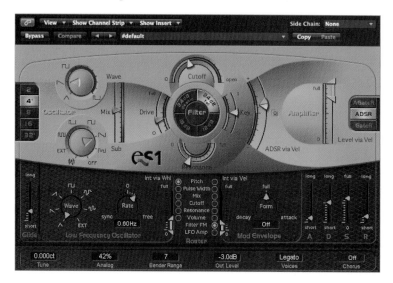

3 Click to open the Settings menu and choose 01 Synth Leads > Vintage Classic.

4 Play your MIDI keyboard to audition the instrument.

Like the vintage instruments that inspired the ES1, the synthesizer has no dedicated effects section. One of the distinct advantages to using software instruments in Logic is the ability to add effects to the generated sound and create new combinations.

5 Click to open the topmost Insert slot pop-up menu in the Arrange channel strip and choose Delay > Tape Delay > Mono.

The Tape Delay plug-in opens.

6   Play your MIDI keyboard to hear the instrument through the Tape Delay plug-in.

The echo time sounds good, but you need fewer repeats at a lower volume.

7   At the far left of the Tape Delay window, drag the Feedback slider down to about 16%, reducing the number of repeated echoes.

8   At the opposite end of the plug-in window, drag the Wet slider down to about 19%, adjusting the amount of wet signal.

9   Play the project to hear the part through the ES1 with the tape delay.

Using the ES2 Synthesizer

The ES2 is a versatile and comprehensive synthesizer capable of a great range of sounds. From large-sounding leads to evolving pads, classic analog waveforms to digital wave-forms and FM, the ES2 offers a wide array of tools for synthesizer enthusiasts.

1   Select the Inst 7 track.

2   In the Arrange channel strip, click the Instrument slot to open the Instrument Plug-in menu and choose ES2 (Synthesizer 2) > Stereo.

The ES2 interface opens.

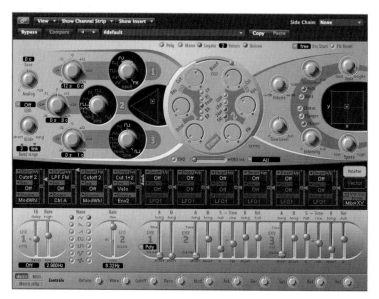

 The Macro controls of the ES2 are new to Logic Pro 8. These appear in their own area at the bottom of the interface and provide easy access to common controls used in performance. Of special note are the Cutoff and Resonance (Reso) controls, which simultaneously affect both of the ES2's filters.

Using Instrument Channel Strip Settings

In the previous ES1 exercise, you added a delay effect to enhance the sound. As the combinations of instruments and effects become more involved, it grows tedious to reinsert every component in the chain each time you wish to use that same sound combination. Using Logic Pro's channel strip settings, you can create and recall settings that contain instrument and effects choices within a single preset.

Logic Pro installs many channel strip settings that fully utilize Logic Pro's effects and instruments to achieve powerful combinations. This is not unlike the technique utilized by hardware synthesizers that can combine synthesized sound with effects sections to create new and exciting sounds. You can think of instrument channel strip settings as a single *patch* that happens to use multiple components.

1 In the Arrange channel strip, click the Setting button to open the Channel Strip Settings menu and choose 05 Synthesizers > 02 Synth Pads > Tsunami Jet.

The following plug-ins are instantiated:

By recalling a single channel strip setting, you instantiated a combination of an ES2 synthesizer with phaser, overdrive, and Channel EQ components to further enhance the sound.

2 Play your MIDI keyboard to hear the combination.

3 Play the project to hear the part through the ES2 combination.

4 Close the ES2 window.

Using Global Tracks to Create a Quick Arrangement

Software instruments offer the malleability of MIDI with real-time generated audio output. You can compose, perform, arrange, and edit as if you were working with external MIDI hardware. This flexibility also carries over to Logic Pro's global tracks (such as the

Chord track and Signature track), which let you graphically view and edit global parameters for the project.

In this exercise, you will use the global tracks to make a quick arrangement using software instruments.

1   Click the Solo button in the Transport bar to turn off Solo mode.

2   Play the project to hear all parts.

> **TIP** If your computer is unable to play the project with all the instruments enabled (due to system overload errors), freeze some of the tracks before playing the project by selecting their respective Track Freeze buttons.

Note that the Signature track at the top of the Arrange area (just below the Bar ruler) is set for D minor, the key of the project. Since the project has a modal feel (Dorian mode on D), let's create a quick arrangement by changing to E-flat minor (transposing up a semitone) at a certain point within the project.

3   Click the disclosure triangle in the Chord track.

4   In the Chord track, use the Pencil tool to insert a chord event at measure 9.

An alert message appears.

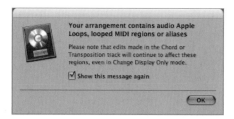

This is a warning to indicate that any changes in the Chord (or Transposition) track will have an effect on Apple Loops, MIDI regions, and aliases. Since this is what you are trying to achieve, it is fine to click OK and close the alert message.

5   Click OK.

The Define Chord window opens.

6   In the Root Note menu, choose D♯ (enharmonic to E♭).

7   In the Chord Type menu, choose Minor.

The topmost window should display E♭ m.

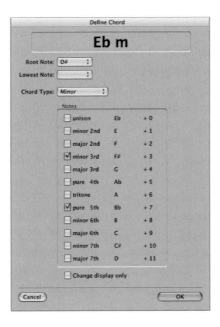

8   Click OK.

The Chord track now has an E♭ minor chord inserted at measure 9.

Note that the Transposition track now displays a +1 event at measure 9, correspon-ding to the chord change (up one semitone).

9   Insert another chord event at measure 13, this time creating a return to the D minor chord.

10   Play the project to hear the new arrangement.

All instruments respond to the transposition as if they were classic MIDI instruments.

NOTE ▶ If you froze the tracks earlier, you will have to refreeze them by de-selecting the Freeze buttons, then selecting them again to effect the key change. This is because when freezing a track, Logic creates and caches 32-bit audio files that are literally a recording of the part (and effects) through the instrument. During playback, this file is read from the disk. If changes are made to the part (such as transposition) after the freeze, you must create new freeze files that incorporate the change.

11 Choose File > Save As.

The Save Document As dialog opens.

12 In the Save As field, enter *04_Software Instr_Finish*.

13 In the file selector box, save the file to Music > Logic 8_BTB_Files > Lessons > Completed.

NOTE ▶ The Include Assets checkbox need not be selected in this situation, unless you want to transport the EXS24 mkII and Ultrabeat samples to another machine or account.

14 Click Save.

15 Choose File > Close Project.

Sound Design with Sculpture

Sculpture, one of the newer instruments offered in Logic Pro 8, represents a unique approach to synthesis. It uses sophisticated algorithms to recreate the way sound is generated in the natural world. Specifically, it simulates the characteristics of a vibrating string or bar. This technique is called component modeling, and it closely mirrors the sound generation found in Logic's vintage keyboard instruments (EVP88, EVD6, and EVB3).

One way to wrap your head around Sculpture is to imagine a synthesizer that lets you control how all the components of a real "physical" instrument interact, and what materials they are made from. In effect, you are building a physical instrument from scratch!

Because Sculpture is so innovative, many people have difficulty approaching it, not knowing how to begin designing sounds and editing settings. In the next exercise, you will walk through the key components of Sculpture and create a sound from scratch.

1   Choose File > Open.

2   In the file selector box, navigate to Music > Logic 8_BTB_Files > Lessons, and open the **04_Sculpture_Start.logic** project.

You will use this project for the exercise.

Understanding the String

In Sculpture, the central synthesis element is called the *string*. This is a bit of a misnomer because the basic physical material can also be similar to a bar (a solid mass). The principle is the same, however: sound is generated only by performing a physical action on, or stimulating, the raw material—striking, picking, blowing, and so on.

1   If you have not done so already, select the Inst 1 track.

2   In the Arrange channel strip, click the Instrument slot to open the Instrument Plug-in menu and choose Sculpture (Modeling Synth) > Stereo.

The Sculpture window opens.

NOTE ▶ Although Sculpture's synthesis model is unique, it still follows the software instrument interface conventions noted earlier: signal flow is from left to right, with modulation at the bottom.

3 Control-click the string (the green horizontal line at the far left) to turn on string animation.

4 Play your MIDI controller.

The string animates, depicting its vibration. This is an effective tool when you're programming sounds with Sculpture, as it provides visual feedback reflecting how your choices are affecting the string.

TIP ▶ When you are using Sculpture for playback (and not editing or programming sounds), it is a good idea to disable string animation because it uses some CPU time to generate the animation. Turn the animation on and off by Control-clicking the string (it is off by default).

Using the Material Pad in the center of the interface, you can construct the string by blending the properties of four basic materials: steel, nylon, wood, and glass.

5 Drag the ball in the Material Pad around the square while playing your MIDI controller. Note how the string animation changes.

The sound also changes as you move the ball, modifying the Inner Loss (damping) and Stiffness (rigidity) of the material.

6   Position the ball about halfway between nylon and steel at the far left edge of the
Material Pad.

The outside ring of the Material Pad contains additional parameters that determine
the sound-making properties of the selected material.

7   Try dragging the Media Loss slider, listening to the sound by playing your MIDI controller, eventually settling on a value of about 0.25.

Media Loss controls the damping of the string caused by its environment. Imagine a
string vibrating in air, water, or pea soup to visualize what this parameter does.

8   Drag the Resolution slider, listening to the sound by playing your MIDI controller,
eventually settling on a value of about 55.

The material's resolution has to do with the number of harmonics generated. The
higher the value, the richer and more complex the sound as more overtones are produced. Be aware that higher resolution values carry a higher CPU load.

9 Drag the Tension Mod(ulation) slider, listening to the sound by playing your MIDI controller, eventually settling on a value of about 0.25.

The Tension Mod control adds pitch displacement of the string to higher note velocities. This is similar to the slight initial pitch change that occurs when you strongly pluck a stringed instrument.

Using Objects in Sculpture

Sculpture has three objects that determine how the string is excited or disturbed (how it is played). Remember that physical instruments need an action applied to the sound-producing material to make a sound: a guitar string needs to be plucked or picked, a violin string needs to be bowed, a marimba bar needs to be struck with a mallet, and so on.

1 Click the 1 button next to the Object 1 controls (at the far left of the interface).

The button turns from blue to gray, indicating that the object is off.

2 Play your MIDI controller.

You shouldn't hear any sound.

Why is no sound produced? This illustrates the dependent physical interaction between objects and strings. Without an object exciting the string, nothing happens, just as in the real world.

3 Turn on Object 1 again by clicking the 1 button.

4 Click the Type button located to the right of Object 1's Strength knob.

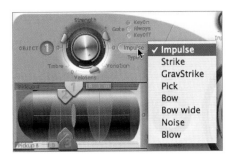

The menu that appears lists various exciter types for exciting the string.

5 Try choosing each exciter type, one at a time, testing each sound by playing your MIDI controller and observing the effect on the string animation.

6 Conclude by choosing the Pick exciter type for Object 1.

Object 1 is now set to simulate the action and sound of a guitar pick acting on a string. The parameters are controlled by the object's Strength knob and surrounding sliders: Variation, Timbre, and, for Objects 1 and 2, VeloSens (velocity sensitivity). The parameters are context sensitive, meaning that the exciter type determines what the controls do. For example, the Timbre slider sets hammer mass when the exciter type is Strike, and bow pressure when the type is Bow.

MORE INFO ▶ See page 461 in the *Logic Pro 8 Instruments and Effects* manual for a chart describing the parameters for each exciter type.

7 Drag the Strength knob and try different values, listening to the result while playing your MIDI controller.

In the case of Pick, the Strength parameter determines pick force and speed.

8 Option-click the Strength knob to return the value to the default.

TIP ▶ You can Option-click most controls in Logic to return them to their default settings.

9   Drag the Variation slider, listening to the sound by playing your MIDI controller, eventually settling on a value of about 0.61.

The Variation control determines plectrum stiffness when the exciter type is set to Pick.

10   Click the 2 button next to Object 2 to turn it on.

11   Click to open the Type menu and choose Disturb.

Note that this menu is considerably longer than the Object 1 menu. Object 2 offers all of the same exciter types as Object 1 but also contains a variety of others, which are referred to as *disturbers*. The nature of a disturber type is not to *start* the string material vibrating (as the exciter types do), but to disturb the vibration in some way through a physical interaction. Therefore, disturbers work in conjunction with exciters to produce a complex result.

12   Play your MIDI controller to hear the result of the applied disturber.

With Disturb chosen, you are introducing a physical object at a fixed distance from the string that keeps it from freely vibrating. Think of an object positioned close to the strings of a guitar so that it is nearly touching. When the guitar strings are plucked, the strings hit the object, creating a buzzing sound.

13 Adjust the Strength of Object 2 to about 0.43, listening to the results by playing your MIDI controller.

Just as they do with the exciter types, so do the Strength, Variation, and Timbre controls modify aspects of the chosen disturber. In the case of Disturb, Strength sets the hardness of the object positioned near the String.

MORE INFO ▶ See page 462 in the *Logic Pro 8 Instruments and Effects* manual for a chart describing the parameters for each disturber type.

14 Click to select the Always button in the Gate settings for Object 2, playing your MIDI controller to hear the result.

The Gate settings determine when the object interacts with the string in relation to the MIDI controller keystroke: on depressing the key (and not when the key is let go), on letting go of the key (and not when the key is depressed), or always.

15 Click the 3 button, and choose Bouncing from the Type menu if necessary.

Notice that Object 3's Type choices are limited to disturbers (no exciters). Bouncing simulates a loose object lying on the vibrating string. Imagine a piece of paper or small wood block lying directly on a guitar's strings to get an idea of what this produces.

16 Set Strength to about 0.11, playing your MIDI controller to hear the results as you adjust the value.

Strength controls the effect of gravity on the bouncing object.

17 Adjust the Timbre slider to approximately –0.22, listening to the results as you do so.

In the case of a bouncing object, the Timbre parameter controls the stiffness of the object.

Now that you have determined the basic sound generation by choosing object types, you can further work with the sound by determining where each object interacts on the length of the string. This is similar to picking a guitar string at the bridge, at the neck, or in the middle.

You can position objects by moving sliders representing each object in the Pickup display.

18 Drag the Object 1 slider in the Pickup display to the right, positioning it in the middle of the string.

19 Drag the Object 2 slider in the Pickup display to the left, positioning it slightly to the right of the left end (a value of 0.03).

20 Drag the Object 3 slider in the Pickup display to the left, positioning it between the Object 1 and Object 2 sliders.

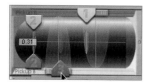

21 Listen to the sound by playing your MIDI controller.

Adjusting the Pickups

Sculpture uses pickups to sense vibrations from the string, functioning identically to an electric guitar's electromagnetic pickups. As it is on an electric guitar, the pickup's location is of importance; different positions along the length of the string create different timbres.

TIP ▶ To hear these subtle differences, play your MIDI controller while you do the following adjustments.

1   Drag the Pickup A slider to the left, roughly between Objects 2 and 3.

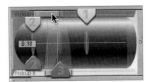

2   Drag the Pickup B slider over Object 1.

The resulting sound emphasizes the Pick exciter, similar to the way the neck pickup works on an electric guitar.

Processing the Sound

Sculpture's extensive processing options allow you to further shape the sound using a variety of means (multimode filter, Waveshaper, stereo delay, and Body EQ). Examine some of the choices, working with the sound you have constructed so far.

1   Turn on the Waveshaper by clicking the Waveshaper button above the Material Pad.

The Waveshaper provides interesting distortion effects, including tube simulation, for harmonically rich results.

2 Drag the Input Scale knob to a value around 0.39.

3 Drag the Variation knob to a value of –0.69.

4 Play your MIDI controller to audition the sound.

You have just applied soft, tubelike saturation to the sound.

Sculpture's Body EQ section utilizes a unique approach to equalization, providing some great sound-shaping possibilities. A standard EQ changes individual frequency bands, but Body EQ also offers spectral models that emulate the resonating properties of specific instruments. These models can be shaped by adjusting formant-related parameters.

5 If Body EQ is not already turned on, click the Body EQ button to the right of the Material Pad.

By default, Body EQ is set to the Lo Mid Hi model, emulating a standard three-band EQ.

6 Click the Model button to open the Model pop-up-menu.

As you can see, the choices range from models of string instruments (guitars, violin, cello, double bass, and so on) to kalimba and various flutes (alto and bass).

7 Choose Dobro Guitar.

The controls change to reflect the formant parameters of the resonating body (Dobro Guitar), and the graphic display to the right now depicts a detailed spectrum.

8   Try playing your MIDI controller to hear the Dobro Guitar spectral model applied to your sound.

In effect, you are coupling the sound generator that you constructed (through the interaction between string and objects) with the resonating body of a Dobro guitar (a metal-body guitar with an acoustic speaker cone).

9   Try changing the three formant controls, which adjust how much the harmonics are emphasized (Intensity), how closely they are spaced (Stretch), and how far their frequency moves up or down (Shift).

Using Modulation in Sculpture

Sculpture's modulation section is extensive, offering everything from low-frequency oscillators (including two jitter generators that produce random variations) to Note On Random modulators and user-created envelopes.

Also of great interest is the Morph Pad, which enables you to morph between parameter settings for the entire instrument. The Morph Pad can be controlled manually, by MIDI controllers, or by its own time-based envelope.

1   If the Morph Pad is not already turned on, click the Pad button in the morph envelope display.

The Morph Pad has five morph points, represented by center and corner points (A, B, C, D). Each point can be thought of as a memory location that stores the parameter settings of everything from string material to object and pickup placement.

Instead of setting each state manually, let's use one of Sculpture's useful features to randomly generate deviants of the original state in each point.

2   Select the 4 Points button located to the left of the Morph Pad.

By selecting this, you are targeting only the four outermost points (A, B, C, D) for randomization, leaving the original (center point) sound alone.

3   Drag the Intensity (Int) slider to the right of the Morph Pad to a value of 25%.

4   Click the Randomize (Rnd) button above the Intensity slider.

To see what just happened, look at how the controls for the various states (points) were affected.

5   Click each point in the Morph Pad (click on the letters), one at a time, looking at how the Material and Object controls change.

NOTE ▶ The small red dot appearing in the controls' graphic readout represents the original state (at the center point within the Morph Pad). Each state, then, is a variation of these original settings, depending on how much randomization (Intensity) was applied.

6   Hold down a note on your MIDI controller, and on the Morph Pad, move the red ball to various points.

The controls (and the sound) change smoothly to reflect the various states.

Saving and Trying Presets

As you can see, Sculpture is a truly exceptional instrument. Let's end this section on Sculpture's unique sound-generation properties by saving the sound you just made as a preset.

1   Click to open the Settings menu and choose Save Setting As.

2   In the Save As field, enter a name that you feel suits the sound you just made.

3   Click Save.

Let's conclude by taking a brief look at some of Sculpture's expertly programmed settings, which show off the diverse capabilities of the instrument. With each of these, try playing your MIDI controller while holding chords and single notes to hear the sound evolve over time. Also try playing with the Morph Pad (if active) and modulation wheel of the MIDI controller, as these are frequently deployed to control sound changes.

Some Presets to Try

Preset Location	Description
07 Blown Instruments > Saturated Air	Highly expressive modeled flute sounds
02 Modeled Pads > Ambient Light	Evolving harmonic pad
10 Motion Sequences > Reverse Rhythms	Rhythmic groove using extensive modulation
13 Warped Sculptures > Marble on a Journey	Randomly bouncing and rolling marble using Morph Pad

Treating Your MIDI Hardware as Software

While it is possible to create entire projects using only built-in instruments, Logic Pro also provides ways to integrate external hardware into the computer recording environment.

Logic Pro has a handy little plug-in that enables you to create a direct connection to an external piece of MIDI hardware as if it were an internal software instrument. The plug-in brings the external device's audio output back into Logic's Mixer for further processing and bouncing, all in real time.

1   Select the Inst 2 track (track 2).

2   In the Arrange channel strip, click the Instrument slot to open the Instrument Plug-in menu and choose External Instrument > Stereo.

This plug-in doesn't do any processing at all, but it functions as a signal router. Basically, it sends MIDI data out to a selected instrument in the Environment representing your external MIDI hardware and receives audio input from a selected input on your audio interface that is receiving the signal from that external MIDI device.

3   Physically patch the audio outputs from your selected MIDI hardware to a pair of adjacent audio inputs on your audio interface (1-2, 3-4, 5-6, and so on).

4   In the External Instrument plug-in, click to open the MIDI Destination pop-up menu and choose GM Device > 1 (Grand Piano).

This menu mirrors the available choices for assigning a MIDI track within the Arrange area. Each enabled channel of the device is represented and may be chosen.

NOTE ▶ For this exercise, you set the MIDI destination to a generic MIDI instrument within the project's Environment. This multi instrument is set to output on all MIDI ports of your interface, so it should trigger all connected MIDI devices. Since only one MIDI device has its audio outputs connected to the audio interface and chosen within the External Instrument plug-in, this will work well for the purposes of this exercise. Within your own project (containing your own MIDI setup in the Environment), however, you would select an instrument representing your individual MIDI hardware.

5   Click to open the Input slot pop-up menu and choose the inputs of your audio interface into which you plugged the MIDI hardware.

6   Play your MIDI controller.

You should hear the output of your MIDI device, which is routed into the Inst 2 channel strip or track.

7   Listen to the sound level and apply additional gain attenuation, if needed, by adjusting the Input Volume slider.

You are now ready to apply additional plug-ins, make volume and pan adjustments, and mix and bounce the MIDI hardware as if it were a software instrument.

NOTE ▶ Faster than real-time freezing and bouncing (offline) is not available to external instruments, as the outgoing MIDI signal and the incoming audio signal must be transmitted to the hardware device in real time. Real-time bounces and freezes work fine.

8   Choose File > Close Project.

An alert message appears asking if you'd like to save the changes done to the project. It is not necessary to save the project file, as no data was actually written.

9   Click Don't Save.

Lesson Review

1. Which direction does signal flow in most of Logic's software instruments?
2. What do Ultrabeat kits contain?
3. Which feature in Ultrabeat is used to compose and play back patterns?
4. How can you create strings of patterns with Ultrabeat?
5. What do multi output instruments do?
6. Sound generation for the EXS24 mkII consists of what three components?
7. Besides offering flexible physical modeling of real-world components, the vintage keyboard instruments offer what additional feature to process the sound?
8. How are software instrument and effects combinations stored for future recall?
9. What is used to quickly create arrangements of both software instrument and classic MIDI tracks?
10. What is Sculpture's basis for sound generation?

11. Besides Sculpture's sound-generation and modulation sections, what other components are used to further process the sound?

12. Which modulation control enables you to program smooth transitions between various parameter states?

13. How can external MIDI hardware be incorporated into Logic's Mixer?

Answers

1. Signal flow moves from left to right in most software instruments, which helps with understanding the instrument as well as locating controls.

2. Ultrabeat utilizes kits that contain individually programmed drum sounds, each with its own unique settings and modulations.

3. Ultrabeat's built-in step sequencer works in conjunction with the Logic project to compose and play back patterns.

4. Ultrabeat's step sequence patterns can be strung together by triggered MIDI notes, or copied to the Arrange window for region-based editing.

5. Multi output instruments (such as Ultrabeat and EXS24 mkII) can route individual sounds to separate channel strips for isolation or further processing.

6. The EXS24 mkII consists of samples organized into sampler instruments that are further shaped by the interface controls.

7. The vintage keyboard instruments have built-in effects processing associated with each instrument.

8. Instrument and effects combinations can be saved and utilized as channel strip settings.

9. Global tracks affect software instruments in the same manner as classic MIDI hardware and can be used to create quick arrangements.

10. Sculpture utilizes a string acted upon by objects as the basis for sound generation.

11. Components such as the Waveshaper, Body EQ, and Delay allow you to further process the instrument in interesting ways.

12. Sculpture's Morph Pad enables you to smoothly move from various states of control settings.

13. External MIDI hardware can be incorporated into the Mixer as a software instrument by using the External Instrument plug-in.

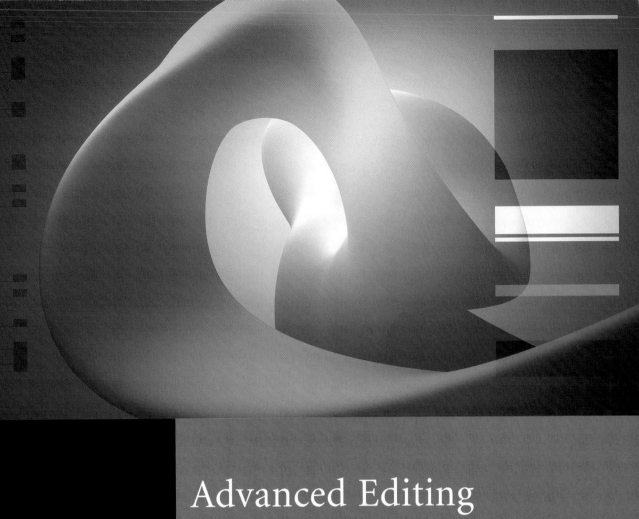

Advanced Editing

5

Working with the Arrangement

A computer-based system offers distinct advantages over other methods of developing and arranging musical material. First and foremost is the ability to work with visual representations of sound, whether as audio waveforms or as graphical data (such as MIDI or notation). You can create detailed edits and work with arrangements by moving sections around as you would text in a word processor. A nonlinear approach to editing lets you jump around in a composition, manipulating multiple aspects of a piece of music and playing back sections for instant feedback.

Many of Logic's features are geared toward manipulating and developing musical material. Lesson 5 focuses on techniques that enable you to efficiently view, organize, and move data within a project.

Creating and Using Markers

Markers serve multiple purposes in a project. They visually identify the sections of a composition, and they also provide navigation points along the Bar ruler. In this way, markers serve as a map that allows you to quickly locate a project's sections for playback, editing, and arranging.

Markers are displayed in the Bar ruler and global tracks area and are created in a variety of ways. In this exercise, you will use several techniques to efficiently create, edit, and view markers; place them within your composition; and add text and color to them for easy viewing.

Adding Markers in the Marker Track

For any given project file, you can easily place and edit markers in the Marker track, one of Logic Pro's global tracks.

Let's start by opening the project file that you will use for this lesson.

1 Go to Logic 8_BTB_Files > Lessons, and open **05_Sintra_Start.logic**.

2 Play the project to familiarize yourself with the material.

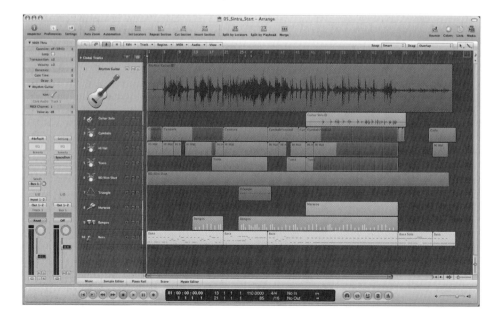

3 At the top of the track list, click the Global Tracks disclosure triangle.

The Marker track appears at the top of the window.

NOTE ▶ This is the only global track component set to be displayed in this project. You can display any of the global tracks by choosing View > Configure Global Tracks.

4 Select the Pencil tool, and click the Marker track at measure 1.

A new marker, Marker 1, is created at measure 1.

NOTE ▶ If you make a mistake, you can erase a marker by clicking it with the Eraser tool.

When a marker is created, Logic automatically assigns a name consisting of the word *Marker* followed by a sequential number. Logic's allocation of marker names is dynamic, always depending on the order of all the markers in a project.

5 Using the Pencil tool, click the Marker track to create another marker at measure 13.

TIP ▶ It is easier to achieve exact placement by dragging in the Marker track until the help tag lists the correct position. Then release the mouse button.

A new marker is created, labeled Marker 2.

6 Using the Pencil tool, insert a marker at measure 5, between the two markers you created.

The new marker is labeled Marker 2, and the following marker is relabeled Marker 3.

You can also use the playhead to determine the point on the Bar ruler where you want a marker to be inserted. In this case, you first have to position the playhead and then create the marker.

7   Press the / (slash) key to open the Go To Position dialog.

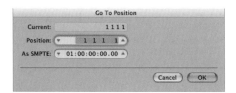

The Go To Position dialog appears, with the Position field highlighted for input.

8   In the Position field, enter *21* and press Return.

The playhead jumps to measure 21.

9   In the Marker track header, click the Create button.

Marker 4 is created at the current playhead position.

TIP ▶ You don't have to stop a project to add markers at a current playhead position. You can use the techniques in this exercise to create markers on the fly, placing them on the Bar ruler during playback. However, accessing this function using the mouse can be awkward when the project is playing. By using the key command Control-K, you can drop in markers quickly as the project progresses.

10 Play the project starting around measure 20, holding down the Control key and pressing the K key when you reach the section change at the downbeat of measure 34.

A new marker (Marker 5) is created at measure 34.

NOTE ▶ Pressing Control-K creates a marker at the nearest bar to the playhead, rounding its placement. If you need to place a marker within a measure or are using absolute time (working with SMPTE), use the key command for Create Marker Without Rounding (Shift-Control-K), or choose Options > Marker > Create Without Rounding. A marker will be placed at the exact spot, rather than being rounded to the nearest bar.

Creating Markers from Regions

Another way to create a marker quickly is by using a region. In this case, the region's start point, end point, and name designate the marker's position, length, and name.

1 Using the Pointer tool, select the Guitar Solo region on track 2.

2 In the Marker track header, click the From Regions button.

A new marker named Guitar Solo is created at measure 44, with the same color as the region.

You can also create a marker by clicking the region and choosing a menu command.

3 On track 10, click the Bass Solo region, and choose Options > Marker > Create by Regions.

A new marker named Bass Solo is created at measure 68.

4 Using any of the above techniques, create a marker from the Coda region (the last region on track 3).

A marker named Coda is created at measure 76.

Adding Marker Text

Markers can display all types of text, such as the name of an associated region or section, and can even serve as a placeholder for musical ideas and production notes. You can enter a name directly on the marker or open a separate window for more detailed text entry.

1   From the Tool menu, choose the Text tool.

2   In the Marker track, click Marker 1.

A text field appears.

3   Enter *Intro*, and press Return.

The marker name changes to Intro.

TIP ▶ Try using the key command for Quick Edit Marker to quickly name markers. You can also choose Options > Marker > Quick Edit Marker, or press Command-Return to quickly name markers.

Let's try a different approach for naming markers, involving the Marker List, a technique that has its own advantages, although it is not as quick as the previous technique.

4   In the Toolbar, click the Lists button to open the Lists area.

5   Click the Marker tab.

The Marker List window uses an Event List format to sequentially display all the markers used in a project. It shows marker position, name, and length and provides a single environment in which to access and edit markers.

6   In the Marker Name column, select Marker 2, and click the Marker Text Area button at the upper left of the Marker List window.

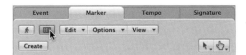

The Marker Text area opens at the bottom of the Marker List, ready for input.

7   Highlight the default text (Marker ##) and enter *Verse 1*.

Marker 2 now appears as Verse 1 in the Marker List and the Marker track.

8   In the Marker List, select Marker 3, and in the Marker Text area, enter *Verse 2*.

By using the Marker List window, you can quickly switch from one marker to another, entering text as needed.

9   Using this technique, name the next two markers (Marker 4 and Marker 5) *Chorus* and *Verse 3*, respectively.

Other information can be entered and displayed in the Marker Text area as well. You can display multiple lines of text in any font that resides in your system, making the Marker Text area a visual notepad. However, sometimes it is more useful to have comments displayed on the marker itself, providing information pertaining to the production.

10 In the Marker List, select the Guitar Solo marker.

11 In the Marker Text area, make sure that the insertion point is placed after the text *Guitar Solo*, then press Return to go to the next line.

12 In the line after *Guitar Solo*, enter *Comped from multiple takes*.

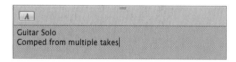

13 In the Toolbar, click the Lists button to close the Lists area.

14 In the Marker track, look at the marker.

The marker inserts a dividing line between the name of the marker, Guitar Solo, and the production notes beneath.

NOTE ▶ The marker displays only as much text as it can fit within the physical space of the marker itself. If you need to display more text, increase the height of the Marker track by dragging down the bottom border separating it from the next track.

Editing Markers

In addition to editing information in the Marker List, you can adjust markers in the Marker track the way you would work with regions in the Arrange area. Common tasks include changing the marker lengths, dragging markers to new locations, and coloring their labels.

The Coda marker you created earlier is a bar too early. Let's move it to correct this.

1   Using the Pointer tool, position the cursor over the middle of the Coda marker.

The cursor turns into a two-headed arrow.

2   Drag the Coda marker one bar to the right (to measure 77).

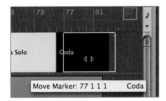

NOTE ▶ You can use the help tag to make sure you are moving the marker to the correct location.

Notice that a small gap appears between the Bass Solo and Coda markers.

You can adjust this by lengthening the Bass Solo marker to fit against the Coda marker.

3   Position the cursor over the right edge of the Bass Solo marker.

The cursor changes to a Resize pointer.

4   Drag the right edge of the Bass Solo marker to extend it to the beginning of the Coda marker (the length should be a total of nine bars).

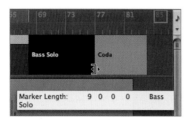

The seemingly simple act of coloring an item can make a big difference when navigating within a project. By coloring a marker, you can quickly discern one section from another.

5   From the Arrange area's local menu bar, choose View > Colors.

The Color palette appears.

6   Select the Intro marker, and select a color in the Color palette.

The marker changes from its gray default to the chosen color.

NOTE ▶ The maker itself remains black until it is deselected. However, you will see the text color change when selecting colors from the Color palette.

7   Select each subsequent marker and apply a color by clicking in the Color palette.

8   Close the Color palette.

Viewing Markers in the Bar Ruler

The Marker track does not have to be visible for you to see the markers you have created. Whenever the Marker track is not visible, the markers are displayed directly under the Bar ruler.

1   Click the Global Tracks disclosure triangle to hide the global tracks.

The Marker track disappears (it is the only global track whose visibility is turned on). All the markers you created in the last few exercises are displayed in the Bar ruler, along with their assigned names and colors.

The markers here are displayed the same way they're displayed in the Marker track, with the exception of the text that you entered for the Guitar Solo marker. When displayed in the Bar ruler, markers are allocated a limited amount of space, which does not allow for extended text.

Navigating the Arrangement

In a nonlinear editor you have the unique advantage of being able to jump around within a project, concentrating on various aspects, regardless of their position in the Bar ruler. To truly benefit from this random access, it is essential to navigate the project in an efficient manner. Quickly getting to where you want to work is paramount, especially when time is limited.

While the basic transport controls work for navigation, they still follow a linear approach modeled on tape-based media. Forward and rewind controls move the playhead from a fixed point in one direction or the other, and you must scroll through intermediary material to reach the edit point.

In this exercise, you take advantage of the nonlinear aspects of Logic, using techniques to navigate the project rapidly while setting yourself up for the edit.

Using Specialized Playback Commands

The basic method of moving nonlinearly within a project is by using the playhead. Jumping to another section is as easy as clicking once in the bottom half of the Bar ruler (below the dotted line). Playback from any point in the project works in a nearly identical fashion—all you do is double-click instead. The two techniques used together enable both quick location and playback.

1   Double-click anywhere in the bottom of the Bar ruler.

    The project starts to play at that location.

2   While the project is playing, click anywhere in the bottom of the Bar ruler.

    The playhead position jumps to that location without stopping playback.

3   While the project is playing, double-click anywhere in the bottom of the Bar ruler.

    The project jumps to that location and stops playback.

    This technique is not very precise for locating starting and stopping points, but it works well for quick navigation when accuracy is not a priority.

However, starting from an exact location is often important, especially when you're isolating specific areas or material in the composition. Let's look at a few of the key commands that help to accomplish this.

4   Choose Logic Pro > Preferences > Key Commands to open the Key Commands window.

TIP   You can open the Key Commands window by pressing Option-K.

5   In the search field, enter *play*.

All commands that have *play* in the name are listed in the Command column (including words that contain this combination of letters, such as *display*).

Several useful playback commands are listed here, many of which are accessible only via a key command. (The "•" preceding a command identifies it as a key-command-only function.)

6   In the Global Commands list, make note of the key commands for "Play from Left Window Edge" (Control-Enter) and "Play from Selection" (Shift-Enter).

You will be using these for playback from specific points in the project.

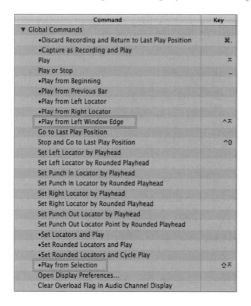

Command	Key
▼ Global Commands	
•Discard Recording and Return to Last Play Position	⌘.
•Capture as Recording and Play	
Play	⌶
Play or Stop	⎵
•Play from Beginning	
•Play from Previous Bar	
•Play from Left Locator	
•Play from Right Locator	
•Play from Left Window Edge	⌃⌶
Go to Last Play Position	
Stop and Go to Last Play Position	⌃0
Set Left Locator by Playhead	
Set Left Locator by Rounded Playhead	
Set Punch In Locator by Playhead	
Set Punch In Locator by Rounded Playhead	
Set Right Locator by Playhead	
Set Right Locator by Rounded Playhead	
Set Punch Out Locator by Playhead	
Set Punch Out Locator Point by Rounded Playhead	
•Set Locators and Play	
•Set Rounded Locators and Play	
•Set Rounded Locators and Cycle Play	
•Play from Selection	⇧⌶
Open Display Preferences...	
Clear Overload Flag in Audio Channel Display	

7 Close the Key Command window.

Before you're ready to try out these playback commands, it is necessary to understand what they do. The Play from Selectio function allows you to select a region or event using its leftmost point as the location to initiate playback.

8 On track 2, select the Guitar Solo region.

9 Press Shift-Enter, the key command for Play from Selection.

The project immediately starts playing from the beginning of the region.

10 Stop playback.

Rather than base the playback location on the start of a region or event, as Play from Selection does, thePlay from Left Window Edge command uses the visible area of the active window to determine its playback start point. Essentially, it uses a "what you see is what you get" approach, starting playback from the leftmost visible point in the window. This is especially helpful when you're zoomed in while editing, as it doesn't require selecting a region or event first and it's independent of zoom level.

11 Using the Zoom tool, draw a selection around the first big transient in the Rhythm Guitar track (track 1), located at the beginning of Verse 1.

The view zooms in horizontally and vertically, displaying a few measures.

12 Press Control-Enter, the key command for Play from Left Window Edge.

The project immediately starts playing from the leftmost point of the visible window area.

13 Stop playback.

> **TIP ▶** As you saw in the Key Commands window, many useful play commands can be accessed via key command only. Try assigning others that mirror your own workflow.

Navigating with Markers

As mentioned earlier in this lesson, markers are extremely useful in helping you locate places in a project. In this way, they can be viewed as navigation points, allowing you to skip to sections where you want to work. In this exercise, you will learn methods of using markers for navigation and for initiating playback.

1   Press 1 to open Screenset 1, returning the project to its original zoom settings.

2   While pressing the Option key, click the bottom half of the Bar ruler in the Verse 1 marker.

The playhead locates to the beginning of the marker (measure 5). This is a quick way to move to the beginning of a section.

By double-clicking while pressing the Option key, you can start playback from the beginning of a marker.

3   Press the Option key and double-click in the Verse 2 marker.

The playhead moves to the beginning of the marker (measure 13) and starts playback.

4   Stop playback.

NOTE ▶ The first technique (moving to a marker) works within the Marker track as well. Unfortunately, however, you are unable to initiate playback by double-clicking when the Marker track is visible.

Using the Marker List to Navigate

Another way to navigate using markers is with the Marker List.

1   In the Toolbar, click the Lists button.

The Lists area opens. Note that the Lists area has its own set of primary and secondary (with Command key) tools. By default, they are Pointer and Finger tools.

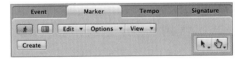

2   Select the Marker tab, if not already showing in the Lists area.

3   Using the Finger tool (by holding down the Command key), click-hold the Intro marker. (Specifically, you should click the word *Intro*.)

The project starts playing from the beginning of the Intro marker and continues playing until you release the mouse button.

4   Release the mouse button to stop playback.

5   Try click-holding other markers with the Finger tool to initiate playback from their positions, releasing the mouse button when you want to stop playback.

This provides a simple way to audition sections in the project, especially when you have many markers that are not in the visible area of the window.

6   In the Toolbar, click the Lists button to close the Lists area.

Using Key and Menu Commands to Locate to Markers

Menu commands (and their respective key commands) also provide an efficient way of jumping from one marker to the next.

1   Click the Global Tracks disclosure triangle to view the Marker track.

The Marker track appears at the top of the window.

2   Choose Options > Marker > Go to Previous, then Options > Marker > Go to Next, observing the results.

The playhead moves from marker to marker sequentially, aligning itself at the beginning. As each marker is selected, it becomes highlighted in the Marker track.

Although the menu commands are readily accessible, the key command equivalents provide the most efficient access to these functions.

3   Try pressing the key commands associated with going to the previous marker (Control–Command–Left Arrow) and going to the next marker (Control–Command–Right Arrow).

With these key commands, you are able to quickly scroll forward and backward by markers along the Bar ruler.

Isolating Material with Cycle Mode

Cycle is an extremely useful mode that enables you to play a section repeatedly. This works well for isolating material in a project, permitting you to focus on the repeated section, editing as you listen.

Cycle works by setting locators (used as start and end points), which can be done manually or automatically. Let's take a look at methods to set locators and to create cycle areas that allow you to isolate material.

1   In the top portion of the Bar ruler, click a position of your choice and drag to the right a few bars.

A cycle area is created.

2   Press Play.

The project starts immediately at the start point of the cycle area, continuing to play until it reaches the end, at which point it loops around again, playing from the start of the cycle.

3   Stop playback.

This technique works for locating to a given point and for playing an isolated passage that has been defined manually. However, precisely positioning the start and end points is difficult and becomes tedious when done around predefined sections (such as markers and regions). To address this, let's look at additional techniques that can automatically set the locators defining a cycle area.

Using Markers to Create Cycle Areas

An interesting thing happens when navigating using the Go to Next/Previous marker key commands: the locators are automatically set around the marker, corresponding exactly to the marker length. You can use this to your advantage, dynamically changing cycle areas that correspond to the sections in the project.

1   With Cycle mode still active, use the key commands for going to the next marker (Control–Command–Right Arrow) and the previous marker (Control–Command–Left Arrow) to move the playhead to the Verse 1 marker.

The locators adapt to the selected marker length, and the cycle area moves in the Bar ruler, matching the Verse 1 marker length exactly.

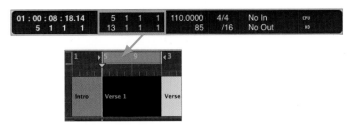

2   Press Control–Command–Right Arrow and Control–Command–Left Arrow as needed to move from marker to marker along the Bar ruler.

The cycle areas adapt to each marker accessed.

As long as Cycle mode is on, the cycle area will relocate to any selected markers, allowing you to effectively concentrate on individual sections in the project.

3   In the Transport bar, click the Cycle button to turn off Cycle mode.

You can also create a quick cycle area with a marker without having to locate to it first. This can be done via a simple drag-and-drop technique.

4   Drag the Guitar Solo marker upward, and release the mouse button when the marker is over the top half of the Bar ruler (where cycle areas are displayed).

A cycle area is created, matching the Guitar Solo marker length and location.

5   In the Bar ruler, click the cycle area to turn off Cycle mode.

This is another way to quickly turn off Cycle mode.

6   Click the Global Tracks disclosure triangle to hide the Marker track.

Setting Locators by Regions or Events

While markers work great for sectional material, you will often want to concentrate on smaller areas in the project. You can accomplish this by setting locators around individual regions or events in the project, and then activating Cycle mode.

1   Select the first region in the Bongos track (track 9).

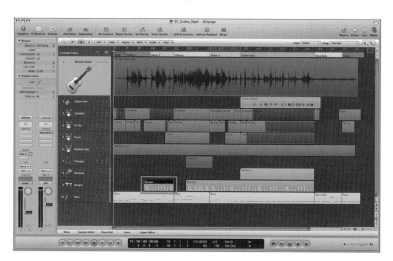

2   From the Arrange area's local menu bar, choose Region > Set Locators by Regions.

3   In the Transport bar, click the Cycle button.

A cycle area is created, matching the Bongos region.

This technique isn't limited to regions: it generally applies to all selected objects (notes, events, and so on) in any editor. Thankfully, a single key command encapsulates all object types, allowing you to execute this command regardless of the editor.

4   Choose Logic Pro > Preferences > Key Commands, or press Option-K, to open the Key Commands window.

5   In the search field, enter *locator*.

All commands that have *locator* in the name are listed in the Command column. Make note of the key command for "Set Locators by Regions/Events," Control-= (equal sign).

NOTE ▶ The Set Locators by Regions/Events key command using the U.S. MacBook preset is Control-' (apostrophe).

6   Close the Key Commands window.

7   Double-click the first Bongos region (the one you selected earlier) to open the Piano Roll Editor.

NOTE ▶ When you double-click a MIDI region, the Piano Roll Editor will open only if you've set it to do so in the Preferences > Global > Editing tab.

8   Use the Pointer tools to draw a selection rectangle around multiple notes in the Piano Roll Editor.

9   Press Control-= (equal sign), the key command for Set Locators by Regions/Events.

The cycle area within the Piano Roll Editor adapts to your selection.

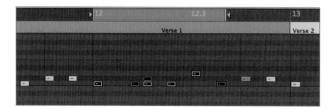

As long as Cycle mode is active, it will adapt to whatever you select when using this command.

Using Skip Cycle Areas

Sometimes it is helpful to skip a section to hear how a project sounds without it. You can do this by creating a *skip cycle*, which lets you omit a passage. Locators are used to determine the position of the skip cycle area, but here they work in reverse, swapping the left and right locators. This technique is especially helpful when trying out transitions between sections.

1 Click the Piano Roll button to close the Piano Roll Editor.

2 In the top half of the Bar ruler at measure 21, drag to the left until you reach measure 13.

A skip cycle area is created, represented by the striped bar at the top of the Bar ruler.

3 Press the Option key while you double-click the Verse 1 marker.

The project plays from the beginning of Verse 1 until it reaches the skip cycle area, then jumps past it, continuing to play from the end point of the skip cycle area.

This is effective for quick designations but suffers from the same problems as manually drawing a cycle area: it's inexact and it doesn't adapt. You can address this with a key command that enables you to create a skip cycle area out of any cycle area (or vice versa).

4 Choose Logic Pro > Preferences > Key Commands, or press Option-K, to open the Key Commands window.

The search field should still have *locator* typed in it, with the Command list displaying all commands with *locator* in the name. Make a mental note of the key command for "Swap Left and Right Locators" (J).

5 Close the Key Commands window.

6 Use the Go to Next/Previous marker key commands to navigate to the Guitar Solo marker.

The skip cycle area changes to a regular cycle area around the Guitar Solo marker.

NOTE ▶ Using the Go to Next/Previous marker commands resets the left and right locators to the marker (in that order), changing the skip cycle area into a cycle area.

7 Press J, the key command assigned to Swap Left and Right Locators.

The cycle area now becomes a skip cycle area.

8 Press the Option key as you double-click the Verse 3 marker to play the project without the Guitar Solo.

The project plays from the beginning of Verse 3 until it reaches the skip cycle area, then jumps past the Guitar Solo, continuing from the Bass Solo until the end of the project.

9 Stop playback, if necessary.

10 Turn off Cycle mode.

Using Zooming

When editing, it is often necessary to work with material at a highly detailed level. Zooming is the act of moving in and out of your arrangement, magnifying your working area to focus on individual aspects of a project.

In this exercise you will use various zoom techniques that improve your ability to view and edit material.

Understanding Zoom Positioning

Before you begin, it is important to understand how Logic uses positioning to determine which visual material is magnified. The goal is to keep the area you are concentrating on visible in the window. This is dictated by either the playhead position or the selected material.

You can see this when executing basic zoom commands such as those controlled by the zoom sliders.

1   Click the background of the Arrange area (where no region is located) to make sure that nothing is selected.

2   Position the playhead at the beginning of the Chorus marker by Option-clicking the marker.

    The playhead locates to the beginning of the Chorus section.

3   At the lower right of the Arrange area, slowly drag the horizontal zoom slider to the right.

    The project zooms in lengthwise, spreading out in both directions but keeping the playhead in roughly the same place within the window.

4   Press 1 to open Screenset 1, returning to the original zoom level.

5   In track 7, select the Triangle region.

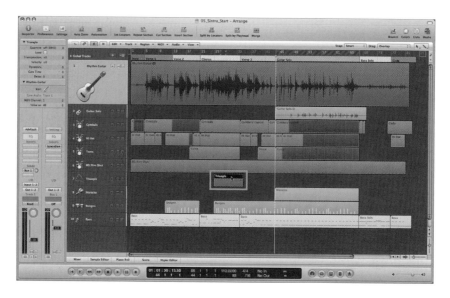

6   Slowly drag the horizontal zoom slider to the right.

The project zooms in, spreading out in both directions, but this time it keeps the left edge of the region in roughly the same place within the window.

What does this mean, and why is this important? In effect, while zooming, the displayed area of the window is justified either to the current playhead position or to a selected region. When you want to zoom in to a given playhead position, you must make sure that nothing is selected before you zoom. If you want to zoom in to an individual region, you need to select it first. This is important to keep in mind while zooming because you may find yourself losing the area that you intend to work with unless you actively choose one of these methods.

Saving and Recalling Zoom Settings

Zooming can be thought of as navigating up and down levels of magnification. Each magnification level can be accessed via the zoom sliders or a key command, and it can also be saved for later use. These zoom steps can also be saved and recalled dynamically while you're working (like saving and restoring screensets), allowing you to return to desired levels of magnification.

Let's explore this technique by assigning a few key commands.

1   Choose Logic Pro > Preferences > Key Commands, or press Option-K, to open the Key Commands window.

2   In the search field, enter *zoom*.

All the commands that have *zoom* in the name are listed in the Command column.

Note the functions relating to saving and recalling zoom settings: Save as Zoom 1, 2, and 3, and Recall Zoom 1, 2, and 3.

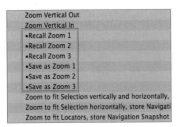

Once they're assigned, you will use these key-command-only functions to save and recall zoom "snapshots" of various levels of magnification.

3   In the Command column, choose "Save as Zoom 1."

4   Click the Learn by Key Label button.

5   Press Command-F1 to assign this key command to Save as Zoom 1.

> **NOTE ▸** The function keys aren't assigned in the default key commands, and they work especially well for zoom settings.

6   In the Command column, choose "Save as Zoom 2."

7   Press Command-F2 to assign this key command to that function.

8   In the Command column, choose "Save as Zoom 3."

9   Press Command-F3 to assign this key command to that function.

Now that you have assigned keys to save three zoom snapshots, let's assign related keys to recall them.

10   Assign Recall Zoom 1, 2, and 3 to F1, F2, and F3, respectively.

> **NOTE ▸** While you're in the Key Commands window, be sure that you have the basic zoom commands assigned (Zoom Horizontal In/Out and Zoom Vertical In/Out). If you don't, assign them to the keys of your choice. By default, these are set to the Control–Right Arrow and Control–Left Arrow keys.

11   Close the Key Commands window.

With this arrangement, the Command key works as a memory toggle, storing settings when it's used in conjunction with the function keys. When the keys are depressed without the Command modifier key, they recall the last zoom level that was saved.

12 Move the playhead to the beginning of the project, and select the Rhythm Guitar track (track 1).

13 Press Command-F1 to save this starting zoom level to the first memory location (Save as Zoom 1).

14 Use the basic zoom key commands (Control–Right Arrow and Control–Down Arrow) to zoom in four steps horizontally and four steps vertically (press each key combination four times).

The project zooms in a modest amount, showing the audio region in track 1 in greater detail.

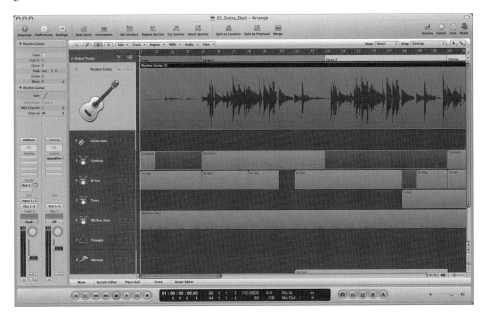

15 Press Command-F2 to save this zoom setting to the second memory location (Save as Zoom 2).

16   Use the basic zoom key commands again to zoom in four more steps vertically and four more steps horizontally (press each key combination four times).

17   Press Command-F3 to save the zoom setting to the third memory location (Save as Zoom 3).

You have saved three zoom settings with varying degrees of magnification.

18   Try pressing F1 through F3 to view the zoom snapshots.

These settings work effectively in conjunction with the zoom positioning techniques discussed earlier, allowing you to quickly view elements of the project at multiple magnification levels.

19   Press F1 to return to the first zoom snapshot.

20   Option-click the Verse 3 marker to go to the beginning of the section.

21   Press F1 through F3, recalling the zoom levels you set earlier.

The selected region (Rhythm Guitar) zooms in, keeping the playhead position within the window.

Zooming In on Regions or Events

Zooming in on specific regions is useful when you need to focus on a particular element in a project. It provides a quick way to resize the visible work area to encompass the entire region or regions.

There are several useful key commands for zooming in on regions, including "Zoom to fit Selection vertically & horizontally, store Navigation Snapshot." This function automatically employs the zoom settings that best fit your selection within the window. The command is also dynamic, using low zoom levels for large regions and high zoom levels for small ones.

Since this has already been assigned to a key combination by default (Control-Option-Z), let's give it a try within the project.

1 Press 1 to open Screenset 1, returning to your original view.

2 On track 8, select the Maracas region.

3 Press Control-Option-Z to activate the "Zoom to fit Selection vertically & horizontally, store Navigation Snapshot" command.

The screen changes size to fit the entire selected region, justifying the selection to the upper-left corner of the work area.

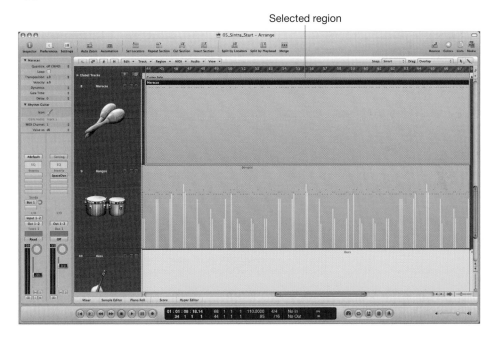

Selected region

4 Control-Option-click anywhere within the Arrange area to return to the original zoom level.

NOTE ▶ Control-Option is a hard-wired key command used to temporarily activate the Zoom tool. Clicking (without dragging) with the Zoom tool will always return to the previous zoom level.

5 In track 1, select the Rhythm Guitar region.

6 Press Control-Option-Z to activate the "Zoom to fit Selection vertically & horizontally, store Navigation Snapshot" command.

The work area changes size to fit the entire region, shrinking the horizontal view while zooming in vertically.

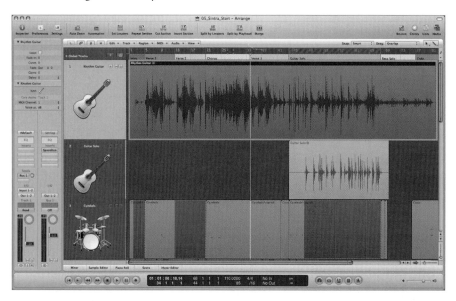

TIP ▶ This technique also works for zooming in on individual events in other editors such as the Piano Roll.

A similar zooming effect can be achieved based on locators rather than regions or events. You need to assign a key command to this function.

7 Choose Logic Pro > Preferences > Key Commands, or press Option-K, to open the Key Commands window.

The search field should still have *zoom* typed in it, with the Command list displaying all commands with *zoom* in the name.

8 In the Command list, choose "Zoom to fit Locators, store Navigation Snapshot."

9 Click the Learn by Key Label button.

10 Press Shift-Control-Z to assign this key command to the function.

11 Close the Key Commands window.

Remember how the locators automatically changed to fit the marker when you used the commands for going to the next and previous markers? You can use this feature in conjunction with the key command you just set, adapting the view to display only the selected section.

12 Use the Go to Next/Previous marker commands to jump to the Intro marker.

13 Press Shift-Control-Z.

The work area is resized horizontally to fit the entire Intro section in the window.

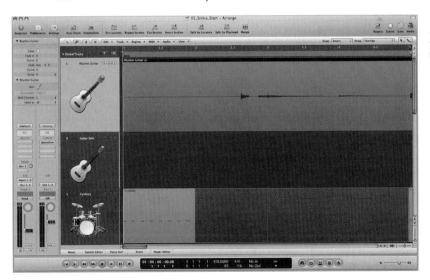

Magnifying the Waveform Without Zooming the Region

Audio is displayed in the Arrange area as waveforms that are constantly redrawn for every zoom level, all the way to single-sample resolution. When the signal level is low, the displayed waveform is quite small and can be difficult to edit.

A good example of this is the Rhythm Guitar region at measure 4. A small waveform is barely visible.

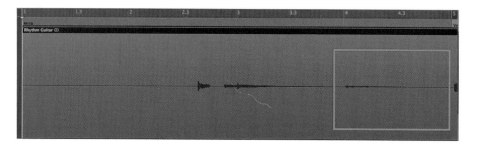

To enable more precise edits, the waveform can be zoomed vertically, independent of the region. Logic has a dedicated Waveform Zoom tool to do just this.

1 At the lower-right corner of the Arrange area, hold down the Waveform Zoom button until a slider appears, then release the mouse button.

2 Once the Waveform Zoom slider is active, drag it up until the small waveform in the Rhythm Guitar region is clearly visible.

The waveform is magnified while the region size stays the same.

This makes the waveform much easier to edit without changing the visible area.

3   Click the Waveform Zoom button to turn off the waveform zoom.

The Waveform Zoom button acts as a toggle between the zoomed view and the original magnification.

The waveform zoom is independent of the screenset and zoom level. It is especially helpful for working with low-signal passages, where you might want the waveform continuously displayed in a magnified state.

Editing the Arrangement

The ability to rearrange the structure of a composition is an essential part of composing and arranging. However, the seemingly simple task of cutting and repeating sections can become overly complicated, and achieving the desired results often entails multiple steps (dividing regions, selecting areas, cutting, pasting, and so on). Fortunately, Logic offers several features that help with editing multiple regions over numerous tracks by combining multiple steps into single commands.

1   Press 1 to open Screenset 1, returning the project to its original zoom settings.

2   Press Control–Command–Right Arrow and Control–Command–Left Arrow (the Go to Next/Previous Marker key commands) as needed to navigate to the Verse 2 Marker.

The cycle area (and locators) adapts to the Verse 2 marker.

3   In the Arrange area's local menu bar, choose Edit > Cut/Insert Time > Snip: Cut Section Between Locators.

NOTE ▶ Depending on your individual setup, a dialog may appear asking if you want to erase the automation data within the selected area along with the edit (this preference can be found in Preferences > Automation). For the purpose of this exercise, it won't matter which option you choose (Don't Erase or Erase). However, it is important to keep in mind that large-scale edits will also affect underlying (and oftentimes unseen) automation information written to the tracks.

Multiple things happen when the command is executed:

▶   All regions that overlap the cycle area are divided to form separate regions within the points specified by the locators.

▶   All material within the cycle area is selected.

▶   The selected regions are deleted and saved to the Clipboard.

▶   The regions immediately after the right locator are moved earlier along the Bar ruler to the location of the left locator.

By performing this edit, you effectively eliminated Verse 2 from the project without forming a gap in the project.

TIP ▶ You can also click the Cut Section button in the Toolbar, or press Control-Command-X.

4   Play the project from Verse 1 to the Chorus, listening to the edit you just made.

Now that you've tried your hand at cutting an entire section, you will perform another common large-scale edit, repeating a section.

5   Use the Go to Next/Previous Marker commands to navigate to the Verse 1 marker and set locators around it.

6   In the Arrange area's local menu bar, choose Edit > Cut/Insert Time > Repeat Section Between Locators.

Similar to Cut Section Between Locators, this command groups multiple functions under one roof, selecting only the region information that lies between the locators and inserting it immediately. The result is that the entire Verse 1 section is repeated, followed by the Chorus section.

7   Play the project, listening to the edit you just made.

8   Stop playback.

Lesson Review

1. How do markers aid in a production?

2. How is changing the text and color of markers useful in a production?

3. Where are markers accessed?

4. How do specialized playback commands function in a production?

5. How are locators set?

6. Zooming justification depends on what factors?

7. How are zoom settings stored?

8. Identify the difference between the Zoom to Fit Selection and the Zoom to Fit Locator commands.

9. How can you magnify the audio waveform independently of the region?

10. How can you edit large areas of a project at once?

Answers

1. Markers can designate section material or serve as navigation points.

2. Changing the appearance of markers (including production notes) helps you easily identify and navigate to sections within the arrangement.

3. Markers can be accessed in the Bar ruler, Marker track, or Marker List.

4. Specialized play commands can effectively aid in quick, nonlinear navigation.

5. Locators can quickly be set by dragging within the Bar ruler or by creating cycle areas for any region, event, or marker.

6. Zooming justification is dependent on playhead position and region selection.

7. Although Logic keeps track of previous magnification levels when zooming, zoom snapshots can be saved and recalled using key commands.

8. Zoom to Fit Selection adapts the viewable area to display selected regions or events. Zoom to Fit Locators allows you quickly display marker areas within the arrangement.

9. Use the Waveform Zoom slider to magnify an audio waveform independently of the region.

10. Locators can be used to edit large areas of the project at once by enabling you to cut or repeat entire sections.

6

Lesson Files	Logic 8_BTB_Files > Lessons > 06_Sintra_Start.logic
Media	Logic 8_BTB_Files > Media > Sintra
Time	This lesson takes approximately 1 hour to complete.
Goals	Solve problems using creative editing techniques
	Create seamless audio edits and transitions
	Create cohesive musical material using existing takes
	Compare takes for inclusion in composite tracks
	Isolate and assemble take material into a composite track
	Use fine-level editing to fix problems in the audio signal

Lesson **6**
Advanced Audio Editing

The flexibility of editing digital audio is one of the distinct advantages of working with nonlinear hard-disk recording systems. The user can precisely fix mistakes, adjust timing, rearrange section material, and combine elements in every conceivable way. What was once incredibly difficult or impossible to do with analog tape is now almost routine if you have the right set of tools and skills.

Modern production is both blessed with and plagued by this flexibility. On the one hand, it allows sophisticated edits to be performed with great accuracy. On the other, falling into obsessiveness is all too easy, and you can worry a track to a lifeless lump of 1s and 0s.

That said, good editing techniques can take your material to another level, turning a raw performance into a polished piece of music. Logic offers many ways to work with digital audio, whether fixing a performance mistake or a recording problem that would ruin an otherwise excellent take, or creating new parts out of an amalgam of tracks.

In this lesson, you will explore techniques for editing digital audio, enabling you to rework raw material with speed and flexibility.

Using Edits to Create Parts

One of the advantages offered by digital editing is the ease with which new parts are created from existing material through copying and pasting. In order to achieve a convincing result, however, it is of equal importance to use judicious edits to assemble the new part as well as create seamless transitions between the constituent building blocks.

1 Choose File > Open.

2 In the file selector box, choose Music > Logic 8_BTB_Files > Lessons and open **06_Sintra_Start.logic**.

> **NOTE** ▶ This is the same project that you used in the previous lesson, but at a different stage of production. You will be using this project file in the following exercises.

Look at the length of the Rhythm Guitar.3 region on track 1. It ends about halfway through the Bass Solo section. This is because the original recorded part from the tracking session did not contain any material for the Bass Solo or Coda sections, which were added later in production. Punching in or adding other recorded material is not an option at this point because the tracking session has long since passed. Instead, let's look at ways to extend the existing material using editing techniques.

3 Use the key command for moving to the next marker (Control–Command–Right Arrow) or previous marker (Control–Command–Left Arrow) to go to the beginning of the Bass Solo section (and to set the locators).

4 Use the "Zoom to fit Locators" key command (Shift-Control-Z) to zoom in to the Bass Solo section (we assigned this in the last lesson).

The window adapts to encompass the Bass Solo section.

5 In the Transport bar, click the Cycle button.

A cycle area is created around the Bass Solo section.

6 In the track 1 header, click the Solo button.

The Bar ruler is shaded in yellow, indicating that Solo mode is turned on.

NOTE ▶ Mute and solo states can be independent for tracks and channel strips, depending on a setting in your preferences (Preferences > Audio > General > Track Mute/Solo). In order for you to see the Bar ruler displaying yellow (Solo mode engaged), you need to have CPU-saving (Slow Response) selected within the Track Mute/Solo menu.

7   Play the project, listening to the Rhythm Guitar track.

8   When you are familiar with the material, click the Stop button.

In this exercise, you will copy and paste the arpeggiated chords at the beginning of the Bass Solo to extend the track through the Coda section. The waveform is rather small in this quiet section, so to make an accurate edit, it is necessary to zoom in on the waveform.

9   Use the Waveform Zoom tool located in the lower-right corner of the Arrange area to magnify the waveform to its maximum resolution.

The waveform is magnified.

10   Using the Scissors tool, click the Rhythm Guitar.3 region at measure 69 (you can use the help tags to position the tool accurately).

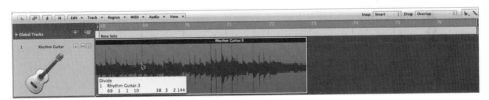

The region divides at measure 69.

NOTE ▶ Logic automatically assigns sequential numbers to newly created regions.

11   Switch back to the Pointer tool.

12   Copy the last region in the track (Rhythm Guitar.5) by Option-dragging it so that it begins at measure 72.

NOTE ▸ Depending on your setup, a dialog may appear asking if you want to copy the automation data within the region. This alert preference can be found in Preferences > Automation. For this exercise, it won't matter which option you choose (Don't Copy or Copy).

The region is copied, creating a new region, Rhythm Guitar.6, which overlaps the previous region at measure 72.

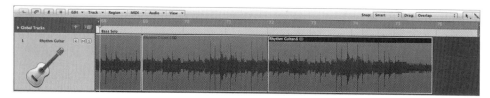

13 Copy the Rhythm Guitar.6 region by Option-dragging it to the right so that it begins at measure 75.

The region is copied, creating a new region, Rhythm Guitar.7, at measure 75.

14 Using the same technique, create a copy of the Rhythm Guitar.7 region to begin at measure 78.

The region is copied, creating a new region, Rhythm Guitar.8, at measure 78.

NOTE ▸ You can use the Zoom Horizontal Out key command (Control–Left Arrow) to see the entire extended part.

Take a moment to observe something important. Look closely at the regions you just moved and copied. You'll notice dotted lines located close to measures 73 and 76. These lines represent the ends of the previous regions that are lying underneath each copied region.

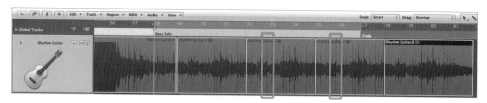

When two regions overlap, the region with the latest start time takes precedence during playback.

15 Using the Pointer tool, select the four copied regions (Rhythm Guitar.5, .6, .7, and .8) by drawing a rectangle selection around them.

You might have noticed that the region lengths seem to shift visually before you release the mouse button. Although the project will play back appropriately, with each region sounding at the right location, it can get visually confusing. You can easily fix this by eliminating the overlaps.

16 From the Arrange area's local menu bar, choose Regions > Remove Overlaps.

Each underlying region is trimmed at the point of overlap.

Using Fades to Smooth Out Transitions

When combining regions, you will often hear a short click at the seam of each edit. This is created by an interruption in the audio waveform at a nonzero point (a point where signal is present). In effect, each region's audio waveform is clipped just shy of the ending or beginning of a sound.

This can be fixed by inserting a crossfade, a technique that automatically performs a quick fade-out and fade-in at the edit point so that the audio interruption won't occur, thereby eliminating the click. Let's take a look at some of the ways in which you can employ fades to smooth transitions.

1 With the four regions (Rhythm Guitar.5, .6, .7, and .8) still selected, press the Set Locators by Regions/Events key command, Control-= (equal sign) (or Control-' (apostrophe) on a laptop).

The cycle area adapts to the newly created passage.

2 Click the Play button to hear the passage with the copied regions.

Listen for short clicks between the edited regions.

3 Stop playback.

4   While holding the Shift key, click the Rhythm Guitar.8 region, deselecting it.

Look at the Region Parameter box, located immediately to the left of track 1. Notice that the box displays "3 selected," indicating that any adjustments made to the region parameters will affect all four selected regions. You will be working with one of these parameters.

5   In the Region Parameter box, click the Fade Out parameter, and choose X from the pop-up menu.

This enables a crossfade option.

Nothing has changed yet within the regions. This is because you haven't determined a length for the fade.

6   Double-click the number 0 to the right of the Fade parameter, and enter *10* in the value field.

The edit seams now display a crossfade (represented by a semitransparent white shape) at each edit point, lasting 10 milliseconds (ms).

7   Play the project, stopping after you've listened to the passage with the crossfades.

The passage plays with smooth audio transitions between the regions.

Now that you've created smooth transitions between the edited regions, you can finish the passage by adding a short fade out to the last region.

8   In the Arrange tools, choose Crossfade Tool.

9   Drag directly over the Rhythm Guitar.8 region, starting at measure 81 and ending slightly after the region end.

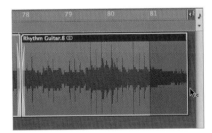

A fade-out is created from measure 81 to the end of the region.

10 Play the project, stopping after you've listened to the passage with the fade-out at the end.

Using Existing Material to Fix Problems

Often, an otherwise perfectly good take might have a small defect such as an instrumental error, an extraneous noise, or even a malfunction in the recording process. By using carefully placed edits, you can substitute a passage of identical material for the problem segment.

1   Using the Go to Next/Previous Marker commands, go to the Verse 1 section.

The cycle area now encompasses the Verse 1 section.

The waveform magnification isn't needed here because the amplitude is at a sufficient level for you to easily see the waveform.

Let's continue by returning the waveform to its normal display state.

2   Click the Waveform Zoom button to return the waveform to its original size.

3   Play the Verse 1 passage.

Verse 1 plays with an audible warble around the fourth beat of bar 7.

The perceived warble was caused by a glitch in the recording process, most likely from the audio interface. All is not lost, however, as the verse is repeated two times with the same musical material.

By finding an identical passage, you can replace the bad section with a copy from a good take. A perfect choice is the equivalent point within Verse 2, starting around the fourth beat of measure 15.

Let's zoom in to this area to make a precise edit.

4   Using the Zoom tool, draw a rectangle selection around measures 15 to 17.

NOTE ▸ Depending on the size of your display, you might need to scroll to the right to perform this selection.

Now you can make the edit. You could do this by cutting and copying, as you did to the tail end of the track; but this requires multiple steps, including cutting around the desired material, copying to the new location, and eliminating the overlaps. Instead, try one of Logic's handiest editing tools: the Marquee tool.

The Marquee tool allows you to select material for editing within regions without having to cut them up. It can work across multiple regions at once or in a single region, depending on the task required.

5   In the Arrange tools, choose Marquee Tool.

6   With the Marquee tool, drag directly over the Rhythm Guitar.1 region, from around 15 3 1 1 to 17 1 1 1.

The selected passage is highlighted within the region.

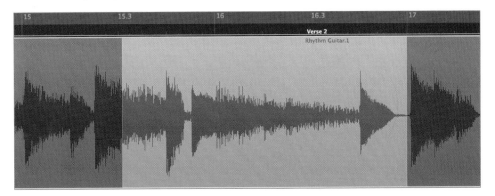

7   Click the Play button.

The project starts playing from the marquee selection, stopping when it reaches the end.

NOTE ▶ The project will always play from the marquee selection when the normal Play command is used, regardless of cycle area or the current playhead position. This feature is handy for quickly locating and auditioning material within regions.

The material to be used for this edit starts at the transient located near 15 4 1 1 and ends right before the transient located just after 17 1 1 1. Your marquee selection was not that precise, but don't worry: Logic allows you to lengthen or shorten a marquee selection by tabbing to nearby transients.

8 Press Shift–Right Arrow to move the left marquee border to the transient at 15 4 1 1.

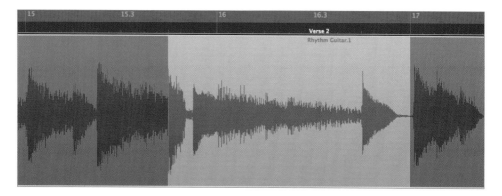

9 Press the Right Arrow key (without holding down Shift) to move the right marquee border to the transient located just past 17 1 1 1.

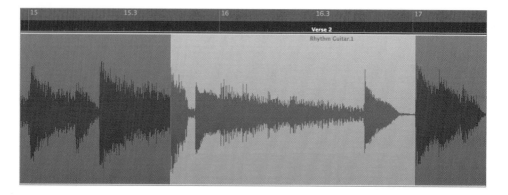

The marquee selection expands to precisely encompass the area you want to edit.

10 Using the Zoom tool, click anywhere in the Arrange area, making sure not to drag.

The window returns to the previous zoom level with the marquee selection still highlighted.

Now that you have selected the material to be copied, you can place it at the desired position. If you were to copy the selection as you did previously (by Option-dragging), the regions would overlap. Instead, you can create a splice without an overlap by using an alternative drag mode. Drag modes are available only in the Arrange area, and they act as preferences for moving regions.

11 In the upper-right corner of the Arrange area, click the Drag pop-up menu, and choose No Overlap.

As the name suggests, No Overlap is used in situations when you don't want to create overlapped regions. In this mode, placing a selected region over another trims the underlying region and eliminates overlaps.

12 Using the Pointer tool, Option-drag the marquee selection to the left, placing it at 7 3 4 238 (use the help tag to help you locate the position).

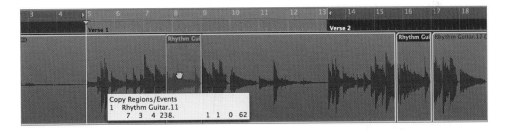

NOTE ▶ When you're dragging regions and events, Logic automatically snaps to a relative position (same bar/beat/division/tick relationship) based on the start point of the selected region or event (in this case, 7 3 4 238). This is usually desirable, as it allows you to align objects with the source material's bars and beats. Snapping to relative positions can be turned off by choosing Snap > Snap to Absolute Value, which will snap the selection to the ruler's bars, beats, division values, and so on, without reference to the source material.

The highlighted passage is copied to the new location, creating a new region at the target position.

13 Using the Pointer tool, click anywhere in the Arrange area to eliminate the marquee selection.

14 Click the Play button.

The edit works well but has an audible click at the first edit point.

15 With the Pointer tool, Shift-click the copied region and the adjacent region immediately to its left.

16 In the Region Parameter box, set a crossfade of 10 ms, as you did previously.

Crossfades of 10 ms are created at both edit points.

17 Click the Play button to hear the material with the crossfades.

18 Click the track's Solo button to turn off soloing.

19 Press the 1 key to recall Screenset 1, resetting your zoom levels to the original state.

> **TIP** ▶ Although selecting across multiple tracks is possible with the Marquee tool, it quickly becomes tedious when you're making frequent edits to multitrack recordings such as drums. Instead, try using the marquee stripe, which creates a marquee selection across all the tracks designated by an area within the ruler. You can turn on this feature in the Bar ruler display menu by choosing Marquee Stripe. An additional lane appears just above the ruler, and you can drag to select an area similar to a cycle area.

Comping Tracks

Comping is the art of compiling a complete track from several raw performances. By using judicious editing techniques, you can assemble a cohesive musical track from the best parts of multiple takes.

In this exercise, you will create composite tracks from various materials and from multiple passes of the same part, drawing on a variety of strategies and techniques.

Understanding Comping Strategies

The process of comping a track demands a certain degree of consistency in the track components. You could assemble a comp from material on separate tracks that is routed to different channel strips, but there is a definite advantage to using the same track and channel strip when creating, editing, and mixing the source material. Using the same channel strip provides identical volume levels, pan positions, bus sends, and inserts, which will help level the playing field when you compare similar material.

The simplest and most efficient way to achieve consistency is to record a take folder on a single track (as described in Lesson 2, "Creating and Managing Takes"). In addition to keeping track material organized, a take folder also provides essential tools for quickly editing and creating a comp.

If a situation arises in which you need to put contributing material on tracks assigned to separate channel strips (such as when individual takes need to be processed differently to better match one another), you will be unable to utilize the comp editing features outlined in this exercise. If this is the case, however, it is still important to have the contributing tracks output to the same pair of channels on your audio interface. That way, you can make sure that your monitoring levels are consistent.

As in all editing procedures, an important aspect of the comping process is deciding how to approach the material that you will use to build a composite track. You should consider some general strategies that can make the process easier and produce a more satisfying musical outcome:

▶ If you have tracked many alternative takes, consider combing through them before you create the comp and isolating the three or four best choices to contribute to the part.

▶ When listening to the passes, judge the amount of editing that would be required to whip them into shape. A natural musical recording with acceptable flaws usually yields better results than a highly doctored track.

▶ Consider how well the material sits with the complete arrangement and with the other contributing tracks. If a part contains dramatic changes in feel or timbre, it will most certainly be harder to create a cohesive part, much less a cohesive composition.

Assembling a Composite Track

In this exercise, you will assemble a composite rhythm guitar track from several takes, isolating and compiling the good bits. In particular, you will be working with the chorus section, which has three takes in the take folder. All parts consist of the same musical material recorded in different passes during the tracking session.

Viewing Tracks for Comping

To accurately edit and assemble the comp from the take folder, it is important to first zoom in and set the cycle area. This allows you to focus on the area you will be working with. Notice that the Rhythm Guitar take folder slightly overlaps the Chorus section (the pickup, or *anacrusis*, to bar 21 is also included in the take).

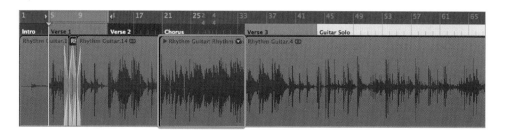

When editing, it is also useful to start playback just before—and to end it just after—the material to be edited, checking the transitions to and from the adjacent sections. For these reasons, it will not be sufficient to use a marker as your target for zooming and setting locators for the cycle area. Instead, first set your locators manually, then use the cycle area as the zoom and playback target.

1   Drag in the Bar ruler to create a cycle area from measure 20 to measure 35.

    NOTE ▸ Cycle mode should still be active from the previous exercise.

2   Use the "Zoom to fit Locators" command (Control-Shift-Z) to zoom in on the cycle area. Now that you've centered in on the part of the Bar ruler you will be working with, take a look at the take folder contents.

3 At the upper-left corner of the take folder, click the disclosure triangle.

The take folder expands to show all three takes within the Arrange area.

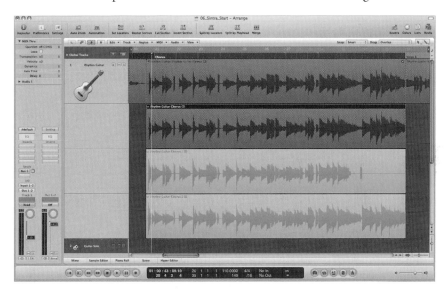

This is a perfect zoom setting in which to assemble the comp, so it is worth your while to save it as a screenset in case your view inadvertently changes.

4 From the Screenset menu, choose Duplicate.

A dialog appears asking for a number and a name for the new screenset.

5 In the Name field, enter *Comp edit view*.

6 Click OK.

Now you can press the 2 key (or from the Screenset menu, choose "2 Comp edit view") to recall these zoom settings.

Comparing Performances

Now that you've isolated your work area, you should listen to each take, separating the wheat from the chaff. As you can see, the first take, Rhythm Guitar Chorus, is highlighted in the take folder and will sound when played back.

> **NOTE ►** Clicking a take within the take folder displays the waveform (color included) in the top track of the take folder, making it active for playback. You did this in Lesson 2.

1 Click Play to listen to the first rhythm guitar take (purple) in the context of the project.

Though not egregious, the performance suffers from subtle deficiencies in the dynamics and timing, which were more skillfully realized in later passes. The ending of the Chorus section, from measures 32 to 34, works well, however, and should be retained, as it provides a smooth transition to the following verse.

2 Click the second take, Rhythm Guitar Chorus.1.

3 Click Play to listen to the second rhythm guitar take (green) in the context of the project.

The material is strong for the third phrase of the Chorus, beginning at the end of measure 24 and going until about measure 27. However, there is a flub near the end of the region resulting from a premature ending of the recording process.

4 Click the third take, Rhythm Guitar Chorus.2.

5 Click Play to listen to the third rhythm guitar take (yellow) in the context of the project.

This take contains a good performance of the beginning and latter parts of the Chorus, with a weaker middle section.

All in all, there is ripe material to choose from if you use phrases, or parts of phrases, from each take to construct a new track.

> **TIP ►** You can select regions from the take folder without opening it by clicking the arrow at the upper right of the take folder to open the Take Folder menu.

Isolating Wanted Material

Selecting desirable material to form the comp can be accomplished in a variety of ways, and the process can quickly become confusing if you don't follow a basic strategy. For this reason, it is advisable to start by selecting a take that will form the majority of the comp material, providing a framework in which to place additional material. In this instance, the beginning and some of the middle sections of the third take (Rhythm Guitar.2) are keepers and will form the majority of the comp.

1 Select the third take, Rhythm Guitar Chorus.2.

The take folder highlights the Rhythm Guitar Chorus.2 take (in yellow).

The next steps are to insert pieces of material from the other takes, one at a time. The ending of the first take sounds satisfactory, so you can do that next.

2 Drag the right-hand border of the first take (Rhythm Guitar Chorus) to the left, stopping just before the large transient at measure 32 (the beginning of the next note).

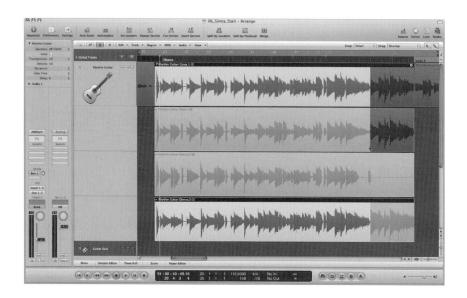

The ending of the third take is dimmed, and the top take track now displays a purple area from measures 32 to 34, representing the first take.

3   In the second take, drag from just before the transient after measure 24, to just before the transient starting on measure 27.

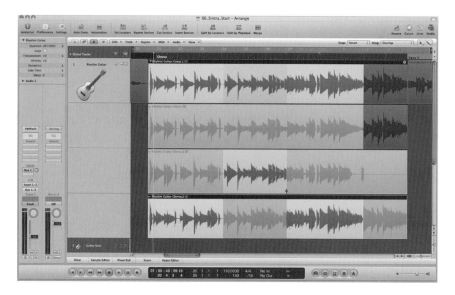

The top take track now depicts the selected areas (waveforms and colors) from each take.

TIP ▶ You can always change the left and right borders of the selected areas by dragging them after they are initially selected. In addition, a selection can be moved forward and backward on the Bar ruler by dragging from the middle of it.

The Chorus is now divided into four distinct phrases.

4   Click the Play button to listen to the comp.

NOTE ▶ Logic automatically creates crossfades between each selected area of the comp. To define the curve and length of a crossfade, choose Logic Pro > Preferences > Audio > General and set the desired values in the "Crossfades for Merge and Take Comping" section.

Creating Alternative Comps

Logic allows you to create multiple comps, storing each for later comparison. These alternative comps are accessed from the Take Folder menu.

1   At the upper right of the take folder, click the Take Folder menu's arrow.

The Take Folder menu appears. As you can see, your completed comp is listed in the menu as Comp 1: Comp 1. Before you make an alternative comp, name the completed comp to avoid confusion.

2   In the Take Folder menu, choose Rename Comp.

The Rename Comp window appears.

3 In the Name field, enter *3_2_3_1* to indicate the order of the takes used in the comp.

4 Click OK.

The take folder now lists the new name, Rhythm Guitar: 3_2_3_1, at the top.

5 Open the Take Folder menu by clicking the arrow.

Notice that a "new comp" option is listed in the menu.

6 From the Take Folder menu, choose New Comp.

Now that you've named the comp and created a slot for the new comp, it is safe to create any additional alternative comps desired.

7 With the techniques you learned earlier in the lesson, try assembling and naming your own comp using material from the take folder.

The Take Folder menu provides an easy way to compare alternative comps.

8 Toggle between the two comps created in this lesson by choosing them in the Take Folder menu.

9 Play the project, comparing each comp created in the lesson with the other.

Flattening the Comp

Now that the comp and an alternative have been completed, the take folder may be closed without a second thought. However, any region-level processing (Region Parameter box settings, Time and Pitch Machine manipulations, and so on) done on the Take Folder will treat the entire region contents as one. When you need to individually manipulate the separate take areas that make up the comp, it is necessary to convert the comp to individual regions. This process is referred to as *flattening*.

1 Open the Take Folder menu by clicking the arrow.

2 Choose Comp 1: 3_2_3_1 to make the original comp active.

3 In the Take Folder menu, choose Flatten.

The selected take areas that made up the comp are converted to individual regions, in the order they were created and with the default crossfades applied (as defined in the General tab of the Audio preferences).

> **NOTE** ▶ The Take Folder menu also includes a "Flatten and Merge" command that converts the take areas of a comp to a single contiguous region by using digital mixdown (a process similar to using the Glue tool or the Merge Regions command on adjacent audio regions). It is not unlike the flatten function in digital graphics applications that merges all visual layers into one.

4   Click the Play button to hear the comp track in the context of the arrangement.

> **TIP** ▶ If you are working on a project in which a take folder was not made, or composite material is located on multiple tracks, all is not lost. You can still pack a new take folder by clicking the associated regions and, from the Arrange area's local menu bar, choosing Region > Folder > Pack Take Folder.

Fixing Problems Using the Sample Editor

Up to now, the exercises have exclusively used the Arrange area for editing. Starting with Logic Pro 8, the Arrange area allows both sample-accurate viewing and waveform editing, just like the Sample Editor. Why, then, do you still need the Sample Editor? The Sample Editor also provides unique editing and file-based processing features (such as the Time and Pitch Machine used in Lesson 3, "Matching Tempo and Pitch") that are indispensable for some tasks.

If you played the entire project during this lesson, you probably noticed the sharp click in the guitar solo. In an otherwise acceptable take, an audible click is evident slightly after measure 61. Using the Sample Editor, you can zoom in and remove the offending spike (most likely caused by a digital clock error during the recording session) by "drawing" it out.

Using the Sample Editor's Waveform Overview

At the top of the Sample Editor is a view of the entire audio region's waveform. The waveform overview acts as a map, always showing the full audio file attributed to the currently selected audio region, regardless of the zoom resolution. Any editing selection or current playback position is mirrored there and in the detailed waveform display. You can also use the overview to navigate the audio file for editing purposes.

1   Press 1 to open Screenset 1.

This returns you to a view of the entire arrangement.

2   On track 2, double-click the Guitar Solo region.

The Sample Editor opens, displaying the Guitar Solo region.

NOTE ▸ Depending on the size of your display's screen, you might need to resize the Sample Editor for maximum viewing by dragging the border that separates the Sample Editor from the Arrange area.

3   Click anywhere in the waveform overview. (Try an area where some signal is present.)

The detailed waveform display updates to show the selected point in the overview, represented by a white rectangle.

The relationship between the waveform overview and the waveform display is interactive, as adjustments made in either area will be represented in both.

4   Press Control–Right Arrow (the Zoom Horizontal In key command) once to slightly enlarge the currently visible selection.

Notice that the dotted rectangle in the overview has shrunk, accurately reflecting the area in the waveform display.

Locating Problem Areas in the Sample Editor

Now that you've been introduced to how the Sample Editor's waveform overview works, let's use it to locate the problematic click.

1 If it is not turned on already, click the Catch button located at the upper left of the Sample Editor.

2 At the top of the Sample Editor, click the Play button to listen to the take.

3 Click the Play button again to stop playback when you hear the digital click right after measure 61.

You can see the click quite clearly as a sharp vertical spike, interrupting the normal audio waveform.

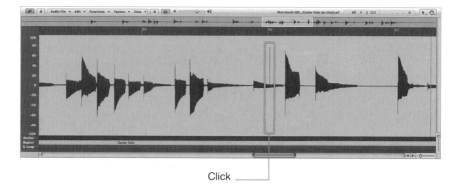

Click

4 In the waveform display, drag to select an area beginning approximately at measure 60 and ending approximately at measure 62.

The selected area is highlighted.

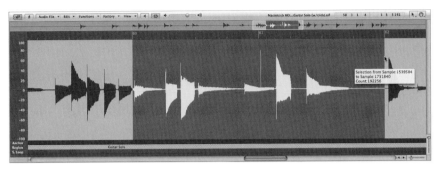

NOTE ► You may need to use the Zoom Horizontal In/Out command to see the entire selection.

5   Click the Loop button next to the Play button to turn it on, if necessary.

Continuously repeating the selected area allows you to concentrate on the click. Now you can zoom in on things a bit.

6   In the waveform display, use the Zoom tool to draw a selection rectangle around the click.

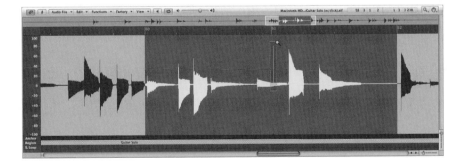

The click's waveform is magnified.

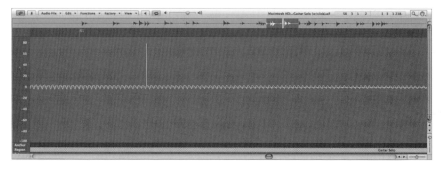

Although the magnification is at a good level, you need to get in even closer to draw out the click.

7   In the waveform display, use the Zoom tool again to draw a selection around the click.

The view is magnified, displaying the click as a sloped rectangle sticking straight up from the surrounding waveform.

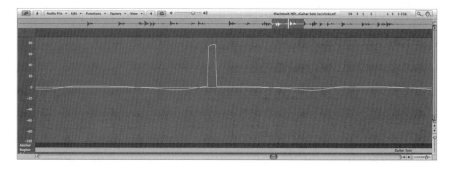

This zoom level will work well for the editing operation. At this magnification, the entire window represents about 130 samples (approximately 3 ms)!

Drawing Out Clicks with the Pencil Tool

Now that the click can be seen clearly, you can use the Sample Editor's Pencil tool to draw out the waveform, smoothing over the click as if it never existed.

NOTE ▶ The Pencil is only displayed when working with high magnification levels.

1   Choose the Pencil tool.

2   Now, draw a line connecting the bottom points of the click rectangle. In effect, you're redrawing the waveform as if it had never been interrupted by the click.

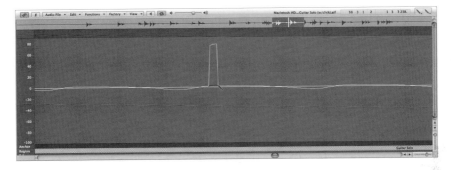

The click is eliminated, replaced by a smooth waveform.

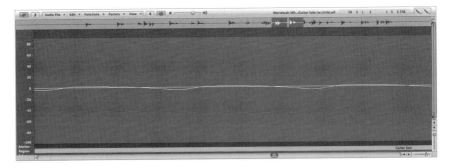

NOTE ▶ You might need two or more tries to do this successfully, as the waveform points must completely connect with each other.

3   Using the Zoom tool, double-click the background of the waveform display to return to the original zoom level.

4   Click the Play button to hear your edit.

The passage plays back without any audible click.

> **TIP** ▶ You can also use this technique with stereo audio files by holding down the Option key when drawing changes, thereby changing both stereo channels.

5   Click the Sample Editor button to close the Sample Editor.

> **TIP** ▶ Instead of using the built-in Sample Editor, you can also set Logic Pro to open audio regions or files within an external sample editor like Soundtrack Pro. To do this, first specify the application you wish to use by choosing Logic Pro > Preferences > Audio > Sample Editor and clicking the Set button under the External Sample Editor heading. Once this path is defined, simply click the audio region or file you wish to edit and choose Options > Audio > Open in [name of sample editor], or use the corresponding key command.

Lesson Review

1.   Which editing technique can be used to extend or repair parts?

2.   How can Logic's dragging behavior be changed in the Arrange area?

3.   What technique is used to smooth out transitions between regions?

4.   What makes up a composite (comp) track?

5.   What is the most efficient way to isolate material to create a comp?

6.   Do you have to manually apply crossfades between the selected areas in the take folder to form a seamless edit?

7.   What is the Sample Editor used for?

8.   How do you eliminate clicks and digital spikes in an audio file?

Answers

1. Parts can be extended or repaired by cutting and pasting similar material.

2. Logic's dragging behavior can be changed to suit the editing need by selecting from the Drag menu.

3. Crossfades are used to smooth out seams between regions and can be placed automatically or manually.

4. A composite track is made up of material taken from contributing takes.

5. Isolating material for a composite track is done quickly by selecting areas in the take folder.

6. Comp tracks made from the take folder use automatic crossfades to seamlessly combine material into a cohesive whole.

7. The Sample Editor allows extremely fine edits and adjustments to an audio region, irrespective of the project's tempo and key.

8. Digital clicks and spikes can be eliminated in the Sample Editor with the Pencil tool.

Taking a Leap of Logic— J.F. Brissette

WHILE THE PERFORMERS of Cirque du Soleil's *O* are swimming, diving, and leaping under the spotlight, a balancing act of another kind takes place in a dimmer corner of their 1800-seat theater at the Bellagio in Las Vegas. Ten times a week, conductor J.F. Brissette simultaneously plays bass, calls cues, and dances on sequence-triggering foot pedals to make sure that every thrilling moment of the aquatic spectacular is supported by an evocative musical score. And while Brissette's juggling act isn't death-defying, it is undeniably agile.

Fortunately, he uses Logic Pro 8 as a safety net.

"Logic is just a joy to use," said Brissette. "I like the ease of use, the whole 'thinking' of the interface, and the way it presents the music to you. With all its software instruments and plug-ins, you don't need a lot of extra gear."

The Montreal-born bassist, arranger, and producer brought Logic to the center ring when he joined *O*.

"In *O*, they were solely using keyboards and their internal sequencers. It was very time-consuming to edit anything. One of the first things I did was to export the MIDI sequences to Logic to work with them. While we still run the show with our main keyboard's internal sequencer, my workflow now includes a complete round-trip between the keyboard sequencer and Logic."

Among the editing tasks that Brissette performs in Logic is the creation of backup recordings of the *O* musicians that can fill in a part in case of emergency. "Unlike a Broadway show, for example, we can't easily find musicians to sit in if one of our musicians gets sick," explained Brissette. "I can transfer live multitrack recordings of the show to my Mac and start cutting them up by song, including the click track, and edit the audio to correspond to each sequence of the show."

Those edited sequences are turned into multiple audio clips, each containing a single instrumental part. During a performance, Brissette can trigger those parts with a foot pedal, while still playing his bass, to provide an instant cyber-sideman substituting for a missing musician. "Nothing can replace the performance of a live musician, but it's nice to have this flexibility when it's called for."

"The third aspect of my Logic use is during stagings and rehearsals," Brissette added. "I can make a new arrangement of a song on the spot. While playing a video of the act with its song playing on my PowerBook, I can work directly with the performers. When someone says, 'Oh cool, could that be a little shorter?'" I can use skip cycle to cut four bars. It all happens in real time with everybody watching."

During a show, Brissette will sometimes record the live performance directly to his PowerBook for reference use. "I use a Logic template with six audio tracks. From my music booth, I can record the band in two tracks, the click track in another, and the ambient mic from the front-of-house console on a fourth track. The fifth track can carry any musician's performance, in case I need to work on something specific or make a 'minus one' recording for them. I usually put my voice on the last track in case I need a version of a song with my [cue] calls. The live recording doesn't skip a beat on the PowerBook."

Brissette ordered Logic Pro 8 "the day after it was announced," but was a little reluctant to reveal his favorite Logic feature. "This sounds a little geeky, but if there were no key commands, I wouldn't be anywhere. I don't like to mouse around. I'm not a mouse guy. If I have to move my mouse more than a few centimeters, that's too much," he joked.

Not surprisingly, when asked to contribute a Logic tip, Brissette mentioned a key command. After bouncing a mix or region in preparation for burning a CD, Brissette adds the bounced file to the Audio Bin, selects it, and presses Shift-Command-R. (You could also choose Audio File > Show Files in Finder from the local menu bar.) The file appears in the Finder where he can drag it to WaveBurner to make a CD.

"I most like the general feeling of being able to do things really quickly in Logic," Brissette concluded. "I like the revamped interface and how they've combined so many things into one window, but longtime users still have the modular environment."

7

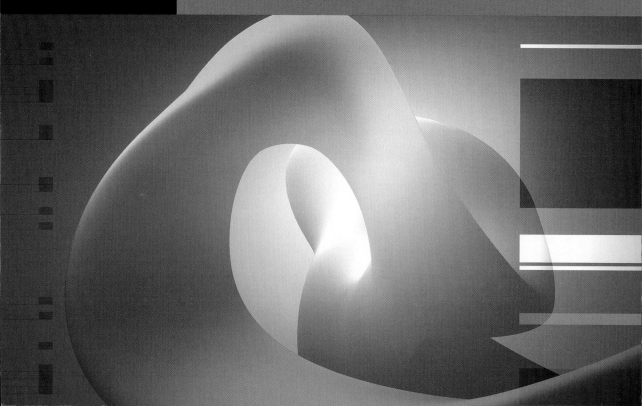

Lesson 7
Advanced MIDI Editing

At its heart, MIDI is a command protocol consisting of status messages that indicate when and how events are performed. While digital and analog audio represent actual sound, MIDI data numerically represents the actions that create or control sound generation. As a result, MIDI editing can be somewhat counterintuitive.

Logic provides similar editing tools and parameters for both MIDI and digital audio input, especially at the region level (for example, for copying and dividing). However, editing the two differs significantly at the finer, note level.

Even considering Logic's powerful digital audio tools, MIDI still has a distinct advantage when it comes to editing, offering extreme flexibility through real-time and nondestructive processing of all data.

In this lesson, you will use several methods of creating expressive musical parts out of existing material, and you will learn selection and editing techniques that enable you to work efficiently at the note level.

Using Loops, Copies, and Aliases

Logic treats all regions—audio or MIDI—in a similar fashion when it comes to duplication. Let's apply digital audio copying techniques from previous lessons to make quick copies of MIDI material in an arrangement.

1   Choose File > Open.

2   In the file selector box, go to Music > Logic 8_BTB_Files > Lessons and open
   07_Sintra_Start.logic.

   For this lesson, you will use the same project you used in the previous two lessons, including all of the earlier edits.

3   If you wish to refamiliarize yourself with the material, play the project.

Using Loops

The Cymbals track (track 3) consists of simple parts that have been created for various sections of the project. With Logic's looping tools, you can fill in some of the parts by extending previously created material.

1   Select the first region in the Cymbals track (track 3).

2   In the Region Parameter box (located at the top of the Inspector), select the Loop checkbox.

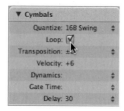

The MIDI region is looped, as represented by the gray boxes following the original region.

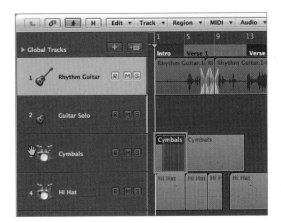

Notice that the loops end at the next region (located at measure 5). When you turn on the Loop function in the Region Parameter box, loops are created to repeat the original region until the loop either runs into another region or reaches the end of the project.

While this works well for quick loops (especially when you're building a backing track), you will frequently need more control over how much of the region is repeated and how often. Loops can be manually drawn to stop at a specific point in time or to play only part of the loop material.

3   Position your pointer over the upper-right corner of the Triangle region on track 7.

The pointer turns into a circular arrow, indicating that it will function as the loop-length editing tool. In this case, the arrangement needs the one-bar triangle part to be extended to 34 2 1 1.

4   Drag the upper-right corner of the Triangle region to the right approximately 10 bars.

Loops are formed as you drag, duplicating the original region. Notice that the loops snap to the bar line when you're dragging (as shown in the help tag), making it impossible to stop the loop at the second beat of bar 34 (34 2 1 1). This is because the snap value is set to Smart by default, which dynamically assigns snap values based on the magnification level (the more you zoom in, the finer the snap grid). In the current screenset, the view is zoomed out to such an extent that the Smart snap function assigns the value to the bar.

Smart snap is convenient for zooming in and out of an arrangement, but it can be inhibiting when making adjustments at levels finer than the bar. There is a quick way to override this, however: changing the Snap mode.

5   Hold down the cursor over the upper-right corner of the original region until the loops disappear, then release the mouse button.

Only the original region is left.

6   In the Arrange area, click to open the Snap menu, and choose Beat.

7   Drag loops from the Triangle region as you did previously, using the help tags to end the loop at 34 2 1 1.

The loops snap to the beat, rather than to the bar, allowing you to stop a loop at the desired beat.

8   Press Shift-Enter (the "Play from Selection" key command) to play the looped triangle part.

9   Stop the playback.

Using Copies

Loops are perfect clones of their source regions. However, they differ from true region copies in their lack of flexibility with regard to placement and content. Loops are always placed adjacent to the original, which makes it impossible to place them at multiple positions in a project. Only copies can be changed independently of the original region; a loop will always reflect the original region's contents.

Copies are best suited for duplicating material from one part of the timeline to another, especially when material needs to be altered independently of its original source. You can use Logic's copying functions to create new material from a copied source.

1   Option-drag the fourth region on the Cymbals track (located at measure 42) to measure 44.

The region is copied to measure 44.

2   On track 3 (Cymbals), click the Solo button to solo the track.

3   Press Shift-Enter to play the project from the copied region.

4   After the copied region has played, click the Stop button.

The Cymbals part consists of steady eighth notes. The project calls for that part to change from eighth notes to quarter notes during the Guitar Solo section, effectively doubling the note lengths as well as changing the placement of notes. What would normally require opening a MIDI editor and selectively deleting and moving individual notes can easily be accomplished with *stretching*, a form of time compression and expression. This technique is identical to one you used earlier on an audio region (in Lesson 3, "Matching Tempo and Pitch").

5   Option-drag the lower-right corner of the new region to the right. Stop when the region length is four bars. The help tag will read 4 0 0 0 for the operation result.

A dialog appears, asking if you want to time stretch the MIDI region.

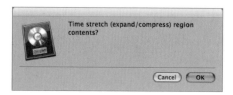

6   Click OK.

7   Press Shift-Enter to listen to the time-stretched region.

The ride cymbal plays at quarter-note intervals over four bars instead of eighth-note intervals over two bars. In effect, you stretched the region to double its length and to double each note value and time placement.

TIP ▶ You can accomplish time compression in a similar fashion by making a region shorter and compressing its events.

Finish by filling in the Cymbals part for the Guitar Solo section with the new region. You can quickly create multiple copies by using the Repeat Regions command.

8   From the Arrange area's local menu bar, choose Region > Repeat Regions.

The Repeat Regions/Events dialog opens. Here you can set the number and placement of copies to be produced.

9   In the Number of Copies field, enter 5.

10   From the Adjustment pop-up menu, choose Bar, if not already selected.

11   Select As Copies.

12   Click OK.

Five copies of the selected region are created, filling the Cymbals track for the Guitar Solo section.

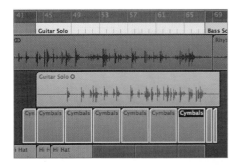

TIP   The useful Repeat Regions command is easily accessed by assigning a key command. Assigning a key command also sets it up for use in the MIDI editors, which have no corresponding command in their local menus.

Using Aliases

In addition to loops and copies of regions, MIDI editing offers another form of replication: aliases.

An alias in Logic functions much as it does in the Finder; it is a reference to another region. It does not contain any actual data and refers to the content of the original item from which it was created.

An alias has the unique ability to update itself when changes are made to the original region. This is especially useful for creating parts that are repeated throughout a project; you only need to alter the original region, and the correction will automatically take effect in aliases throughout the composition.

This function will prove useful for duplicating the cymbals material from one verse to another, while still allowing for additional changes.

1 In the Cymbals track, Shift-Option-drag the second region (located at Verse 1) to measure 13 (located at Verse 2).

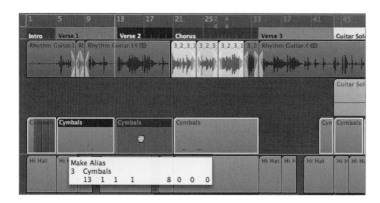

An alias is created at measure 13.

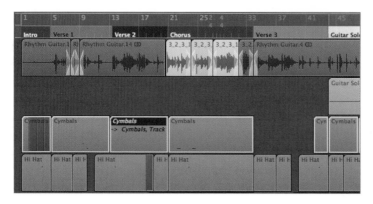

NOTE ▶ The name and information displayed in the alias is italicized. The information listed after the arrow in the alias refers to the region name and track number from which it was derived.

2   From the original Verse 1 section, create an additional alias by Shift-Option-dragging the region to measure 34.

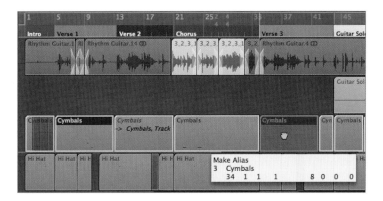

To better understand how aliases function, you can perform a small edit on the original MIDI region.

3   Press Control–Command–Right Arrow/Left Arrow to locate the playhead to the Verse 1 marker.

4   Select the original Cymbals region from which you produced the aliases.

5   Open the Piano Roll Editor by clicking the button at the bottom of the Arrange window.

You might need to scroll down a bit to see all the MIDI events within the regions.

TIP ▶ You can set a preference to open any editor when you double-click a MIDI region. Go to Logic Pro > Preferences > Global, and click the Edit tab. Your editor choice can be selected from the "Double-clicking on a MIDI region opens" pop-up menu.

6   Press Control-Enter (the "Play from Left Window Edge" command) to play the region contents.

7   Stop playback after you've heard the contents of the region.

8   Using the Mute tool, mute the two notes at the fourth beat of measure 9.

> **NOTE** ▸ You might need to resize the window or use the zoom commands to view the entire region contents.

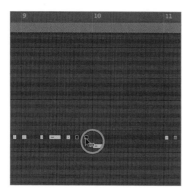

The notes are dimmed and will be muted on playback.

9   Press Control-Enter to play the part with the muted notes.

10   Stop playback.

11   Close the Piano Roll Editor by clicking the button at the bottom of the Arrange window.

12   Select the alias you created at measure 34 (Verse 3).

13   Press Shift-Enter to play the selected alias.

The alias plays with those two notes muted. By creating aliases, you were able to change the original part and keep the corresponding parts updated.

> **TIP** ▸ When you select an alias and open an editor, Logic asks you if you want to open the original region, or turn the alias into a "real copy" to edit independently from the original. If Original is chosen, then the original region is displayed in the editor. This allows you to quickly make alterations that affect the original and all of the related aliases.

14   In the Cymbals track, click the Solo button to turn off soloing.

Demixing MIDI Regions

It is not unusual to record MIDI drum parts by triggering multiple sounds in a single pass, creating a single region containing both the kick drum and snare parts. This technique can help create a track that locks into a groove. However, having the kick drum and snare in the same region can make it more difficult to edit those parts, as any modifications done to the region will be applied to both parts.

Because a MIDI file transmits a stream of commands with discrete events, it allows for some fancy editing functions. One such function is *demixing*, which enables you to divide a MIDI region into components based on specific criteria. You can try this on the bass drum–rim shot part, splitting them into separate tracks for independent editing.

1   In the Arrange area, select the BD/Rim Shot region in track 6.

2   Open the Piano Roll Editor by clicking the button at the bottom of the Arrange window.

    The Piano Roll Editor displays the content of the selected region (you might need to scroll down to better view the region contents).

    Within the Piano Roll Editor, you can see the bass drum (C1) and rim shot (C♯1) parts represented as notes.

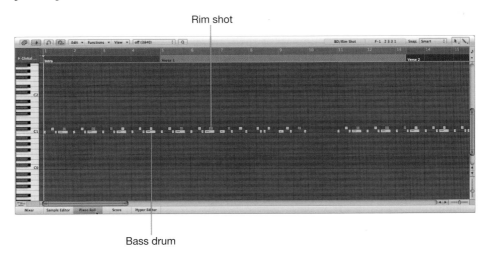

Rim shot

Bass drum

You can separate the two parts using a feature accessed from the Arrange area.

3   Make sure the Arrange area has key focus by clicking the top part of the area or by pressing the Tab key.

4   Use the Zoom Vertical Out command (Control–Up Arrow) to view all tracks.

5   From the Arrange area's local menu bar, choose Region > Split/Demix > Demix by Note Pitch.

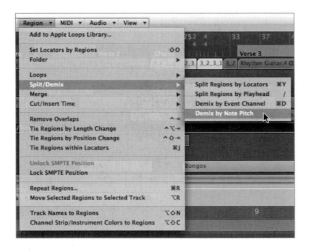

The region on track 6 disappears and is replaced by two new tracks with corresponding regions.

6   Click the background of the Arrange area to deselect any regions.

7   Click the region in track 7.

The Piano Roll Editor displays the bass drum events (C1).

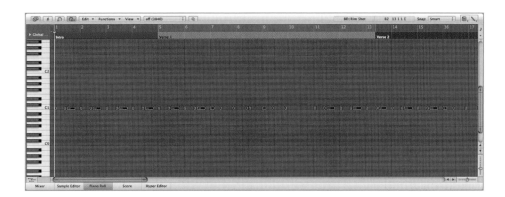

8   Select the region in track 8.

The Piano Roll Editor displays the rim shot events (C♯1).

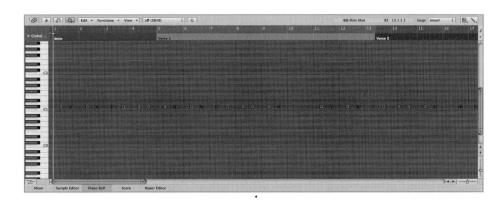

When using the Demix by Note Pitch function, a new MIDI track and a new region are created for every note number found. In addition, the newly created tracks are automatically assigned to the same instruments as the ones in the original MIDI region. For easier identification, name the new tracks and regions with their corresponding instruments.

9   Press the number 1 to recall Screenset 1.

10   Double-click the name on track 7 (BD/Rim Shot), enter *Bass Drum*, and press Return.

11   Double-click the original name on track 8 (BD/Rim Shot), enter *Rim Shot*, and press Return.

12 Drag a selection rectangle around both regions.

13 From the Arrange area's local menu bar, choose Region > Track Names to Regions.

The regions assume the names of their corresponding tracks.

> **TIP** ▶ You can view more than one region's note data within the same Piano Roll Editor. The Piano Roll Editor (and other editors as well) will automatically display all regions that are selected. This can get a bit confusing when you're working with lots of events, so it helps to display each region's events with separate colors. To do this, first make sure that each region is colored differently in the Arrange area, and then, in the Piano Roll Editor's local menu bar, choose View > Region Colors.

Working with Region Parameters

MIDI regions are data containers that hold various types of MIDI events. The events in a MIDI region can be altered individually using one of Logic's MIDI editors (Piano Roll Editor, Event List, Hyper Editor, Transform window, and so on), or altered all at once using the Region Parameter box.

The Region Parameter box gives you access to a variety of parameters that affect the data in MIDI regions. These functions invite experimentation, as they are entirely nondestructive, and the MIDI data can be returned to an unaltered state at any time. Think of these parameters as filters that can be applied to single or multiple MIDI regions in varying degrees of intensity, without permanently altering the data.

Earlier, you used the Loop function in this box to create multiple iterations of a selected region. In this exercise, you will use more of the settings in the Region Parameter box to work with the Bass Drum and Rim Shot regions that you split apart in the previous exercise.

1 On the Bass Drum track (track 7), click the Solo button.

> **NOTE** ▶ Mute and solo states can be independent for tracks and channel strips, depending on a setting in your preferences (Preferences > Audio > General > Track Mute/Solo). In order to independently solo the separate drum tracks assigned to the Inst 1 channel (tracks 3–8), you need to have CPU-saving (Slow Response) selected in the Track Mute/Solo menu.

2   On track 7, select the Bass Drum region (make sure that no other region is selected).

Look at the Region Parameter box. Notice that the top of the box reads "Bass Drum," the name of the region you selected. This signifies that any alterations within the box will affect the Bass Drum region only.

Transposing Regions

Note events in any MIDI region can be transposed all at once by changing the Transpose parameter in the Region Parameter box. This is most effective with pitched material, but it is also handy for changing sample selection in drum parts.

In the EXS24 mkII drum kit used in the current project, the bass drum contains the same audio sample mapped across a range of two adjacent keys (B0 and C1). The EXS24 mkII pitch-shifts these samples accordingly, producing bass drum sounds that vary slightly in pitch. The project currently uses the higher of these two choices (C1) but would benefit from a slightly deeper bass drum. By transposing the Bass Drum region down a semitone, you can change all MIDI notes contained in the region to B0, triggering the lower of the two bass drum samples.

1   Play the soloed Bass Drum track.

2   Next to the Transpose parameter, double-click the 0, and enter –1 (minus 1) in the text box. Press Return.

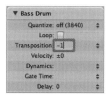

3   Play the Bass Drum track again, listening to the slightly lower pitch.

Changing Velocities in a MIDI Region

The Region Parameter box also provides a quick way to alter note velocities within a MIDI region. You can boost or reduce velocities, adding a numerical value to or subtracting a value from each event.

The bass drum part is a little loud in the Chorus section. Rather than dynamically change the volume level in the mixing stage, you can make a velocity adjustment to the MIDI note events in this section. This provides a more musical result, as lower velocities trigger different, softer bass drum samples with less attack. When you reduce the event velocities, the sound not only gets quieter but also changes its timbre, much as a real drum does when struck with less force.

To affect only the events within the Chorus section, it is necessary to divide the Bass Drum region, isolating the events that need to be adjusted.

1   Use the Go to Next/Previous Marker key commands (Control–Command–Right Arrow/Left Arrow) to locate to the Chorus section.

2   In the Arrange area's local menu bar, choose Region > Split/Demix > Split Regions by Locators.

The Bass Drum region divides at the borders of the Chorus section.

TIP ▸ Logic provides quick access to this command in the Toolbar with the Split by Locators button.

3   Use the Play from Selection key command (Shift-Enter) to listen to the bass drum part. Stop playback when finished.

4   In the Region Parameter box, double-click the Velocity parameter, and enter –18 in the text box. Press Return.

5   Press Shift-Enter to listen to the results of the velocity adjustment.

Compressing or Expanding the Dynamics of a Region

The Dynamics parameter in the Region Parameter box also acts on MIDI note velocities but—instead of adding or subtracting a fixed value—it scales the difference between the highest and lowest velocity values.

In this way, it functions similarly to the way a compressor or expander acts on the dynamics of an audio signal, increasing or decreasing the dynamic range for the selected MIDI region. When applying a value larger than 100 percent, the differences between "soft" and "loud" notes are increased (as they would be by an expander), and they are decreased with values of less than 100 percent (as they would be by a compressor).

1   On the Bass Drum track, click the Solo button to turn off soloing.

2   On the Rim Shot track (track 8), click the Solo button.

3   In the Toolbar, click the Lists button.

     The Lists area opens with the Event tab selected by default.

4   Select the Rim Shot region (track 8).

5   Press Shift-Enter to listen to the rim shot part.

The Event List displays the MIDI events in the Rim Shot region, and the Region Parameter box displays "Rim Shot" at the top.

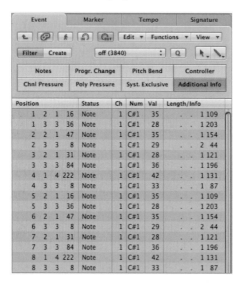

Look at the numbers displayed in the Val(ue) column, which indicate the velocity of each note. Although the range is not wide, the dynamics could use a little velocity compression to achieve a more consistent sound.

6   In the Region Parameter box, click to open the Dynamics pop-up menu and choose 75%.

7   Play the project, listening to the rim shot part.

The dynamics are evened out, with a reduction in the range between the highest and lowest values.

8   Close the Event List by clicking the Lists button in the Toolbar.

9   Click the Solo button on the Rim Shot track to turn off soloing.

Using Gate Time to Alter Articulation

The Gate Time parameter directly affects the length of MIDI events, but not in the way that you might expect. Instead of uniformly decreasing or increasing the length of all MIDI events within a region, the Gate Time parameter changes notes by a percentage of their lengths, thereby allowing you to adjust the articulation of a performance from, say, staccato to legato.

The first region on the Bass track needs a little tightening up, as the longer notes sustain a bit too long, bleeding into the shorter ones. By adjusting their lengths with the Gate Time parameter, you can reduce the length of the longer notes and get a more articulate performance from the shorter ones.

1   Click the Solo button on the Bass track (track 12).

2   Select the first region in the Bass track so it appears in the Region Parameter box.

3   Press Shift-Enter to listen to the region.

   To clearly hear the effect of the Gate Time parameter, you can test an extreme setting and observe the results.

4   In the Region Parameter box, click to open the Gate Time pop-up menu and choose Fixed.

5   Press Shift-Enter to listen to the region.

The bass part is performed extremely staccato, truncating the ends of each MIDI event. Obviously, this hasn't improved the piece, so you need to make a more subtle adjustment.

6   Click to open the Gate Time pop-up menu, and choose 50%.

7   Press Shift-Enter to listen to the region again.

All events are adjusted to 50 percent of their length, creating an articulate performance.

8   Stop playback.

9   On the Bass track, click the Solo button to turn off soloing.

Using Delay to Adjust the Feel

The Delay parameter is used to move a region forward or backward in time by small increments. By choosing a positive value, you can delay the playback of a region, achieving a laid-back or dragging feel. Negative values push the region earlier, creating a rushing or driving feel in relation to the beat.

The current project's musical material warrants a laid-back groove, especially in the drum tracks, so you should apply a delay setting to the rim shot to better fit in the pocket created by the other instruments.

Delay settings can be displayed in ticks (the smallest possible bar subdivision or system quantization), note values, or milliseconds. Most people who have worked with digital delay devices are used to thinking in terms of milliseconds, so switch the default setting of ticks to milliseconds before changing the Delay setting.

1   Play the project, listening to how the rim shot works with the rhythm section.

2   In the Arrange area's local menu bar, choose View > Delay in ms.

3   With the Rim Shot region selected, click the arrows to the right of the Delay parameter to open the Delay pop-up menu, and choose 1/192 = 11.3.

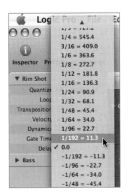

By selecting this value, you are delaying the playback of the Rim Shot region by a 1/192 note, or 11.3 milliseconds.

4   Play the project from the beginning, listening to how the rim shot now Plays in the arrangement.

> **NOTE** ▶ Settings made in the Region Parameter box, with the exception of Loop and Quantize, aren't displayed in the editors. The changes take effect during playback. These changes can also be written permanently to the region: In the Arrange area's local menu bar, choose MIDI > Region Parameters > Normalize Region Parameters.

Quantizing Regions

Just as musical rhythm is expressed in relation to the grid formed by beat and meter, so sequencers map MIDI event timings to a grid determined by a base resolution provided by the software application. To ensure that the placement of an event in time is as accurate as possible, Logic offers a resolution of a 1/3840 note (one tick).

This division allows for a vast range of rhythmical placement, but there will be occasions when you need to adjust the accuracy of events in relation to more musical divisions (eighth notes, sixteenth notes, triplets, and so on). This can be done with *quantization*, which compares events to a chosen resolution and then corrects their time placement by moving them to the nearest position on a beat/time grid.

Logic offers multiple ways of quantizing events, including adjusting the data in the Region Parameter box. In this exercise, you'll check out the aural and visual effects on note events when quantizing.

1   In the Arrange area, select the Bass Drum track (track 7) in the track list.

All three regions on the track are selected.

Region parameters can be applied to single regions and also to multiple regions simultaneously. Take a look at the Region Parameter box. Instead of displaying the name of the individual selected region, the box displays "3 selected," indicating the number of selected regions that will be affected by parameter adjustments. In addition, an asterisk, instead of a value, is placed next to the Velocity parameter, because one of the selected regions already has a value for velocity. If you were to enter another setting here, the region with the preexisting setting would retain it and add the new value.

TIP ▶ You can override such an offset by pressing Option while changing the value. This eliminates any relative adjustment so that all regions have the same value.

2   At the bottom of the Arrange window, click the Piano Roll Editor button.

3   While keeping your eye on the bass drum part in the Piano Roll Editor, click to open the Quantize menu and choose 8F Swing.

The events shift in the Piano Roll Editor.

4   Click the Metronome Click button in the Transport bar at the bottom of the window.

5   Play the project, listening to the quantized bass drum part against the metronome.

The feel is completely transformed from a somewhat straight pattern to a swing feel, in which every other note is delayed.

While applying a swing feel illustrates the power of quantization, it definitely does not work with this project.

NOTE ▶ If the click is too loud or soft, you can adjust the metronome volume within the Project Settings (File > Project Settings > Metronome).

6   From the Quantize menu, choose 1/16-Note.

7   Click the Metronome Click button to turn off the metronome.

8   Play the project, listening to the bass drum part with the new quantize setting.

> **TIP▶**   The settings in the Region Parameter box can also be applied to incoming MIDI signals. This is done by changing settings without selecting a region (the box reads "MIDI Thru" instead of a region name). This feature can be useful for transposing incoming notes up or down an octave, thereby increasing the range of a small MIDI controller. In this case, the events are recorded as played, but the region containing the events inherits the same parameter settings as MIDI Thru.

Using the Extended Region Parameters

So far, you've performed straightforward quantization, aligning all notes in a region to a selected value. However, strict quantizing can sometimes make things sound too mechanical. Unless a performance is especially sloppy, you might want to apply quantization only partially, maintaining the original feel but moving notes in closer alignment to the timing grid.

Among the extended region parameters, you will find many ways of applying quantization to a selected region.

1   In the Arrange area, select the Rim Shot region.

2   Choose View > Extended Region Parameters.

The Region Parameter box expands to display the extended region parameters.

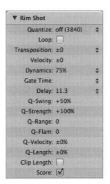

An additional eight parameters are listed in the Region Parameter box, mostly applying to quantization (the Q signifies this). In the box, you can also see the Delay and Dynamics settings that you applied earlier.

Use this box to further refine the Rim Shot region by applying some of its quantization settings. While working with the extended region parameters, keep an eye on the Piano Roll Editor to observe the changes that take place.

3   In the Piano Roll Editor, use the Zoom tool to zoom in to measure 3.

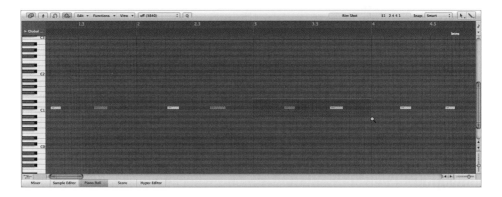

4   In the Region Parameters box, choose 1/8-Note from the Quantize pop-up menu.

The notes align to the grid, which can be easily seen in the Piano Roll Editor.

Quantize off   Quantize 1/8-Note

While some slight timing discrepancies are present in the rim shot performance, you will want to retain the original feel and use quantization only to move inaccurate events closer to the grid instead of aligning them perfectly. This can be done by entering a value other than 100% (which is full quantization) for the Q-Strength parameter.

5   In the Region Parameters box, double-click next to the Q-Strength parameter, and enter *78* in the text box. Press Return.

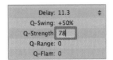

The inaccurate note events shift slightly forward, toward the grid line.

Quantization strength set to 78%

By limiting quantization strength, you are moving events toward the grid without perfectly aligning them. Think of this as applying weight to the Quantization parameter, wherein any value above 0 percent pushes the affected notes toward the value specified.

6   Play the project, listening to the quantized region in context of the full arrangement.

> **TIP** Try exploring the extended region parameters to create musical parts. You can find a good explanation of all extended quantization parameters in Chapter 19 of the *Logic Pro 8 User Manual.*

Working with MIDI Note Events

Let's continue developing the material by editing at a finer level: individual MIDI events. While you can do this in any of Logic's MIDI editors, the Piano Roll Editor works particularly well for quickly selecting and viewing region contents.

In this section, you will extend and refine a percussion part, creating a musical performance from a static one.

1   Press Control–Command–Right Arrow/Left Arrow to locate to the Guitar Solo section.

2   In the Transport bar, click the Cycle button to turn on Cycle mode.

A cycle area appears around the Guitar Solo section.

3   In the Arrange area, select the Maracas region on track 10.

The region's content is displayed in the Piano Roll Editor.

4   If needed, assign key focus to the Piano Roll Editor by clicking the top part of the area or by pressing the Tab key.

5   In the Piano Roll Editor, zoom out to display about five or six measures.

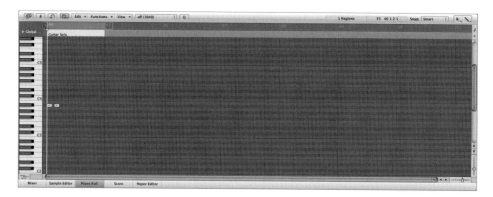

Repeating Note Events

As you can see in the Piano Roll Editor, only two maraca notes were input for the Guitar Solo section. With techniques similar to those you used previously to duplicate regions, you can quickly repeat groups of notes, extending a part.

1   In the Piano Roll Editor, select the two events by around them with the Pointer tool.

The notes play as they are selected. You can quickly create a part by duplicating these two notes using a command similar to the Repeat Regions command that you learned earlier in the lesson. As you might have noticed, you cannot access this function from a menu in the Piano Roll Editor (or any other MIDI editor, for that matter). This is because the menu command that you used in the Arrange area applies to regions only, not to individual events. Fortunately the key command (Repeat Regions/Events) covers both regions and events selected within a MIDI editor.

2   Press Command-R (the Repeat Objects key command).

The Repeat Regions/Events dialog appears.

3   In the Number of Copies field, enter *15*.

4   Set the Adjustment pop-up menu to Beat.

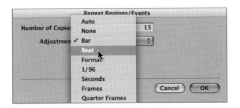

By choosing Beat in the Adjustment menu, you are specifying that the newly created copies should be placed at the beat, instead of applying the bar justification you used earlier when copying regions.

5   Click OK.

The events are repeated, aligned to the beat, filling up four measures.

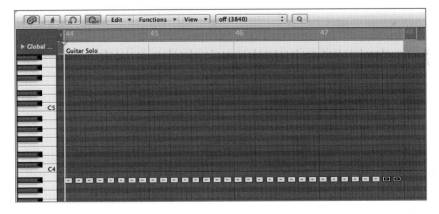

NOTE ▶ The region containing the events also expands from one to four bars, adapting itself automatically to the newly created content.

6   In the Arrange area's track list, click the Solo button to enable solo for the Maracas track (track 10).

7   Play the project, listening to the maracas part.

Selecting Events for Editing

To efficiently work with note events, you need to use a variety of selection techniques to edit only the data you wish to change.

As you most likely heard when playing the repeated notes, the part sounds quite static. This is understandable, since it consists of one repeated note with the same velocity value. To create a more realistic part, it is necessary to modify the velocities, add accents, and alter dynamics to breathe life into it. Let's explore some of the selection techniques offered in Logic Pro to edit notes independently and in groups.

1   In the Piano Roll Editor, choose the Velocity tool.

2   Click the first note in the passage and drag downward, reducing the velocity to 70 (use the help tag to guide you).

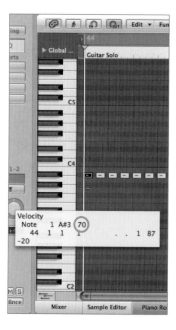

As the note event reduces its velocity (changing from yellow to green), you can hear the sample change to one with a softer attack. This softer sound will work best for the desired maracas part.

TIP ▶ If you don't want notes to sound when selected in any of Logic's MIDI editors, click to disable the MIDI Out button at the upper-left side of the editor.

You can make a similar velocity adjustment to the remaining notes in the region without affecting the first note. Instead of drawing a selection rectangle around all of the events except the first, you can use one of Logic's specialized commands to select all the notes that are not currently selected.

These useful selection commands are available within any MIDI editor by choosing Edit in the local menu bar, and they can be accessed at any time while editing.

3   From the Piano Roll Editor's local menu bar, choose Edit > Toggle Selection.

All the notes that were not selected are now selected, and the original selected event is deselected.

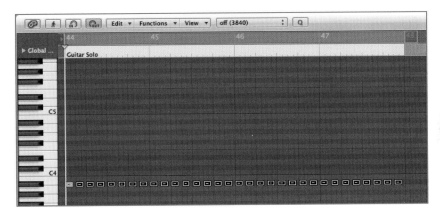

Using the Toggle Selection command, you are able to access the unselected events without having to change tools.

4   With the Velocity tool, drag any of the selected notes downward to a value of 70.

You can continue working with the dynamics of the maracas part by adding accents to beats 2 and 4 throughout the passage.

5   Click the background of the Piano Roll Editor to deselect the notes.

6   Hold down the Shift key, and using the Pointer tool, select the notes occurring on 44 2 1 1 and 44 4 1 1.

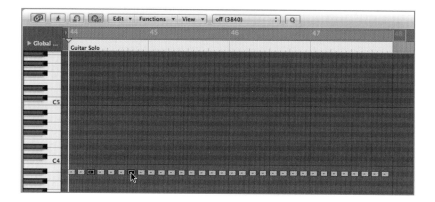

You've selected the beats you want to work with, but only for the first bar. To perform the edit for the entire region, you still have to select the equivalent beats within each measure. This could be accomplished by Shift-clicking each note in succession, but that would get tedious. Instead, you can use one of Logic's selection functions to select the desired beats all at once.

7   From the Piano Roll Editor's local menu bar, choose Edit > Select Equal Subpositions.

The note events occurring at beats 2 and 4 are selected for each bar of the passage.

8   Using the Velocity tool, drag one of the selected notes upward until the velocity reaches a value of 101.

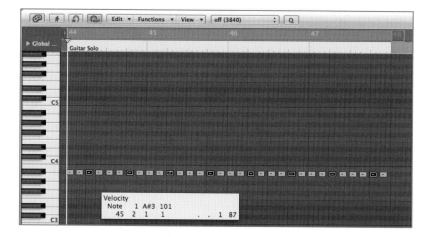

All the selected notes change velocity simultaneously, creating an accent on beats 2 and 4 for the entire region.

9 Play the project, listening to the Maracas track with the velocity changes.

It's still a little loud overall, so reduce the velocities of all the notes. In this case, all events are triggered by the same pitch (A♯3). You can quickly select all events of the same pitch by clicking the equivalent note on the keyboard.

10 In the onscreen keyboard at the far left of the Piano Roll Editor, click the key that is immediately next to the notes within the editor (A♯3).

The note sounds, and all A♯3 notes are selected within the Piano Roll Editor. This provides a quick way to select all note events of a given pitch without having to change tools.

TIP ▶ This technique is also a quick way to audition sounds.

11 Using the Velocity tool, drag the first note event downward, reducing the velocity to 65.

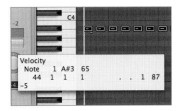

This is a relative adjustment; all velocities are reduced by a value of 5, including the accents, which now have a velocity value of 96.

Using Transform Functions

Transform functions are powerful selection and processing tools that allow you to manipulate all types of MIDI information in almost all conceivable ways. Each function employs a set of conditions and operations to specify exactly what data is selected and how it will be manipulated.

The functions can range from the simple to the complex. In this exercise, you will learn how to both use one of the many preset transform functions, as well as create a custom transform set that can be used within your projects.

These functions are accessed in the Transform window, which can be opened from the Window menu or accessed within any editor through the Functions > Transform menu.

1 In the Piano Roll Editor, choose Functions > Transform > Humanize.

The Transform window opens.

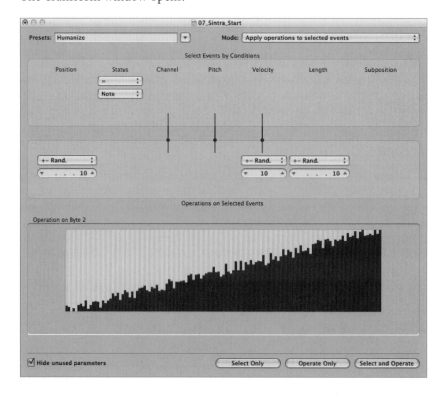

The Humanize function applies a slight randomization to events, creating a looser and more natural-sounding performance.

The Transform window is divided into three main sections: Select Events by Conditions, Operations on Selected Events, and Operation on Byte 2. While these headings might sound a little confusing, they can be explained in a straightforward manner.

Basically, to use the Transform functions on MIDI data, you must indicate exactly what you wish to affect within the Select Events by Conditions section. Here, you specify the criteria of the desired target, whether you want a simple selection based on event type (or status) or a complex selection having multiple conditions (for example, events that have a specific length, position, and value).

The Operations sections indicate how you want to modify the selected MIDI events. This can be almost any kind of MIDI transformation you can dream up, even converting one type of event to another for further processing. With the Humanize transformation, for example, selected notes are randomized in position, velocity value, and length. Each transformation has a specific extent assigned to it, which can be anything from a single number or note to a range of operations. Here, the position, velocity and length of the selected note events are randomized within a positive or negative range of 10 ticks.

The Operation on Byte 2 section is a graphical representation of the transformation itself and directly depicts the values for byte 2 of the MIDI event chosen in the Status column. (A MIDI channel voice message consists of a status byte followed by one or two data bytes.) In the case of note events, byte 2 is velocity; for controllers it is the value for the assigned controller.

All of this translates to a function that slightly varies note events, imparting a looser, more human feel.

2   At the bottom of the Transform window, click the Select and Operate button.

The note events displayed in the Piano Roll Editor change slightly in position, length, and velocity.

3   Close the Transform window.

4   Play the project, listening to the "humanized" part.

All that's left to complete the maracas part is to repeat the region throughout the Guitar Solo section. This can be done quickly by using the Repeat Regions/Events command you used earlier, creating multiple aliases.

5 Close the Piano Roll Editor.

6 With the Maracas region still selected, bring up the Repeat Regions/Events dialog by using the key command (Command-R).

7 In the Number of Copies field, enter 5.

8 From the Adjustment pop-up menu, choose Bar.

9 Click to select As Aliases or Clones.

10 Click OK.

Aliases of the Maracas region are created throughout the Guitar Solo section.

11 Click the Solo button to turn off soloing for the Maracas track (track 10).

12 Play the project, listening to how the maracas part works with the arrangement.

Creating New Transform Functions

You probably noticed when navigating through the Transform menu that Logic offers numerous preset transform functions. These functions are capable of accomplishing many common MIDI editing tasks in an efficient manner. However, there will most likely be a time that you will need to create your own transform set to address a specific need, whether it be the quick selection of specific MIDI data for editing, or selecting and performing an operation on the MIDI data via a single step.

1 In the Arrange area, click the Solo button for the Bongos track (track 11).

2 Select the first region in the Bongos track.

3 Use the Set Locators by Regions/Events key command (press Control-=, or Control-' on a laptop) to set the cycle area around the first Bongos region.

4 Open the Piano Roll Editor, displaying the contents of the Bongos region.

As you can see in the Piano Roll Editor, a few note velocities are quite low (displaying as purple), resulting in dynamics that are a tad too soft.

5 Play the Bongos region, stopping playback after you have had a chance to become familiar with the material.

For this exercise, you will be creating a transform function that will selectively boost only the MIDI velocities of these lightly played notes (that is, the notes with a velocity range of 1 to 20), evening out the dynamics of the performance.

Creating a new transform set is done within any open Transform window, whether opened within a MIDI editor, or from the main Window menu.

6 Choose Window > Transform.

The Transform window opens, displaying the last selected preset (in this case, Humanize).

7 Click the disclosure triangle next to the Presets menu in the upper-left corner of the Transform window, and choose **Create Initialized User Set**.

A dialog appears asking if you'd like to create a new transform set, or rename the current one.

8 Click Create.

A new, blank transform set is created.

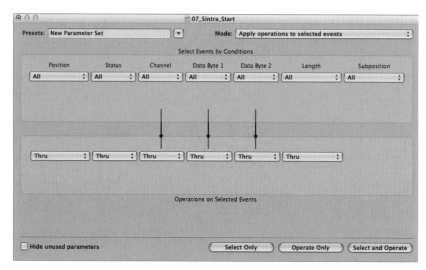

Notice that many more parameters are accessible (via pop-up menus) than there were when you opened the Humanize preset. This is because preset transform functions open with unused parameters hidden from view, presenting only the relevant parameters for selection or operation.

TIP ▶ Preset transform functions will display all parameters if you deselect the "Hide unused parameters" checkbox in the lower-left corner of the Transform window. Having all parameters displayed allows you to further extend the capabilities of the preset by adding more selection and operation data.

9   Select the text in the Preset menu ("New Parameter Set"), and enter *Velocity Booster*. Press Return.

A dialog appears asking if you'd like to rename the current, empty set or create a new one.

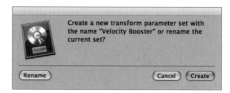

10 Click Rename.

When you create a new transform set, it is advisable to start off by defining just what you want to transform. In the Select Events by Conditions area, "All" is displayed by default for every parameter, signifying that no discrimination will be made when selecting MIDI data (all event types, positions, and channels will be selected). In order to narrow the focus of the selection, you need to specify the relevant parameters instead of leaving them in their default state.

It is best to start defining selection criteria by choosing the MIDI event type, which is done from the Status menu.

11 Click the Status pop-up menu and choose = (equal sign).

A new menu is created just below the option you chose, allowing you to specify the event type.

12 Click the new pop-up menu, and choose Note.

By specifying Note as the Status parameter, you are excluding all events but MIDI notes in the selection. This is still far too general a selection. The goal of the transform function is to select only the MIDI notes whose velocities range from 1 to 20. In order to do this, you need to define further criteria within the selection parameters.

13 Click the Velocity pop-up menu and select <= (less than or equal to).

A value field appears below the menu. Entering a number within this value field defines a selection less than or equal to the inputted number.

14 Double-click the number in the value field and enter *20*. Press Return.

Now that your selection criteria are defined, you can specify what will happen to the selected data when the operation runs. This is done by choosing operations from the parameter menus in the Operations on Selected Events area.

15 In the Velocity column in the Operations on Selected Events area, click the pop-up menu to view the list of operations that can be performed (do not choose anything as of yet).

As you can see, there are many possibilities, providing numerous ways to transform MIDI data in simple to complex ways.

NOTE ▶ Definitions of the available operations are provided on pages 478–480 of the *Logic Pro 8 User Manual.*

16 Choose Add from the Velocity pop-up menu.

A value field appears below the Add menu. Any number entered into this value field will be added to the related parameter defined within the Select Events by Conditions area.

17 Double-click the Add value field and enter *10*. Press Return.

You have now created a new transform set that, when activated, will add 10 to the velocity values of MIDI notes with velocity values of 20 or less.

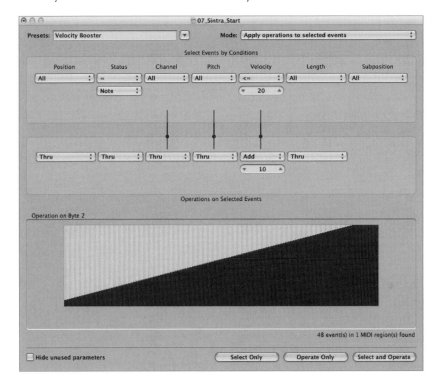

18 Click the Select and Operate button at the lower-right corner of the Transform window.

All MIDI notes with velocity values of 20 or less (the purple ones) are increased in velocity (and are displayed as dark blue).

19 Play the project, listening to the newly transformed MIDI data.

20 Stop playback.

NOTE ▶ If you want to select only specific MIDI data without processing, click the Select Only button. Likewise, you can also choose to process only previously selected MIDI data by clicking the Operate Only button, bypassing the selection criteria altogether.

Applying New Transform Sets

All newly created transform sets are immediately available within any MIDI editor's Functions > Transform menu. This puts your transform set creations within easy reach whenever you are editing MIDI data.

1   Close the Transform window.

2   Close the Piano Roll Editor.

3   In the Arrange area, select the second region on the Bongos track.

4   Open the Event List, this time by using the key command (the E key).

5   From the Event List's local menu bar, choose Functions > Transform > Velocity Booster.

The Transform window opens, displaying the transform set you created earlier.

6   Click the Select and Operate button.

All MIDI notes with velocity values of 20 or less are selected within the Event List and increased in velocity by 10.

7   Close the Transform window.

8   Close the Event List.

9   In the track list, click the Solo button on the Bongos track, disabling it.

10 Turn Cycle mode off.

11 Play the project from the beginning, listening to the newly transformed material within the context of the project.

12 Stop playback.

13 Save the project as **7_Sintra_Finished** to the following location: Music > Logic 8_BTB_Files > Lessons > Completed.

TIP ▶ Newly created transform functions are saved in the project file itself. In order to be able to use your newly created transform functions in other projects, you need to import them first. You can do this by choosing File > Project Settings > Import Settings, and making sure that the Transform Sets checkbox is selected. Then select the project file where the new transform set resides, and click the Open button.

Lesson Review

1. What are the differences between loops, copies, and aliases when you're duplicating material?

2. What does demixing a MIDI region do?

3. What does the Regions Parameters box do?

4. What does the Toggle Selection command do within a MIDI editor?

5. What does the Select Equal Subpositions command do within a MIDI editor?

6. Where can you access the Transform functions?

7. How are the Transform functions useful?

Answers

1. Loops are used to quickly duplicate material and can be manually drawn out for exact placement. Copies are used for duplicating material from one part of the project to another and for altering material independently of its original source. Aliases are used for duplicating material that needs to automatically update when the original is edited.

2. Demixing separates combined parts recorded within a single MIDI region into individual regions for further editing.

3. The Region Parameters box allows real-time control over various playback parameters, enabling you to transpose and adjust the feel of events within a MIDI region.

4. The Toggle Selection command selects all regions (within the Arrange area) or events (within a MIDI editor) that are not currently selected and deselects any regions or events that are selected.

5. The Select Equal Subpositions command selects all regions or events with a similar bar or beat relationship to the selection.

6. The Transform functions can be accessed via the main Window menu, or via the Functions > Transform menu within all MIDI editors.

7. The Transform functions contain many helpful operations for processing MIDI data, including boosting selected note velocities and Humanizing.

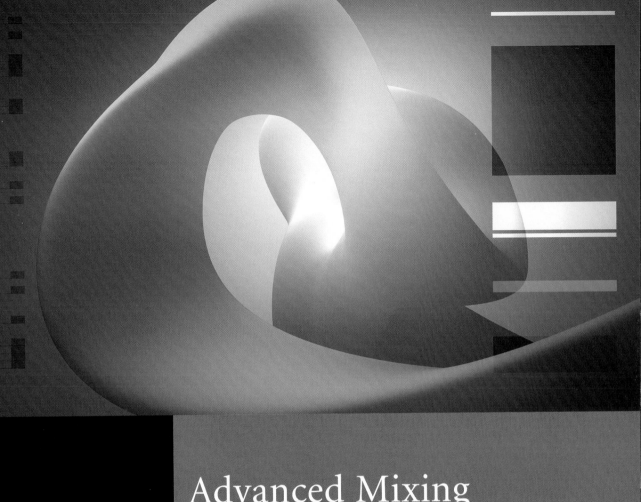

Advanced Mixing

8

Time   This lesson takes approximately 90 minutes to complete.

Goals   Use Mixer views to navigate in a mix

Create a dedicated alternative Mixer view to access frequently used channel strips

Create a vocal signal chain using effects processors in a channel

Create a send effect using aux channels

Control the balance and imaging width of a stereo signal

Change the plug-in order in a signal chain

Use channel strip settings to save an effects chain

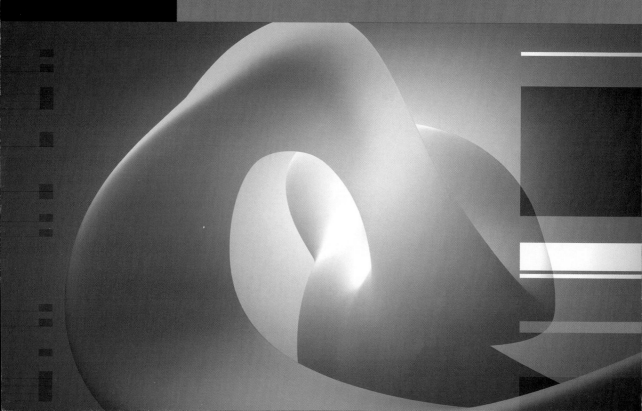

Working with Mixer Channels

At the heart of any mixer is the channel. All signals are routed through channels, modified by effects processing, and ultimately brought together in a mix.

In Logic, mixer channels are based directly on objects in the Logic Environment, each channel dedicated to a specific type: MIDI, audio, or software instrument. These channels are accessed via Logic's integrated Mixer, which shows them in an organized display.

Each channel offers a set of controls for working with the signal throughput. Among these controls are inserts for applying effects processing to the signal path, and sends for feeding a controlled amount of the signal to another Mixer channel.

In this lesson you will use the Mixer to efficiently view and access the Mixer channels and apply effects processing in the signal chain. In addition, you will manipulate the order and placement of plug-ins in Logic's Mixer.

Using the Mixer

The Mixer has three display modes that access the channels of a mix: Single view, Arrange view, and All view. Understanding how the three differ will help you navigate through your mix efficiently.

In this first exercise, you will open the project file to use throughout the lesson.

1   Choose File > Open.

2   In the file selector box, go to Music > Logic 8_BTB_Files > Lessons and open **08_I Was Raised_Start.logic**.

3   Play the project to familiarize yourself with the material, clicking the Stop button when you are finished.

Using Arrange View

The Mixer's Arrange view is often referred to as an adaptive mixer. In this display mode, Logic creates a Mixer setup adapted from the Arrange area's track list, reflecting aspects such as track order, track names, and assigned colors. The Mixer's Arrange view will reflect the Arrange area's track list, even when new tracks are created and reordered.

Arrange view will probably be the view you use most often when mixing, as it allows you to focus on those elements that are directly involved with the project's arrangement.

With the project open, you can observe firsthand the relationship between the Arrange area and the Mixer's Arrange view by rearranging the track order for a more ergonomic mixing setup.

1   Open Screenset 2.

This screenset contains an open Mixer with a small Arrange area (based on the template you created in Lesson 1, "Speeding Up Your Workflow").

2   In the Arrange area, use the vertical scroll arrows at the far right or the up and down arrow keys on your keyboard to examine the tracks in the arrangement.

NOTE ▶ If you are using a smaller screen resolution than 1140 x 900, it is possible that the vertical scroll arrows will be hidden from view. If this is the case, use the Up and Down Arrows to scroll through the track list instead.

There are 29 tracks displayed vertically in the track list.

3   In the Mixer, use the scroller to examine the channels used for the project.

This is a fairly large session, with 37 channel strips displayed side by side. Notice that the first 29 channel strips correspond to the tracks listed in the Arrange area's track list, in both order and number.

NOTE ▶ The aux, output, and master channel strips are included because they are a part of the signal chain used by the Arrange area's tracks (including sends and returns, and master bus). You can hide them by deselecting Add Signal Flow Channel Strips in the Mixer's View menu.

4   In the Mixer, try selecting different tracks by clicking the name at the bottom of each channel strip.

When a channel is selected, it is highlighted with a light green border. Note that the same track is highlighted in the Arrange area, which automatically scrolls to display the track selected in the Mixer.

5 In the track list of the Arrange area, try selecting other tracks.

When a track is selected in the Arrange area's track list, the Mixer automatically scrolls to display the corresponding channel.

6 In the Mixer, select track 25, the drum overheads channel (Drum_overhds).

Note that this channel is located between the Snare and Toms_rack channels. It would be more conveniently located in the Mixer next to the other stereo drum tracks (Drum_intro and Loop).

You can move the track in the Arrange area while observing the changes in the Mixer.

7 In the Arrange area's track list, drag the track downward, dropping it after the Toms_floor track.

The track order changes in both the Arrange area and the Mixer, and the Drum_overhds track is inserted between the Toms_floor and Loop tracks.

Arrange area track list   Mixer

Using the Channel Strip Filters

The channel strip filter buttons, located at the upper-right side of the Mixer, define the types of channels displayed in the Mixer. They can be selected singly or in combination. When the filter buttons are used in Arrange view, the display will show only the tracks in the Arrange area that are of the selected types defined by the filter buttons. By default, all the filter buttons are selected, thereby displaying every type of channel available in a given view.

1   Click the Audio channel strip filter button to turn it off.

All audio channels in the arrangement are hidden, leaving a single instrument channel, plus the aux, output, and master channels used by the Arrange area tracks.

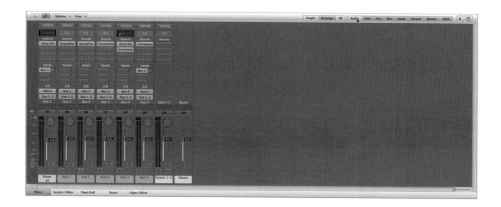

2   Click the Audio button again.

All channel types are now active, and the complete arrangement is visible.

Using All View

The Mixer's All view displays all the channels available in the project. All view has a direct connection to Logic's Environment; a channel has to exist in the Environment to be displayed in All view.

Since the tracks displayed in All view correspond to Environment channels and not to tracks in the Arrange area, you can use this view mode to look at channels—such as output and master channels—that are not otherwise contained in your arrangement. As in Arrange view, channels in All view are displayed via the channel strip filter buttons. The channel strip filter selections made for the Arrange and All views are independent, and they remain intact even when you toggle between the display modes.

Rather than use All view to display multiple (or all) types of channels, it is most useful to dedicate All view to a single type of channel, such as output channels. All view then becomes an "alternative" Mixer that provides quick access to a frequently used channel type in a mix.

In this exercise, you will set up All view as a dedicated output mixer.

1   In the Mixer menu bar, click the All button.

By default, all filter buttons are turned on, displaying all channel types available in the project's Environment. To view only channels of a specific type, you need to disable all channel strip filter buttons for channels that you do not wish to view. This can be time consuming, but Logic supplies a single-action shortcut.

2   In the menu bar, Option-click the Output button.

All channels disappear and are replaced by the output channels (four stereo channels) available to the project.

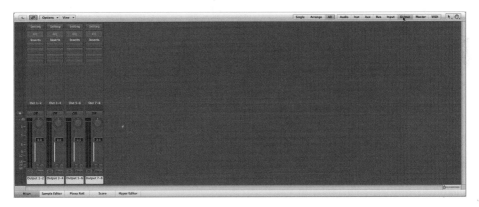

NOTE ▶ You need to have an audio interface with at least eight outputs for the output channels to appear active (having a fader, pan control, inserts, and so on). Otherwise, the output channels will appear labeled but blank.

Option-clicking a channel strip filter button displays only the selected channel type. You can add other channel types to the view by clicking (without Option) additional filter buttons.

3   Click the Master button to turn it on.

The master channel is added to the mixer.

4   Click the Arrange and All buttons to toggle between the view of the output and master channels (All view) and the tracks used in the arrangement (Arrange view).

Notice that the display modes remember the channel filter settings you last assigned, even when switching between Arrange view and All view.

> **TIP** ▶ The channel strip filter settings are saved in the screenset, so you can make this a part of the permanent Mix setup.

This setup enables you to conveniently access individual outputs on your audio interface as you adjust volume levels, apply signal processing, or perform bounces.

Using Single View

Single view essentially limits the Mixer display to a single isolated channel and its signal path. This offers an effective way to trace the signal flow from track to output, including all send destinations (aux channels). While Single view can be left enabled as you select source channels via the Arrange area's track list, it makes more sense to treat it as a temporary view state that can be toggled on and off while you're mixing in the other view modes. This allows you to quickly focus in on, and make adjustments to, a single channel's signal flow, then return to working on the total mix.

1   If Arrange view is not already selected, click the Arrange button in the menu bar.

2   Click the Violin1 channel strip (track 11).

3   Click the Single button.

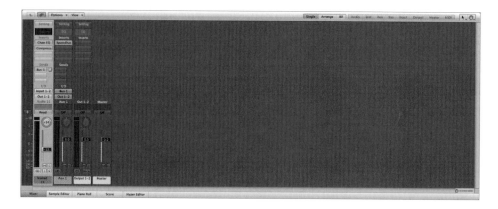

The complete signal flow stemming from the Violin1 channel is displayed, including the send destination (Aux 1) and the output and master channels.

4   Click the Arrange button to return to the overall mix.

Using Insert Effects

Processors such as equalizers, de-essers, and compressors are commonplace in the majority of mixing scenarios, most often inserted directly into a channel's signal path. Logic offers many flavors of equalization and dynamics processing in the form of individual plug-ins, each suited for specific tasks and functions.

In this exercise, you will use Logic's Channel EQ, DeEsser, and Compressor plug-ins to process the lead vocal track, exploring the unique properties offered by each plug-in.

1   In the Mixer, select the Vox_Lead channel (track 1).

2   Click the Vox_Lead channel's Solo button.

3   Press Control–Command–Right Arrow/Left Arrow (Go to Next/Previous Marker) to locate the playhead at Verse 2.

4   In the Transport bar, click the Cycle button to turn on Cycle mode.

5   In the Arrange area, drag the cycle area's right border to the right so that it encompasses the Chorus 1, Verse 3, and Chorus 2 sections.

This will enable you to have a varied selection of vocal parts.

6   Play the project, listening to the soloed lead vocal to get an idea of what you will be working with.

7   Stop the project playback.

Using the Channel EQ

The Channel EQ, part of Logic's suite of equalizers, is the default equalizer for use in channels. This high-quality plug-in offers eight frequency bands, with an integrated Fast Fourier Transform (FFT) analyzer and an intuitive graphical interface.

1   In the Vox_Lead channel (track 1) at the far left of the Mixer, double-click the EQ area.

The channel's Channel EQ plug-in opens.

NOTE ▸ When you double-click the EQ area, the Channel EQ will instantiate on the first available Insert slot. The Channel EQ can also be instantiated on the Insert slot of your choice if you click the Insert slot and choose EQ > Channel EQ > Stereo/Mono/Multi Mono (depending on the channel format) from the pop-up menu.

You can start by using the built-in Analyzer to look at the vocal signal.

2   Play the project.

3   While the project is playing, click the Analyzer button (at the left of the Channel EQ window).

The signal's frequency content appears in the central EQ display, represented by an animated line that updates in real time to reflect the signal's frequency curve.

The Channel EQ window is multifunctional. The signal's frequency curve is continually displayed, and you are able to make changes by graphically drawing in the EQ curve. This greatly helps to identify and correct problem spots in the signal.

4   Click the first band button to turn on the low-cut filter.

A gray frequency curve is shown at the far left of the EQ graphic display, representing the range of the low-cut filter.

NOTE ▶ The low-cut and high-cut filters (band buttons 1 and 8) are not turned on by default when the plug-in is opened.

5   Position the pointer over the gray curve.

The band changes to a light red color, as does the numerical display for the band, located just below the curve in the Parameter section.

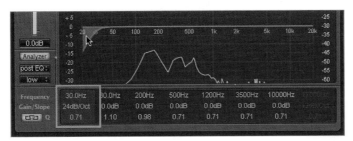

Parameter section

NOTE ▶ This highlight color corresponds to parts of the frequency spectrum: red for lows, yellow for low-mids, green for high-mids, and blue for highs.

6   Drag the red EQ curve to the right, until the Frequency field in the Parameter section reads *112Hz*.

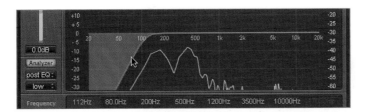

This gradually reduces the frequencies below 112 Hz.

7 In the EQ graphic display, position your pointer just below the 0 dB line at the 200 Hz range.

A yellow dot, called the pivot point, appears at the pointer position. The corresponding numerical display within the Parameter section is also highlighted in yellow, indicating the band you have chosen (the third band from the left).

8 With the yellow pivot point and band illuminated, drag the area just below the 0 dB line down and slightly to the right while watching the numerical display in the Parameter section. Release the mouse button when you reach a Frequency setting of 245 Hz and a Gain setting of −11.0 dB.

TIP You can also create or adjust the EQ curve by dragging any number in the Parameter section for the corresponding band.

A parametric EQ curve is created, with the center of the band at the pointer position.

This creates a substantial frequency cut in the 245 Hz range, but its bandwidth is a bit too narrow. You can change the bandwidth, or Q, by dragging the pivot point up to tighten the bandwidth and dragging it down to broaden the bandwidth.

9 Drag the dot (pivot point) down to broaden the bandwidth until you reach a Q value of 0.20.

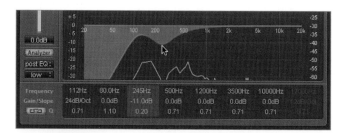

NOTE ▶ When instantiated, the Channel EQ activates Gain-Q coupling by default. Represented by a Link button in the lower-left corner, Gain-Q coupling automatically adjusts the bandwidth (Q) when you raise and lower the gain for an EQ band. This preserves the perceived bandwidth of the bell-shaped parametric curve. You can disable this function by clicking the Link button.

10 In the graphic display, position your pointer over the 3500 Hz range.

A green pivot point appears at 3500 Hz, and the corresponding numerical display is highlighted in green.

11 Using the techniques that you just learned, create a Frequency setting of 2450 Hz, a Gain setting of +3.5 dB, and a Q setting of 0.71.

A parametric EQ curve is created, with the center of the band at the pointer's position.

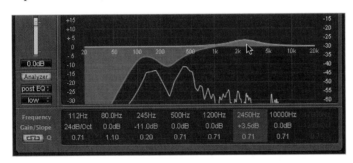

TIP ▶ You can return each bandwidth component to its default values by Option-clicking the corresponding numerical setting within the Parameter section.

You now have an EQ curve that enhances the lead voice.

12 Click the Pre/Post EQ button (on the left below the Analyzer button), changing the display setting of the Analyzer to "pre EQ."

By toggling between the two display modes, you can compare the frequency spectrum with and without the EQ curve applied.

13 Click the Analyzer button, disabling the frequency display.

TIP ▶ When you no longer need the Analyzer to set the EQ curve, turn it off to save valuable CPU resources.

14 Stop the project playback.

15 Close the Channel EQ window.

Using the DeEsser

The lead vocal now sounds considerably less muddy, but it also has noticeable sibilance. You can utilize Logic's DeEsser processor to detect and compress the offending frequency, reducing the sibilance of the vocal.

1   Click the second Insert slot on the Vox_Lead channel, and choose Dynamics > DeEsser > Mono from the pop-up menu.

> **TIP** You can also click a plug-in name in the pop-up menu to insert it, rather than choosing the format (mono, stereo, or 5.1) within the subsequent menu. When doing so, Logic automatically selects the format that best matches the channel.

The DeEsser plug-in opens.

The DeEsser plug-in is a compressor that rejects a specific frequency band for as long as a threshold level is exceeded. It accomplishes this by locating the problem frequency with the Detector and reducing the same frequency band (or a different band) with the Suppressor.

Logic's DeEsser has an extremely flexible monitoring system that allows you to listen to various functions of the DeEsser at work. This enables you to home in on the offending band quickly and easily.

2 Play the project.

3 While the project is playing, click the Monitor pop-up menu (the default is Off) at the lower-left corner of the plug-in interface and choose Det. (for Detector).

The sound output immediately changes because you're now monitoring the signal through the Detector's frequency range. You will use this to help identify the offending frequency of the sibilance.

4 Drag the Detector Frequency knob, listening to the vocal as the frequency band sweeps.

5 Stop dragging the Detector Frequency knob when you hear the "sizzling" sounds emphasized, at about 8800 Hz.

Now that you've set the frequency band that will trigger the DeEsser, you can set the Suppressor to reduce the same band (most common) or to suppress a different frequency band when the DeEsser is active.

6 Drag the Suppressor Frequency knob, matching the Detector Frequency setting of 8800 Hz.

After isolating the frequency of the sibilance, you're ready to set the threshold at which gain reduction is applied. You can do this most effectively by monitoring the Detector Sensitivity knob, which dictates the threshold at which the DeEsser begins to work.

7 Click the Monitor pop-up menu and choose Sens. (for Sensitivity).

Because the Sensitivity control occurs after the Detector Frequency control within the DeEsser's internal signal flow, the monitored sound consists only of audio in the selected band, with enough gain to get through the Sensitivity circuit. The result is short sibilance bursts. With this Monitor mode, you are trying to listen only to the offending sound.

8 Drag the Sensitivity knob down, reducing its value to 42.0%.

You should hear only sibilance.

9 Click the Monitor pop-up menu and choose Off.

The sound changes because you're monitoring through the entire DeEsser audio chain. Now that you have successfully isolated the offending frequency, you're ready to apply gain reduction by using the Strength knob.

10 Drag the Strength knob up to a value of –11.0 dB.

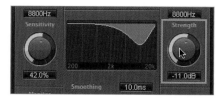

This should reduce the isolated frequency without compromising the full bandwidth signal.

11 Drag the Smoothing slider to the right until you reach a value of 37.5 ms.

This smoothes the attack and release of the DeEsser, creating a subtler effect.

12 While the project is playing, observe the Activity light at the lower right of the plug-in.

This indicates when the DeEsser is actively clamping down on the offending frequency.

NOTE ▶ You can observe the DeEsser in action at the end of Verse 2 and 3, where the lyrics contain a great deal of "s" sounds.

13 Close the DeEsser window.

14 Stop the project playback.

Using the Compressor

Logic's Compressor plug-in provides effective dynamic control and is particularly well suited for processing vocals. By inserting the Compressor into the signal chain after the Channel EQ and DeEsser, you can tighten up the dynamics of the corrected sound, producing a fuller, more robust result.

1 Click the third Insert slot of the Vox_Lead channel and choose Dynamics > Compressor > Mono from the pop-up menu.

The Compressor plug-in window appears.

The Compressor plug-in is a multimode dynamic processor with a built-in side chain and limiter. New to Logic Pro 8 are multiple circuit types based on various gain-control elements inspired by compressor designs both vintage and modern. From colored to transparent sounds, the Compressor offers processing that is well suited to the diverse mixing needs of modern production.

For the Vox_Lead track, a Field Effect Transistor (FET) compressor circuit is a good choice. A FET compressor is often used on vocals for its ability to respond quickly to a signal and create a clean and punchy sound.

2   Click the Circuit Type menu, and choose FET.

Listen to the vocal track while adjusting the Threshold and Ratio controls to govern how and when compression is applied to the incoming signal.

3   Play the project.

4   Drag down the Compressor Threshold slider to a value of –26.5 dB.

5   Drag the Ratio slider to a value of 6.6:1.

The Gain Reduction meter at the top of the plug-in window gives you a visual display of how the Compressor is working with the signal. It reads around –4 dB on average levels and around –12 dB for peaks.

This works pretty well, but the gain reduction is happening a bit fast, creating a slightly unnatural sound for the vocal part. You can address this by increasing the attack to delay the start of the gain reduction induced by the Compressor.

6   Drag up the Attack knob to a value of 19.0 ms.

Although the speed with which a compressor responds to an incoming signal is important, no less important is the speed at which it releases that signal. Release performance and settings can greatly color sound, depending on the dynamics of the original signal and can sometimes lead to undesirable "pumping" and "breathing" effects. To create a more transparent sound, Logic's Compressor contains an Auto mode, in addition to the manually adjusted Release knob. When Auto mode is enabled, the release time is automatically increased as volume peaks go above the threshold setting, dynamically adjusting to the audio material.

7   To the right of the Release knob, click the Auto button.

Now that you've dialed in the basic compression settings, you should apply makeup gain to compensate for the inherent gain reduction caused by the compression process.

8   Drag up the Gain slider to a level of 8.0 dB.

The volume level of the output signal is now roughly equivalent to that of the input signal, and the signal reflects the obvious dynamic smoothing that the compressor provides.

Using a Plug-in's Extended Parameters

Many of Logic's plug-ins (both instruments and effects) offer extended parameters that are hidden from the standard interface by default. These settings are worth exploring and are easily accessed by clicking the disclosure triangle at the lower left of the plug-in interface.

The Compressor parameters you just set sound great but could benefit from a little coloration to make the result sound more like the pleasing harmonic distortion associated with tube-based audio hardware. You can add this coloration using the Output Distortion parameter located within the Compressor's extended parameters.

1   At the lower left of the Compressor's interface, click the disclosure triangle.

The extended parameters appear at the bottom of the plug-in window.

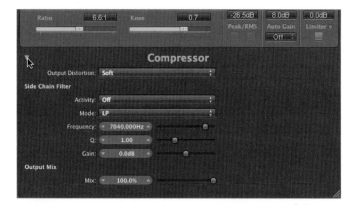

2   From the Output Distortion menu, choose Soft. While subtle, the Soft setting introduces gentle audio clipping at the output, which is quite pleasing to the ear.

3   Click the Solo button to unsolo the Vox_Lead channel and listen to the effects processing applied to the track within the context of the mix.

4   Close the Compressor window.

5   Stop the playback.

Using Send Effects

You can continue working with the lead vocal channel by applying some reverb. You could insert a reverb effects processor into the channel as you did with the EQ and dynamics plug-ins and then adjust the plug-in mix between the direct and processed signal to achieve satisfactory results. However, a much more efficient approach is to set up the reverb plug-in on an aux channel that can receive a signal from any channel.

With the reverb set up in such a manner, controlled amounts of signal from individual tracks can be sent to the aux via the sends on their respective channels. The audio signals are processed with the effect and mixed with the stereo output.

This carries the additional advantage of saving considerable CPU power, because a single instantiation of the effect processor is inserted, instead of the same plug-in being inserted on every channel that needs processing.

The current project already uses send effects in such a manner, instantiated on multiple aux channels within the Mixer (as mentioned earlier in "Using Arrange View").

1   If necessary, scroll to the right to see the five aux channels in the Mixer.

The first three aux channels contain reverb send effects that complement selected instruments in the mix (piano/strings, drums, guitars). So far, a send effect has not been created for a vocal reverb, which usually demands its own type of reverb processing. For this exercise, you will be creating a new reverb send effect that complements the lead vocal you've been working on.

Creating a new aux channel for a send effect is easy, as the aux channel is automatically created when you enable a new send selection on the track.

2 On the Vox_Lead channel, click the top Send slot, and choose Bus > Bus 6 from the menu.

If you look at the aux channels you viewed previously, you'll notice that a new aux channel (Aux 6) has been created, with Bus 6 set in the Input slot. You next need to insert the reverb send effect on this new aux channel, then adjust the send level on the Vox_Lead channel, moving back and forth while you adjust both the reverb settings and the send level to create a satisfactory sound. What could potentially be extremely nonergonomic (especially on a smaller monitor) is made easy by using Single view, learned earlier in the lesson.

3 With the Vox_Lead channel selected, click the Single button.

The Mixer displays the Vox_Lead, Aux 6, Output 1-2, and Master channel strips, representing the complete signal flow stemming from the lead vocal track.

The newly created aux channel (Aux 6) is now within easy reach of the source channel (Vox_Lead). Notice that the created aux channel is mono. This is because Logic automatically sets the format (mono, stereo, or 5.1) to match the source channel. In this situation, a stereo reverb send effect is desired, so you will need to change the format before you instantiate the plug-in.

4   On the Aux 6 channel strip, click the Format button to change the track from mono (single circle) to stereo (two overlapping circles).

The channel becomes stereo, with two level meters side by side.

5   On the Aux 6 channel strip, click the top Insert slot and choose Reverb > Space Designer > Stereo from the pop-up menu.

The Space Designer plug-in window opens.

Space Designer is a convolution reverb that uses a special audio recording of a real acoustic space (or an effect processor) to apply reverb by means of a real-time process. Think of it as a reverb sampler that imposes its sonic signature on a track.

Space Designer comes with a wealth of these acoustic space recordings, called impulse responses (IRs), on which it bases its processing. IR files, as well as any processing parameters, are stored in the effect settings.

6   Click the Settings menu at the top of the window (which now reads "#default"), and choose 01 Large Spaces > 03 Plate Reverbs > 02.6s Vocal Plate.

> **NOTE** ▶ If you have created custom presets of your own, Logic will list the installed factory presets in a folder named Factory. If you do not see the 01 Large Spaces folder, look in the Factory folder, and then continue along the file path specified above.

The IR takes a moment to load. After loading, you can see the visual representation of the IR, which, in this case, was sampled from an electronic reverb processor's plate algorithm.

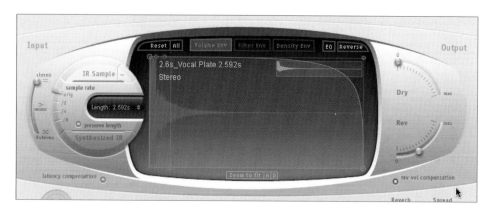

7   At the bottom of the IR waveform display, click the A button.

This button allows you to zoom in on the attack area of the IR's waveform display. The magnification helps you see how the signal will be affected by the reverb sample.

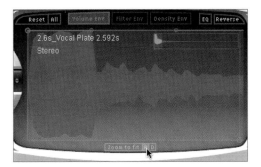

NOTE ▶ If you look closely at the zoomed IR waveform, you'll notice that the reverberation signal occurs immediately (it starts at the far left).

Space Designer offers additional processing of the IR signal via an extensive array of editing parameters. These parameters range from settings found on traditional reverb units to control settings specific to working with volume and filter envelopes.

When using reverb on vocal tracks, it is often desirable to complement the sound with predelay to separate the original signal from the reverb tail.

8 At the lower right, drag up the Pre-Dly (Predelay) knob to a value of 61 ms.

Now that you've completed some basic adjustments to the Space Designer reverb, you can send a controlled amount of the lead vocal signal to the send effect for processing. You do this by means of adjusting the send level on the output channel strip.

Once a send destination has been assigned, the corresponding Send knob appears next to the Send slot. By adjusting the Send knob, you can choose the amount of signal sent to the chosen destination (in this case, Aux 6).

9 Click the Solo button on the Vox_Lead channel.

10 Play the project.

11 While listening to the lead vocal track, drag up the Send knob, setting a value of −14.9 (dB).

NOTE ▶ When you solo a track assigned to an aux, Logic automatically keeps the effects return channels (aux channels) open. This automatic mute suppression allows you to hear the soloed track with the send effects applied. The same applies when you solo an effect return signal. The channels fed into the effect are muted, but their effect sends remain open, ensuring that the effect continues to receive a signal.

12 Stop the playback.

13 On the Vox_Lead channel, click the Solo button to unsolo the channel.

14 Click the Cycle button to turn Cycle mode off.

15 Close the Space Designer window.

MORE INFO ▶ The distributed audio processing feature in Logic Pro allows you to expand the processing capacity of your Logic Pro system by offloading calculations for software instrument and DSP effects to additional Macintosh computers that are connected by Gigabit Ethernet. This is effective when you need additional processing horsepower for CPU-intensive software synthesizers or plug-ins such as Sculpture or Space Designer. For more information on how to set up a distributed audio processing system, refer to page 99 in the *Logic Pro 8 User Manual*.

Panning Stereo Tracks

Logic's Mixer channels offer true stereo functionality without requiring the user to dedicate two tracks (a left and a right channel) for playback. This provides playback of interleaved stereo files, stereo software instruments, and stereo busses through a single mixer channel, providing ease of use when working with stereo sources.

On stereo channels in the Mixer, the Balance control balances the relative levels of the left and right signals that make up the stereo signal. Adjusting the balance of a stereo track reduces one side in favor of the other.

For example, imagine a stereo drum overheads track that has the hi-hat on the left side of the spectrum and the ride cymbal on the right. If the Balance control for the track is turned to the left, then the right side of the signal diminishes, losing the ride. If the knob is turned to the right, the opposite happens, reducing the hi-hat signal in favor of the ride.

While this stereo balance function provides considerable ease of use, it also represents a limitation when it comes to the placement of a sound in the stereo field of a mix. It is often necessary to reposition the center of a recorded stereo signal within the mix while maintaining or changing the spread (stereo width). Fortunately, Logic offers a handy plug-in, the Direction Mixer, that does this on any stereo track. This plug-in allows for a more focused sound, as you are truly panning a stereo signal instead of adjusting the signal level of the left and right sides.

1   Click the Arrange button.

All active channels in the project's arrangement are displayed in the Mixer.

2   On the Piano channel strip (track 14), click the second Insert slot, and choose Imaging > Direction Mixer > Stereo from the pop-up menu.

The Direction Mixer plug-in window opens.

The Direction Mixer plug-in offers the panning functionality described above by means of the Direction parameter. Graphically, the Direction knob is quite different from the Pan control used on mono tracks. Values within the range of –90 to +90 degrees represent the full stereo field, while greater and lesser values (from +90 to +180 or from –90 to –180 degrees) bring the middle of the signal back toward the center, but with the left and right sides reversed. At +180 (or –180) degrees, the signal is dead center, but with the left and right sides inverted.

3 Drag the Direction knob up to set a value of +51.

This places the center of the Piano signal slightly to the right side of the mix.

In addition to positioning the middle of the stereo signal across the stereo field, you can use the Direction Mixer plug-in to widen or tighten the spread of the stereo base by adjusting the Spread parameter. A setting of 1.0 maintains the width of the original signal, while lower settings bring the sides toward the center, decreasing the spread.

4 Drag one of the Spread sliders to set a value of 0.8.

This will tighten up the stereo signal so that it doesn't take up quite as much width in the stereo mix.

5 Click the Solo button for the Piano channel.

6 Press Shift-Enter (the Play from Selection command) to play the project from the beginning of the Piano part.

7 While the project is playing, click the Bypass button on and off to hear the Piano track with and without the Direction Mixer.

Notice that with the Direction Mixer active, it feels as though the piano is sitting to the right of the vocalist, but the stereo image is not compromised. If you had used the main Balance control to do the same thing, you might have lost the sound of the low notes on the piano, because they are normally heard in the left side of the stereo image.

8   Make sure the Direction Mixer plug-in isn't bypassed.

9   Stop the project playback.

10   Close the Direction Mixer window.

11   On the Piano channel, click the Solo button to unsolo the channel.

12   Play the project again, this time listening to how the Piano track fits within the stereo mix.

> **NOTE** ▶ The Direction Mixer plug-in also decodes MS (middle-side) encoded stereo recordings. Once the MS mode is engaged (by clicking the MS button), you can alter the stereo signal with the Spread and Direction controls as you would with standard left-right stereo signals.

Switching the Contents of the Plug-in Window

Accessing the multitude of active plug-ins in a project can be a clumsy process requiring the opening and closing of each plug-in window. Menus in a plug-in window provide a simpler way to navigate around active plug-ins, allowing you to view any plug-in in the same window regardless of its channel or its order in the signal chain.

This navigation technique also helps when you're copying presets from one location to another and identical processing is required. The two violin tracks are a good example of this, since they could both benefit from similar EQ and dynamics processing. In this exercise you navigate from the Violin1 channel to the Violin2 channel using the plug-in window menus, copying and pasting settings from one plug-in to another.

1   In the Mixer, look at the two adjacent Violin tracks (tracks 11 and 12).

Notice that they have identical plug-ins at the same Insert slots in the channels. However, the Violin1 plug-ins have customized settings, which you will copy to Violin2.

To use this plug-in settings technique, you need to have a plug-in window open.

2   In the Violin1 channel (track 11), double-click the Channel EQ plug-in to open the plug-in window.

The EQ curve indicates a subtle dip at around 395 Hz and a smaller boost at around 3450 Hz.

3   At the upper right of the plug-in window, click the Copy button.

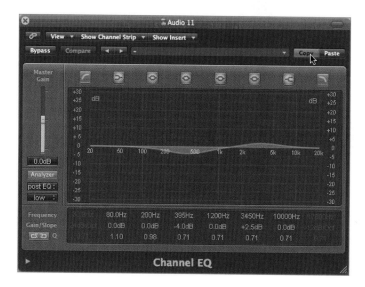

Now that you have copied the EQ plug-in settings from Violin1, you can paste them into the Channel EQ in the Violin2 channel. You will use the two "Show" pop-up menus located at the top of the plug-in window to view the Channel EQ setting for Violin2 in the same plug-in window.

The Show Channel Strip menu accesses the same numbered Insert slot on any channel that has an active plug-in.

NOTE ▶ The list displayed in the Show Channel Strip pop-up menu corresponds to the channel type and number, not to the channel order in the Mixer. Channel type and number are displayed in the Mixer in the middle of each channel strip. This makes Violin1 Audio 11, and Violin2 Audio 12.

4   Click the Show Channel Strip pop-up menu button, and choose Audio 12 (Violin2).

The Violin2 Channel EQ settings (default) are now displayed in the open plug-in window (identified as Audio 12).

5   Click the Paste button (next to the Copy button).

The plug-in settings from Violin1 are pasted into the Channel EQ of Violin2.

6   Click the Show Channel Strip menu button, and choose Audio 11 (Violin1).

This returns you to the Violin1 Channel EQ. Let's move on to display the Compressor plug-in, located in the second Insert slot for the channel. Each Insert slot for a single channel can be accessed by the Show Insert pop-up menu.

7   Click the Show Insert menu button and choose Comp.

The Compressor interface now appears in the plug-in window.

8   Click the Copy button.

9   Click the Show Channel Strip menu button and choose Audio 12 (Violin2).

The Compressor inserted in the second Insert slot on the Violin2 channel is displayed in the plug-in window.

10   Click the Paste button.

The plug-in setting from Violin1 is pasted onto the Compressor of Violin2.

11   Close the plug-in window.

Changing Plug-in Locations

As anyone who has worked with effects processors knows, where you place an effect is as important as what effect is chosen. Inserting effects at different places in the signal chain can lead to different results depending on the processing involved.

Changing effect placement is easily done in Logic's Mixer by dragging with the Hand tool. You can try this by changing the order of the lead vocal signal chain that you created earlier, placing the EQ after the Compressor.

1   Solo the Vox_Lead channel by clicking the Solo button.

2   Click the Cycle button to turn on Cycle mode.

This will bring back the cycle area you created earlier when auditioning the lead vocal.

3   Choose the Hand tool.

This tool allows you to grab and move plug-ins in this window.

> **TIP** ▶ By default, you switch from the Pointer tool to the Hand tool in the Mixer by pressing Command as you click.

4   Drag the Channel EQ in the first Insert slot on track 1 (the Vox_Lead channel), placing it in between Insert slots 3 and 4 (a yellow line will appear between Insert slots 3 and 4).

The signal chain reflects the new order, inserting the Channel EQ (including the settings) after the Compressor.

NOTE ▶ When dragging plug-in locations with the Hand tool, pay special attention to the area where you release the mouse button, as this affects placement in the signal chain (top to bottom). To aid in this, a light yellow rectangle or line is displayed indicating where the plug-in will be placed. With careful placement, you can put plug-ins above or below the others (indicated by a yellow line) in the signal chain, and even swap locations (an empty target slot will be indicated by a yellow rectangle).

5   Play the project and listen to the lead vocal channel with the new plug-in order.

6   While it's playing, drag the Channel EQ plug-in back to the first Insert slot.

The plug-in changes position, even when the project is playing.

7   Stop the playback.

TIP ▶ This technique also works for dragging Insert plug-ins from one channel to another. If you do this, make sure to keep format (mono, stereo, or 5.1) compatibility between the two channels in mind. You can even copy plug-ins from location to location by pressing the Option key while dragging.

Using Channel Strip Settings

Chains of multiple plug-ins (and their settings) can be saved and recalled as channel strip settings. This enables you to apply commonly used chains of effects in any project far more quickly than individually inserting each plug-in and its settings.

You used channel strip settings via the Library earlier in the book to open a software instrument that was coupled with a chain of effects (Lesson 4, "Working with Software Instruments"). This time, you'll save the lead vocal effects chain as a channel strip setting for future use.

1   Click the Setting button at the top of the Vox_Lead channel strip, and choose "Save Channel Strip Setting as" from the pop-up menu.

A window opens with a file selector box.

2   In the Save As field, enter *I Was Raised Vox*, and click Save.

This will save the signal chain to a folder reserved for audio channel strip settings. The chain can be recalled on any audio channel.

TIP ▶ Channel strip settings can be applied to channels of a different kind by pressing Option while opening the Channel Strip Settings menu.

Lesson Review

1.   Explain the difference between the Mixer's Arrange, All, and Single view modes.

2.   In the Channel EQ, what feature enables to you to visualize both the pre- and post-processed signals to identify and correct frequency-specific problems?

3.   In the DeEsser, what features help to identify and reduce signal sibilance?

4. Which insert plug-in allows the smoothing of a signal's dynamics and the ability to impart subtle coloration?

5. Which send effect modifies how a signal interacts with an impulse response, simulating the placement of a signal within an acoustic space?

6. Which insert plug-in aids in accurate stereo placement within a mix?

7. A plug-in's Show Channel Strip and Show Insert menus allow what?

8. Which tool allows you to change the insert order, thereby affecting signal flow?

9. How are channel strip settings used?

Answers

1. The Mixer's Arrange view adapts to the Arrange area's track list, and vice versa. The All view mode displays all the channels existing in a project's Environment, and it can be used to create an alternative mixer with commonly accessed channels. The Single view displays the entire signal flow from a selected channel, including send channels and output.

2. The Channel EQ's built-in Analyzer can help identify and correct problem bands in a signal's frequency spectrum.

3. The DeEsser plug-in can be monitored at multiple points to identify and reduce signal sibilance. It accomplishes this by locating the problem frequency with the Detector and reducing the same frequency band (or a different band) with the Suppressor.

4. Logic's Compressor plug-in does so with different circuit types and harmonic distortion.

5. The Space Designer convolution reverb.

6. Stereo tracks can be accurately balanced and their images adjusted by means of the Direction Mixer plug-in.

7. A plug-in's Show Channel Strip and Show Insert menus allow navigation from plug-in to plug-in within the same window, making it easier to copy and paste settings between plug-ins.

8. The Hand tool allows you to change the insert order by dragging and dropping plug-ins within a single channel, or from channel to channel.

9. Channel strip settings can store commonly used effects chains for use in any project.

9

Lesson Files	Logic 8_BTB_Files > Lessons > 09_I Was Raised_Start.logic
Media	Logic 8_BTB_Files > Media > I Was Raised
Time	This lesson takes approximately 1 hour to complete.
Goals	Create submixes for processing multiple channels
	Label and rename tracks for easy access
	Create channel groups to link the controls of multiple channels
	Incorporate external effects processors into Logic's Mixer

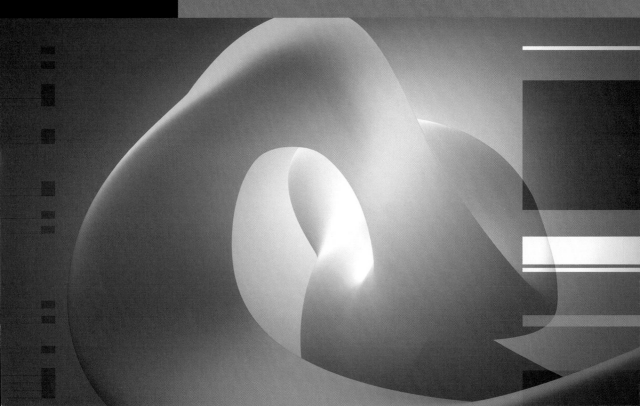

Lesson 9
Controlling Signal Flow

In the software world of Logic, a signal is routed from one channel to another via the send and input/output fields in each channel. Signals are often sent to multiple destinations simultaneously and can even interface with external devices by leaving the audio interface and coming into it again.

In this lesson, you will use the Mixer to route an audio signal to Logic's audio channels and accomplish specific mixing tasks. You will also integrate external effects processors into your signal flow, interfacing the physical world with the virtual one.

Using Aux Channels as Submixes

In addition to acting as effects returns (as in the previous lesson), aux channels can act as submix channels, enabling you to feed the output of multiple audio channels to a single fader. Using an aux channel for a submix allows you to work with multiple routed channels as a single set while retaining the relative differences of individual channels.

A common use for a submix is to apply a single effects-processing chain to multiple tracks (such as those for backing vocals or drums). This eliminates the need to assign the same effects chains to several tracks separately and also saves valuable CPU power.

In this exercise, you will assign backing vocals (tracks 2–10) to a shared aux channel, creating a submix that applies the same signal processing to all the tracks at once.

1   Choose File > Open.

2   In the Open window's file selector box, go to Music > Logic 8_BTB_Files > Lessons and open **09_I Was Raised_Start.logic**.

The project opens to the Mixer/Arrange area screenset you used in the previous lesson.

3   Drag over the track names of the backing vocal tracks (tracks 2–10) in the Mixer.

The channel strips are selected as you drag over them.

4   Click any selected track's Output slot, and choose Bus > Bus 7.

All the Output slots in the selected channel strips change to Bus 7.

> **TIP** ▶ This technique also works for assigning send destinations on multiple tracks.

5   On any of the selected channels, double-click the Output slot.

The Mixer automatically locates to a newly created aux channel (Aux 7).

> **TIP** ▶ This navigation shortcut also works with Send slots.

Logic automatically creates a new aux channel when you select an unused bus as an output. This is similar to what happened when you created a new send effect in the previous lesson.

To differentiate between the submix channel and the other aux channels, it's a good idea to give the submix channel a more descriptive name and assign it a new color. Doing so also makes the submix channel easier to locate in the Mixer layout and in the menus that access aux channels (such as the Send and Output menus).

6   Double-click the name of the newly created aux channel strip (Aux 7) and enter *BkVox Sub*. Press Return.

The Aux 7 channel is renamed BkVox Sub.

7   Select View > Colors from the Mixer menu bar.

The color palette appears.

8 Choose a color by clicking any color square within the palette. When you've chosen it, close the Colors window.

By setting the selected tracks to output directly to an aux channel, you can process the full signal of the combined channels using the aux channel's Insert slots (applying EQ, de-essing, compression, and so on). Let's try this by instantiating a Channel EQ onto the newly created submix.

NOTE ▸ This form of processing is referred to as *serial processing*, because the entire output of one or more channels is fed in a series directly into another channel.

9 On the BkVox Sub channel, click the top Insert slot and choose EQ > Channel EQ > Stereo from the pop-up menu.

A Channel EQ is instantiated and ready for use.

10 In the Settings menu, choose 05 Voice > Backing Vocals.

At this point, you could easily continue to apply additional processing to the backing vocals (such as de-essing and compression), which would affect all the signals at once.

11 Close the Channel EQ window.

12 On the BkVox Sub channel, click the Solo button.

NOTE ▸ When an aux channel is soloed, Logic uses automatic mute suppression on the tracks that feed the aux. This allows you to hear the contributing signals without having to find the separate channels and solo each of them.

13 Press Control–Command–Right Arrow/Left Arrow (the Go to Next/Previous Marker command) to locate the playhead to the Refrain section.

14 In the Transport bar, click the Cycle button.

15 Play the project, listening to the backing vocals as sent through the EQ on the aux channel.

16 While it's playing, drag the BkVox Sub channel's volume fader up and down.

All backing vocal tracks change their volume, adjusted by a single fader.

17 Return the volume to 0.0 (dB) by Option-clicking the fader.

18 Stop the project playback.

Setting up the aux channel as a submix allows you to control the volume of all partici-
pating tracks while maintaining the relative volume levels set by each track's fader.

Applying Send Effects to Submixes

The submix channel you just created also works well for assigning a group of channels
to a common send effect, such as reverb. Conveniently, aux channels also contain sends,
which allow you to assign the submix containing the backing vocals to any send effect
configured on the other aux channels.

1 On the BkVox Sub channel, click the top Send slot and choose Aux 6 from the
pop-up menu.

NOTE ▶ The name you just assigned to Aux 7 is listed here in parentheses.

Aux 6 is the vocal reverb that you set up in the previous lesson.

2 Play the project.

3 On the BkVox Sub channel, drag up the Send knob, listening to the backing vocals
as you adjust the amount of signal sent to the vocal reverb to taste.

4 Stop the project playback.

NOTE ▶ This routing is frequently referred to as *parallel routing,* wherein the signal is split (via the send) and fed to separate channels.

5   On the BkVox Sub channel, click the Solo button to take it out of Solo mode.

6   Play the project, dragging the fader on the BkVox Sub channel to adjust the volume level of the backing vocals.

7   Stop the project playback when you are happy with the volume level of the backing vocals in relation to the overall mix.

TIP▶ The methods of signal routing described in these exercises invite experimentation! Try combining both methods to create interesting signal processing chains.

Using Mixer Groups

A *group* is used to link similar controls (panning, volume, and so on) in different channels. This creates a direct relationship among all the channels in the group assignment. As a result, when you adjust the parameters on one channel, the same parameters are adjusted in all of the group's channels.

Assigning channels to groups is similar to using aux channels as submixes. Both techniques enable you to simultaneously adjust the output of multiple channels while maintaining the relative levels of the individual tracks.

However, the two techniques differ profoundly in function, as aux channel submixes directly control the signal flow, while groups affect channels and tracks.

Assigning Channels to Groups

In this exercise, you will assign similar backing vocals to a group, linking together specific properties that you can control in the Mixer.

1   On the Harm1 channel (track 2), click the Group slot (see below) and choose Group 1 from the pop-up menu.

A yellow 1 appears in the Group slot, and the Group Settings window opens.

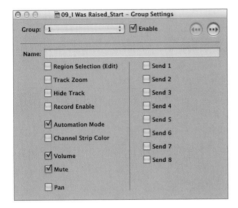

In this window, you can set the channel properties to be linked.

NOTE ▸   In addition to sharing channel strip parameters, groups can share attributes such as viewing and recording settings in the Arrange area, the channel strip color, and the Automation mode.

2   Select the Send 1 checkbox.

This links the topmost Send knob for the group.

3   In the Name field, enter *HrmVox*, and press Return.

4   Close the Group Settings window.

1: HrmVox now appears in the Group slot on the track. This signifies that the channel is assigned to Group 1.

5   On the Harm2 channel (track 3), click the Group slot, and choose Group 1 from the pop-up menu.

The Harm1 and Harm2 channels both display *1: HrmVox* in the Group slot.

TIP ▶ You can assign the most recently selected group to any channel by Option-clicking its Group slot.

Now that you have assigned the two channels to a group, you can adjust both tracks simultaneously.

In this mix, the harmony vocals (Harm1 and Harm2) need additional reverb processing to create a more reflective sound. Both tracks are outputting to the BkVox Sub (Aux 7) and then to Aux 6 for processing; but they also have sends set for Aux 3 (a longer, more reflective reverb).

Since the two channels are similar in character and material, it is desirable to have the same send level for both sent to this longer reverb. Because Send 1 was selected in the HrmVox Group Settings window, changing either channel's Send 1 value will also cause the other to change.

6   Use Control–Command–Right and Left Arrow keys to set the locators around the Chorus 2 section.

Due to the unusual signal routing in the current tracks (combined parallel processing and series routing), automatic mute suppression will not work to isolate both reverbs and source signals. However, you can still accomplish this by using the Track Solo buttons in the Arrange area's track list.

NOTE ▶ In order for this to work, you need to have Track Mute/Solo set to CPU-saving (Slow Response) within Preferences > Audio > General.

7 In the Arrange area, click the Solo buttons for the Harm1 (track 2) and Harm2 (track 3) tracks.

> **TIP** ▶ You can quickly solo or mute multiple tracks by dragging over the buttons in the track list.

8 Play the project.

9 While listening to the playback, drag up the Send knob on either of the channels, applying additional reverb to your liking.

Both Send knobs move as you adjust one or the other.

10 When you are finished setting the reverb level for the channels, stop the playback.

Temporarily Disabling a Group

It is often necessary to adjust individual channels of an assigned group without affecting the entire group. At these times, you can temporarily disable the group by means of a *group clutch*. The group clutch works like an automobile's clutch, temporarily taking the group "out of gear" while letting you perform the necessary adjustments.

In the current project, the Harm2 channel is a little too loud to blend with the part sung on the Harm1 channel. To change the fader without affecting the other channel, you need to engage the group clutch, make an adjustment, and then reengage the group by turning off the group clutch.

The group clutch can be activated via a menu selection in the Mixer's local menu bar (Options > Group Clutch) or a key command (Command-G). As you will probably be performing this most often during playback, the keyboard shortcut makes for a more ergonomic mix process.

1 Play the project, listening closely to the HrmVox group.

2 Press Command-G, the group clutch key command.

The Group display turns from yellow (active) to gray (inactive), indicating that the group clutch is engaged.

3 Drag the Harm2 fader down to −16 (dB).

4   Press Command-G again.

The group display turns from gray (inactive) to yellow (active), indicating that the group clutch is disengaged.

5   With the song still playing, turn off soloing on the Harm1 and Harm2 tracks by clicking their Track Solo buttons in the Arrange area.

The entire arrangement can now be heard.

> **TIP** ▶ You can quickly turn off soloing in all the tracks in the Arrange area by clicking the Transport Solo button in the Transport bar.

6   In one of the HrmVox group channels, drag up the fader to adjust the level of the group in relation to the mix (to about –7.6 dB and –12 dB, respectively).

Both faders move in tandem, maintaining the relative gain between them.

7   Stop the project when you are happy with the volume level of the harmony vocals in relation to the overall mix.

Incorporating External Effects Processors

Although software effects processors can offer distinct advantages over external processors, having high-quality hardware processors in the signal chain can uniquely improve the sound. External effects processors are easily incorporated into Logic's software Mixer with a "helper" plug-in that manages the flow to the processor from the audio interface's inputs and outputs.

With the I/O plug-in, you can treat the external processor almost as if it were itself a plug-in, inserting it into a channel or applying it as a send effect in Logic's Mixer. To illustrate this technique, you will insert an imaginary hardware reverb unit as a send effect.

To enable the integration in this exercise, you need to physically send a signal from your audio interface to your hardware processor and back again. This is done by connecting an open pair of outputs from your audio interface into the stereo inputs of the hardware reverb, and connecting the stereo outputs of the hardware reverb back to an open pair of stereo inputs on the audio interface.

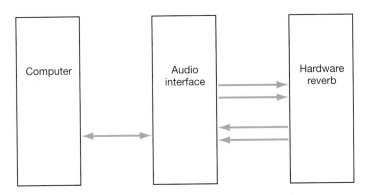

If you have a hardware reverb processor, try this by connecting the equipment according to the above diagram, using inputs 5–6 and outputs 5–6 of your audio interface. If not, follow along with an "imaginary" external processor connected.

> **NOTE ▶** If your system configuration does not include as many as six inputs and six outputs, you cannot complete this exercise.

Once this physical cabling has been completed, you need to create a new aux channel to feed the external hardware.

1   Select Options > Create New Auxiliary Channel Strips.

The New Auxiliary Channel Strips dialog appears.

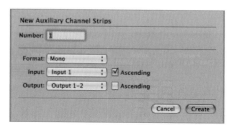

In this dialog, you can specify the number, format, and I/O configuration of the aux channels you've created.

TIP ▶ New auxiliary channels are easily created by clicking the + button at the far left of the Mixer.

2   From the Format menu, choose Stereo.

3   From the Input menu, select Bus > Bus 8.

4   Click Create.

A new aux channel, Aux 8, is created in the Mixer.

5   Double-click the track name for Aux 8, and rename it *Ext Verb*.

NOTE ▶ Naming aux channels that feed external hardware is useful to differentiate them from Logic's internal send effects.

If this channel is to function as a send effect, you'll need to route to the external effects processor. This is done via the I/O plug-in.

6   In Aux 8, click the top Insert slot, and choose Utility > I/O > Stereo.

The I/O plug-in window opens.

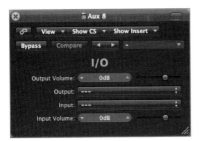

The next step is to assign the appropriate inputs and outputs of the audio interface to access the hardware processor. This is done via the Input and Output menus.

7   Click the Output menu and choose 5–6.

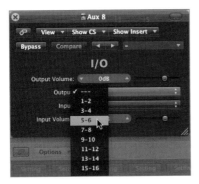

8   Click the Input menu and choose 5–6.

You can now send signals to the hardware reverb inserted on Aux 8 using the same means you would use for any send effect: the channel Send menu.

9   In the Guitar_riff1 channel (track 19), click the top Send slot, and choose Bus > Bus 8 from the pop-up menu.

NOTE ▶ As when reverb plug-ins are inserted as bus effects, the wet-dry ratio on the external hardware reverb should be set to 100% wet.

10 Solo the Guitar_riff1 channel by clicking its Solo button.

11 Press Control–Command–Left Arrow to locate to the Intro section.

The cycle area now encompasses the Intro section.

12 Play the project.

13 While the project is playing, on the Guitar_riff1 channel, drag up the Send knob to adjust the amount of signal sent to the hardware reverb on Bus 8.

14 Raise the return level by dragging the Aux 8 channel fader up until you can hear the effect.

> **NOTE** ▶ All external hardware processors are different. You might need to adjust the send and return levels in Logic to achieve optimum gain staging. You can also apply additional signal gain going to and from the external effects processor by dragging the Output Volume and Input Volume sliders on the I/O plug-in. When using this setup, do not change Logic's master channel strip fader or master fader in the Transport bar, as this changes the volume level of all output channels and, therefore, your send levels to the external hardware.

15 Stop the project playback.

> **TIP** ▶ The I/O plug-in can also be used as an insert effect, sending signals to and from external effects processors such as hardware compressors, EQs, stomp boxes, and so on.

Lesson Review

1. What is the most efficient way to apply effects processing to multiple channels at once?

2. How do you link the controls of multiple channels while mixing?

3. How do you temporarily disengage a group?

4. How do you insert an external effects processor into the signal chain?

Answers

1. Use aux channels as submixes to apply effects processing to multiple channels.

2. Use groups to link the controls of multiple channels while mixing.

3. Engage the group clutch (press Command-G or, in the Mixer's menu bar, choose Options > Group Clutch).

4. Insert external effects processors into the signal chain using the I/O plug-in.

10

Lesson Files	Logic 8_BTB_Files > Lessons > 10_I Was Raised_Start.logic
Media	Logic 8_BTB_Files > Media > I Was Raised
Time	This lesson takes approximately 1 hour to complete.
Goals	Automate mixes offline
	Edit automation data
	Assign a MIDI keyboard control to automation parameters
	Input real-time automation using a mouse and a MIDI hardware controller
	Write automation data for an entire group at once

Lesson 10
Automating the Mix

A good mix is a performance of sorts. Like an instrument in an ensemble, each element of a mix speaks its part clearly and expressively, complementing the other elements. This is a dynamic process, frequently involving the continuous adjustment of individual signals as a project progresses.

In this lesson, you'll use automation to craft a mix, manually drawing in automation data as well as entering data in real time with a MIDI controller. You will also learn various methods for editing automation data, including techniques to get the most from the data that is already entered.

Working with Offline Automation

To create a dynamic-sounding mix, you have to be able to control audio signals over time. Adjusting volume, panning, or even plug-in parameters through the course of a project is an important part of breathing life into a mix.

While the mouse is suitable for setting controls, you will quickly discover that it is not the ideal tool for performing common mixing moves (such as dragging sliders and faders). The ability to click only one thing at a time is a major hurdle you must overcome to effectively refine your mix.

Logic's comprehensive track-based automation system offers help, allowing you to change over time the settings of virtually all channel-related software controls. These movements can be recorded offline with a mouse in non–real time or in real time with a dedicated hardware MIDI control surface or a MIDI controller. Whichever entry method you use, the automation data can easily be edited and manipulated after the initial input, giving you control over all the sonic elements in a composition.

You start by opening the project file used in this lesson.

1   Choose File > Open.

2   In the Open window's file selector box, go to Music > Logic 8_BTB_Files > Lessons and open **10_I Was Raised_Start.logic**.

3   Play the project if you need to familiarize yourself with the material you will be mixing.

Understanding the Automation Interface

In Lesson 8 you applied some effective dynamic processing to the lead vocal, but it still needs basic level adjustment to sit comfortably in the arrangement. While the vocal's volume level is adequate for the Verses, the vocal quickly becomes lost in the denser Chorus and Refrain sections and requires a boost in gain.

In this set of exercises, you will use offline automation to manually input automation data that controls the lead vocal's volume level. In order to work with offline automation, you need to display track automation data in the Arrange area.

1   If it is not selected, select the Vox_Lead track (track 1) in the track list.

2   In the Arrange area's local menu bar, choose View > Track Automation.

The header of the selected track displays the automation menus.

Automation Parameter menu

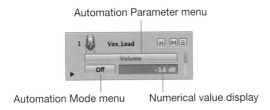

Automation Mode menu   Numerical value display

NOTE ▶ By default, Volume is displayed as the active automation parameter when you view track automation for the first time.

The track displays a thin black line and a yellow number representing the volume setting for the channel (−3.6 dB). The numerical value of the active automation parameter is also displayed below the Automation Parameter menu and is represented by the fader immediately to the right.

Value fader

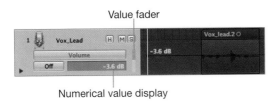

Numerical value display

When track automation is active, an automation area highlighted in dark gray is displayed over the track. You will input your offline automation data by clicking in this semitransparent area.

The track automation view can be saved in the screenset. Since you will be working exclusively with automation in the next few exercises, it is a good idea to lock this to Screenset 1.

3   Choose Screenset > Unlock, then Screenset > Lock (choose Unlock to disable the lock, and choose Lock to lock it with the new changes).

Creating Automation Nodes

To provide accurate input when working with offline automation, you need to view the area you will be working with at a fairly high level of magnification.

1   Create a cycle area from measure 18 to measure 73.

2   Press Control-Shift-Z (the "Zoom to fit Locators" key command) to magnify the area designated by the cycle area.

3   Press Control–Down Arrow to vertically expand the view as far as it will go.

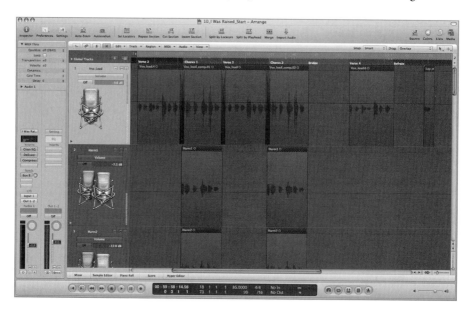

The Pointer tool has multiple functions for inputting automation data offline. Without a key modifier, the Pointer tool creates points, called *nodes*, when you click in an automation track. Used with the Shift key, it enables you to select the nodes for adjustment or editing in the automation track.

You can start creating offline automation by increasing the lead vocal's volume level in the Refrain section.

4   Using the Pointer tool, click the automation line around measure 65.

The black line turns yellow, showing that automation is now active, and a small node is created with the current volume setting (–3.6 dB).

When you graphically make an entry in the automation track, the automation mode automatically changes to Read, enabling the track to follow the volume level adjustments you create.

5   Click the automation line between the node you just created and the next region.

Another node is created, displaying the same value.

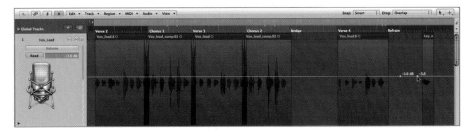

NOTE ► You can delete an individual node by clicking it (without dragging).

6   Drag up the node you just created to a value of +1.7 dB.

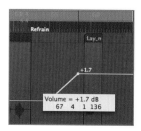

NOTE ▶ The first node indicates where you want the change in value to start, and the second indicates where you want it to end.

The Chorus 1 section also needs a volume boost that doesn't affect the level of the Verses. You will ramp up the volume at the beginning of the section, which requires two nodes, and ramp it down at the end, which requires another two nodes. Rather than create the nodes one at a time, you can use a handy feature that lets you automatically create a pair of nodes at each end of a selected region.

7   Click the top area of the Vox_lead_comp.01 region to select it.

8   Choose Options > Track Automation > Create 4 Nodes at Region Border.

Four nodes are created: two overlapping nodes at each end of the selected area.

Notice that the automation line and the nodes within the selected region (and before it) are white. This is because the automation area is selected (along with the nodes) and is ready to be edited. To increase the volume level, you simply drag the selected line up, adjusting the automation.

TIP ▶ You can quickly make adjustments to adjacent nodes without selecting them first by dragging the line between them.

9   Drag up the selected automation line between the nodes, increasing the gain to –1.1 dB.

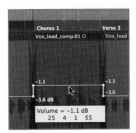

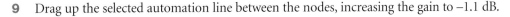 **TIP** ▶ You can also quickly create nodes and adjust automation by using the Marquee tool. Start by using the Marquee tool to select the area you wish to edit, then use the Pointer tool to drag the selection up or down to adjust the automation level.

Copying the Automation Data

You need to raise the volume in the Chorus 2 section as well. You can easily do this by copying the previously created automation nodes. To make a selection of multiple nodes within the automation track, you must Shift-drag around the targeted area.

1   Holding down the Shift key, draw a selection rectangle around the four nodes used in the Chorus 1 section.

   NOTE ▶ Make sure you draw the selection rectangle within the automation area, as you could inadvertently select a region along with the automation nodes.

   The four nodes are selected, along with the area between them.

2   Option-drag the selected area, positioning the copied set of nodes to the same relative location around the Chorus 2 section (starting around 40 4 4 151).

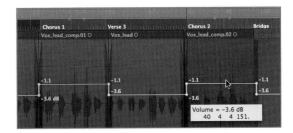

The automation nodes you created for Chorus 1 are copied to Chorus 2.

> **TIP** ▶ If you wish to copy automation data while maintaining the relative positions of the nodes in the bars and beats grid, try choosing Snap Automation in the Arrange area's Snap menu. When Snap Automation is turned on, all created nodes and edits are snapped to the grid. This is especially useful for creative automation (such as automation of a software instrument filter) that repeats on specific beats or at other intervals.

3 Play the project, listening to the automated changes in volume level in the Vox_Lead track and observing the fader movement in the Arrange channel strip.

4 Stop the playback.

Using Curves

Now turn your attention to the Crunch_Gtr1 and Crunch_Gtr2 tracks in the Bridge section. These two tracks are double-tracked takes of the same part.

1 Press the number 1 to open Screenset 1.

The magnification level returns to the original level.

2 Press Control–Command–Right Arrow/Left Arrow (the Go to Next/Previous Marker key commands) to locate to the Bridge section.

The cycle area adapts to encompass the Bridge section.

3 In the track list, select the Crunch_Gtr1 track.

The region within the Bridge section becomes selected.

> **NOTE** ▶ When a cycle area is active, clicking the track list will select only the regions that lie within the cycle area's boundaries.

4 Using the Zoom tool, draw a selection rectangle around the two regions in the Crunch_Gtr1 and Crunch_Gtr2 tracks that occur during the Bridge section.

The window zooms in vertically and horizontally, displaying the two Crunch_Gtr tracks.

5   Play the project, listening to the two Crunch_Gtr tracks in the mix.

The levels for both tracks are too hot and would benefit from a slight dynamic build during the last strummed chords. You can fix the problem by creating an automated level increase for the first of the two tracks.

6   Click the Solo button for the Crunch_Gtr1 track.

7   On the Crunch_Gtr1 track, click the automation line at around 47 3 1 1.

A node is created with a value of −3.8 dB (the current fader position).

8   Create another node after the one you created and before the Crunch guitar 1 region.

9   Drag the node you just created down to a value of −8.8 dB.

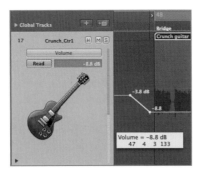

10   Create a node right before the last chord (around 54 1 1 1).

11   Create another node at the end of the strummed chord (around 55 1 1 1).

12   Drag the node you just created up to a value of −4.6 dB.

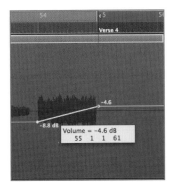

So far, you've created a quick 5 dB dip in volume level, followed by a more gradual level increase during the last strummed chord. You can further refine the gradual level increase by applying a curve to the line.

Logic offers four kinds of automation curves: convex, concave, and two types of S curves. You can apply these by holding down the Control and Option keys while dragging the line between two nodes. The direction you move your mouse while pressing the keys determines the kind and amount of curve that will be applied between the nodes.

13 Control-Option-drag the line between measures 54 and 55, trying out each of the four curve shapes (drag up, down, left, right) one at a time.

The line changes to a convex shape when dragged up, a concave shape when dragged down, and different S shapes when dragged left and right.

14 Control-Option-drag the line to the right, creating a gentle S-shaped curve.

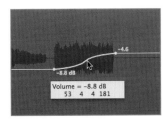

15 Create a node by clicking the automation line at 56 3 1 1.

16 Drag the node you just created down to a value of −8.8 dB.

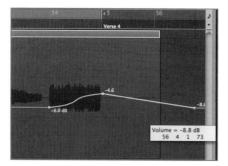

This brings the level back down in preparation for the next exercise.

17   Play the project, listening to the automated changes in volume level for the Crunch_Gtr1 track and observing the fader movement in the Arrange channel strip.

18   Stop the playback.

> **NOTE ▶** Using Shift and Control-Option in combination with the Pointer tool provides a speedy way to access the many automation editing functions in Logic. However, if you prefer, Logic has dedicated tools for editing automation and adjusting curves (the Automation Select and Automation Curve tools), which are available in the Arrange area's Tool menus.

Copying Automation Data Between Tracks

Now that you've automated volume levels for the first of the Crunch_Gtr tracks, you can apply the same settings to the other take (Crunch_Gtr2) by copying and pasting the entire automation track.

1   Press the 1 key to open Screenset 1, returning to the view of the entire arrangement.

2   Hold down Shift and drag to select all the nodes in the Crunch_Gtr1 track.

> **NOTE ▶** It is important to include the node located at the beginning of the project for this technique to work.

3 Press Command-C to copy the automation.

4 Select the Crunch_Gtr2 track.

5 Press Command-V to paste the automation.

The automation that you previously created now appears on the Crunch_Gtr2 track. Since you did not enter these nodes manually, Read mode was not automatically enabled for this track. You need to make sure to enable Read mode to ensure that the copied track automation will be performed.

6 For the Crunch_Gtr2 track, click the Automation Mode menu, and choose Read.

7 On the Crunch_Gtr1 track, click the Solo button to turn soloing off.

8 Play the project, listening to the automated volume level changes in the guitar tracks during the Bridge section.

9 Stop the playback.

> **TIP** ▶ Automation data can also be copied and pasted within the Automation Event List. This list cannot be accessed via the standard Event List within the Lists area, but only by using a key command. The default command is Control-Command-E.

Scaling Automated Values

Often you'll want to boost or lower levels for an entire track proportionally while maintaining the automation shape and node relationships. In the current project, the Crunch_Gtr tracks have the correct dynamic shape but need to be boosted a few decibels in the mix.

Instead of selecting each automation node and dragging the nodes to adjust the levels (similar to the way you previously adjusted the gain), you can scale the existing values up and down using the value fader with the Command key. In this exercise, you can try your hand at scaling the relative values of the volume automation data.

1 Select the Crunch_Gtr1 track by clicking within the track header.

2 In the Crunch Gtr1 track header, Command-drag the value fader up and down, observing the changes to the automation.

Notice how the difference in levels between the nodes becomes greater as you scale up, and how the node levels move closer together when scaling down. When you adjust the levels for the entire automation track at once, all the values are changed proportionately by a percentage.

3   In the Crunch_Gtr1 track, Command-drag the value fader until the first node of the track reads –2.4 dB.

4   Do the same for the Crunch_Gtr2 track, Command-dragging the value fader to set the level to –2.4 dB.

5   Play the project, listening to the Crunch_Gtr tracks.

6   Stop the playback.

Automating an Effect Bypass

One advantage of offline automation is its precise timing. When placing a node in the automation track, you can determine its exact location along the Bar ruler by dragging it as you would any event.

Listen for specific points in the Crunch_Gtr tracks that could use some precise automation.

1   Drag the lower-right corner of the cycle area, extending it to measure 57.

2   Play the project, listening carefully to the Crunch_Gtr tracks during the end of the Bridge section and at the beginning of the following verse.

You can distinctly hear the reverb tail continue from the last strummed chord of the Bridge into Verse 4. While this makes perfect sense from an engineering perspective, it does not fit the aesthetic of the project. All instruments stop precisely at the end of the Bridge section, leaving the voice and piano exposed. By using automation, you can bypass the reverb at this point, eliminating the hanging tail that overlaps the verse.

Adding Channels to the Track List for Automation

To automate the reverb bypass, you must first determine which reverb effect is being fed by the Crunch_Gtr tracks. This can be done by tracing the signal flow in the Mixer.

1   Press the 2 key to open Screenset 2.

2   With either of the Crunch_Gtr tracks (tracks 17 and 18) selected, click the Single button in the Mixer's menu bar.

Both Crunch_Gtr tracks output to Aux 4, a submix channel that has a Channel EQ and a SilverVerb plug-in inserted. The reverb is what needs to be automated.

This submix channel exists only in the Mixer as part of the signal flow. It is not represented in the Arrange area, where offline automation is performed. To perform the offline automation of a plug-in on an aux channel, you must add it to the Arrange area's track list.

3   Select the Aux 4 channel.

4   In the Mixer's local menu bar, choose Options > Create Arrange Tracks for Selected Channel Strips.

5   Press 1 to open Screenset 1.

A new track, Aux 4, is created in the Arrange area and positioned below the Piano track.

6   Within the track header, drag the Aux 4 track down, positioning it below the Crunch_Gtr2 track.

This is where you will automate the reverb bypass that will apply to both Crunch_Gtr tracks.

7   Using the Zoom tool, draw a selection rectangle around the two Crunch guitar regions in the Bridge section as well as in the track below (Aux 4).

The magnification level expands, allowing you to view the selected area for both the Crunch_Gtr tracks and the Aux 4 track.

8   In the Aux 4 track, click the Automation Parameter menu, and choose Main > Insert #2 Bypass.

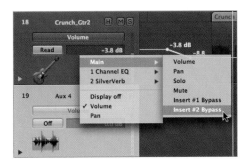

Insert #2 Bypass corresponds to the SilverVerb plug-in in the second Insert slot in the Aux 4 channel.

9   In the Aux 4 track, click the top of the automation track close to measure 55.

A new node is created, displaying *Bypassed*.

10 If necessary, drag the new node so that it occurs just after the last bit of the waveform in the Crunch_Gtr tracks (around 55 1 1 114).

11 Play the project to hear the automated bypass silence the reverb.

12 Stop the playback.

Performing Real-Time Automation

In real-time automation, you can replicate your physical gestures, whether they involve dragging a mouse or manipulating a hardware control surface that sends messages to Logic. Logic's automation is sample accurate, so it captures the precise movements of channel controls—movements that can be recalled during playback.

There are three modes for writing real-time automation: Write, Touch, and Latch. They are available on any channel or Arrange area track. These modes are active whether or not Logic is in Record mode, and they can write automation whenever Logic's Transport is running.

Write mode is rarely used because it deletes all previously recorded automation data under the playhead position as it moves forward. (There are times when this is useful, however.) Thus, you should most often use Touch or Latch mode when writing automation data, as the existing data, if any, is read until a channel control is "touched." This allows you to update the existing data as well as overwrite it when needed.

The difference between Touch and Latch modes is best understood by using them. To get a feel for the difference, you will try both modes while writing some real-time automation data in the blank space before the first region in the Piano track.

1   Press 1 to open Screenset 1.

The magnification level returns to its original view.

2   Press Control–Command–Right Arrow/Left Arrow (the Go to Next/Previous Marker key commands) to locate to the Intro section.

The cycle area adapts to encompass the Intro section.

3   Press Control-Shift-Z (the "Zoom to fit Locators" key command) to zoom in to the Intro section.

4   Select the Piano track (track 14).

5   Click the Solo button to hear the Piano track isolated within the mix.

6   Click the Automation Mode menu, and choose Touch.

You will be using the mouse for data entry, dragging the Arrange channel strip volume fader to create the automation while Logic is playing. Don't worry if you aren't able to do everything in the first seven bars: Cycle mode will be on, repeating the section as many times as you need to complete the steps.

7   Play the project.

8   While the project is playing, drag the volume fader in the Arrange channel strip all the way up, and release the mouse button.

The fader returns to the state at which you started.

9   While still playing the project, change the automation mode to Latch.

10 Drag the fader all the way down, and release the mouse button.

The level stays where you left the fader and is "latched" into place.

11 Stop the playback.

The main difference between these two modes is what happens after the mouse button is released. When you're in Touch mode, the automation returns to the value at which you started. When you're in Latch mode, the value remains where you left the control.

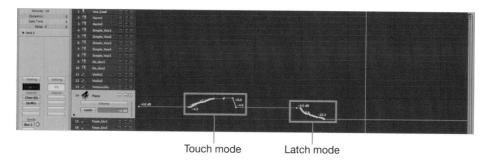

Touch mode   Latch mode

Try recording an entire pass for the Piano track using Latch mode. The piano part could use a decrease in volume level of around 2 dB for the Verse 2 through Bridge sections.

12 Control-Option-click the background of the Arrange area to return to the original zoom level.

13 Click the cycle area to turn Cycle mode off.

14 Click Stop to locate to the beginning of the project.

15 On the Piano track, click the Solo button to turn off soloing.

16 Set the Arrange channel strip fader for the Piano track to around –4.6 (dB).

This will be the level at which you will start recording automation.

NOTE ▶ Because Touch and Latch modes write only when a control is active, you can overwrite any existing data by holding down the fader as the project plays over the automation data. To overwrite the automation you performed earlier, you will need to hold down the fader for the Piano track, and release the mouse button only after passing over the area.

17 Start by click-holding the fader, then play the entire project, riding the Piano track's volume level by dragging the volume fader in the Arrange channel strip down to –6.7dB for the Verse 2 through Bridge sections.

18 Stop the playback when finished.

You should have recorded an entire pass of real-time automation for the Piano track.

If you are happy with this pass, it is a good idea to switch the automation mode to Read so that you won't inadvertently overwrite your changes.

19 Switch the automation mode to Read.

> **TIP** ▶ You can delete the currently displayed automation data by choosing Options > Track Automation > Delete currently visible Automation Data of Current Track (or press Control-Command-Delete). You can also quickly delete all automation written to a track, regardless of what automation parameter is displayed, by choosing Options > Track Automation > Delete All Automation Data of Current Track (Shift-Control-Command-Delete).

Using Automation Quick Access

To truly benefit from using real-time automation, you need to control the channel with something other than the mouse. A hardware control surface that is designed to integrate with Logic's Mixer would provide the best control for real-time automation, but any MIDI controller will do.

Automation Quick Access allows you to assign any knob, fader, or wheel on your MIDI controller to the currently visible automation parameter on a track. Although this lets you use your MIDI hardware to write real-time automation, it is limited to automating only one parameter at a time.

While a fader control (available on many MIDI keyboards) is more appropriate for controlling volume level, in this exercise you assign the modulation wheel on your MIDI keyboard, as this is more widely available on MIDI hardware.

1 Choose Logic Pro > Preferences > Automation.

The automation preferences are displayed, with the Automation Quick Access settings located at the bottom of the window.

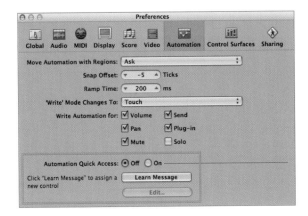

2   Click Learn Message.

3   Move the modulation wheel on your MIDI keyboard up and down.

     A help tag appears, indicating that the assignment has been learned.

4   Click Done, which has taken the place of the Learn Message button.

5   Close the Preferences window.

6   Select the Kick track (track 23).

7   In the Automation Parameter menu, choose Pan.

     The Pan setting is displayed in the automation track.

8   Move your MIDI keyboard's modulation wheel.

     The Pan setting changes with your movements.

9   In the Arrange channel strip, Option-click the Pan knob to reset the value to 0.

10   Click the Automation Parameter menu, this time choosing Volume.

     The volume level is displayed in the automation track.

11 Move your MIDI keyboard's modulation wheel again.

The volume level changes with your movements.

Notice how the modulation wheel changes function depending on which automation parameter is active. That is the nature of Automation Quick Access. It allows you to access whatever automation parameter is currently displayed on the selected track.

TIP ▸ Logic supports many leading hardware control surfaces with little or no setup, but you can also assign multiple parameter controls to respond to MIDI messages sent from any generic MIDI hardware controller (keyboard, control surfaces, and so on). To do this, use the mouse to jiggle the onscreen knob, slider, or fader that you want to automate to make sure that it is selected as the last active control. Then, choose Logic Pro > Preferences > Control Surfaces > Learn Assignment. Finally, send the chosen MIDI message from the hardware device by jiggling the desired hardware control until a message appears stating that the assignment has been learned. Repeat with additional controls to create comprehensive control maps that link Logic to external MIDI control devices.

Automating Groups

Now that you've assigned your controller using Automation Quick Access, you'll use the modulation wheel to write real-time automation, riding the level of the drums throughout the project. To aid in doing this, the drum channels have been grouped to link the channel parameters. This enables you to record automation data for all the tracks in a group at the same time by controlling a single channel.

1 Press 2 to open Screenset 2.

2 In the Mixer, scroll to the far right to view the drum tracks.

Note that the drum tracks have been assigned to group 7, named Drums.

3   With the Kick track still selected in the Arrange area, move your MIDI keyboard's modulation wheel.

All the drum channel faders move in relation to the Kick channel.

NOTE ▶ Although Automation Quick Access is used primarily in the Arrange area, the last selected automation parameter for the selected track (in this case, Volume) is remembered, enabling you to adjust levels in the Mixer.

In addition to linking controls such as those for volume, pan, and sends, you can also link the automation mode for the group. This lets you switch automation modes for all the channels in a group at once.

NOTE ▶ The automation mode can be linked or unlinked by accessing the group settings (click the Group slot and choose Open Goup Settings from the pop-up menu). The automation mode is turned on by default when you create a new group.

4   On the Kick channel, click the Automation Mode menu, and choose Latch.

All the channels in the Drums group change to Latch mode.

Now you are ready to record an automation pass for the entire Drums group at once. Set the initial levels and locate to the beginning of the project in preparation for recording the real-time automation.

5   Using your modulation wheel, set the level of the Kick channel to −15 (dB).

6   Click Stop to locate to the beginning of the project.

7   Play the project, using the modulation wheel to ride the volume levels for the Drums group during playback, creating a mix to your liking.

8   Stop the playback when you're finished.

9 On the Kick channel, click the Automation Mode menu and choose Read.

The automation mode for all the channels in the Drums group changes to Read. Look in the Arrange area to see the automation data that you just wrote.

10 Press 1 to open Screenset 1.

You can see the automation data written to the Kick track, but the other drum tracks are too small for you to see their automation. You need to enlarge the track display.

11 Shift-click tracks 24 through 29 (Hat, Snare, Toms_rack, Toms_floor, Drum_overhds, and Loop) in the track list.

The regions on each selected track are highlighted.

12 Press Control-Option-Z (the "Zoom to fit Selection" key command) to zoom in to the selected regions (the Drums group tracks).

You should now see the Volume automation data displayed for every track.

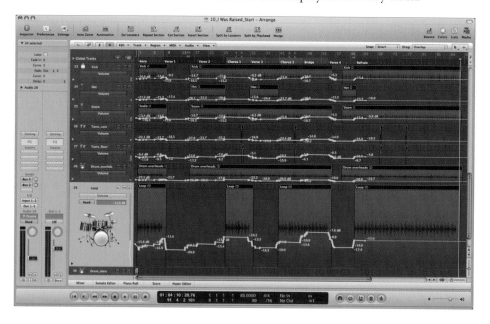

NOTE ▶ Any edits made to individual automation tracks within a group will be reflected by the other tracks as well. This enables you to quickly create offline automation, as well as edit real-time automation for groups while working on a single track.

Lesson Review

1. How is offline automation created?

2. How is automation edited and copied?

3. How are automation curves used?

4. How is automation data scaled?

5. What is the difference between Touch and Latch modes?

6. How is Automation Quick Access used?

Answers

1. You create offline automation by clicking in the automation track.

2. You can edit and copy automation data within the automation track the same way you would work with event data.

3. Automation curves can be used to create more dynamic changes in volume levels.

4. You can scale automation data by Command-dragging the value fader for the automation parameter.

5. While both Touch and Latch automation modes write data when controls are active and read data when no controls are "touched," they behave differently when the channel controls are released. When you're in Touch mode, the automation parameter returns to the value at which you started. When you're in Latch mode, the value remains where you left the control.

6. Automation Quick Access is used to assign automation to a slider or knob on a hardware MIDI controller.

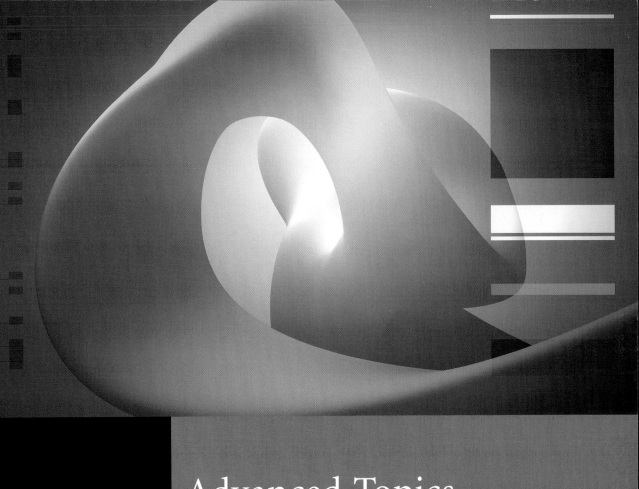

Advanced Topics

11

Lesson File	Logic 8_BTB_Files > Lessons > 11_MIDI Processing.logic
Media	Logic 8_BTB_Files > Media > Environment
Time	This lesson takes approximately 90 minutes to complete.
Goals	Use and create layers in the Environment
	Understand MIDI signal flow within the Environment
	Create objects for processing MIDI data
	Create serial and parallel routing for complex real-time processing
	Trigger MIDI regions with touch tracks objects

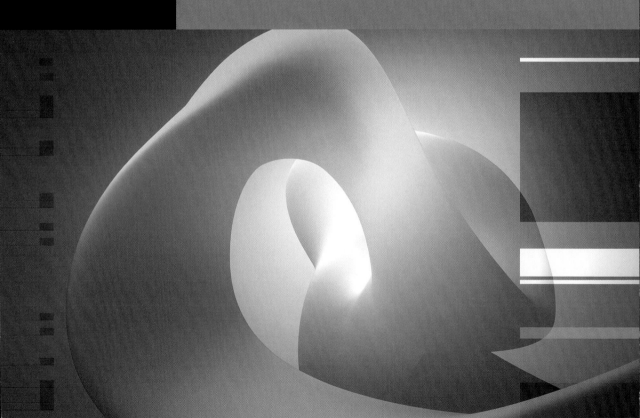

Lesson 11
MIDI Processing in the Environment

From the very beginning, the Environment has set Logic apart from other sequencers. The Environment is often thought of as a virtual studio, containing objects that represent your audio channels and MIDI devices. However, the Environment is much, much more, enabling you to process data from MIDI and software instruments in real time by creating complex signal routings and transformations to augment your music.

In this lesson, you will explore useful MIDI processors in the Environment, creating signal routings to affect MIDI input in a variety of ways.

> **NOTE** ▶ You will need to set the "Display Middle C as" preference to C3 (Yamaha) to accurately follow the directions in this exercise (and others throughout the book). This command can be found in the Preferences > Display > General tab.

Navigating Within the Environment

The Environment is tucked neatly away within its own window, which can be accessed like any other, via the main Window menu. Like other windows, the Environment window can be part of a screenset, which helps to keep things organized.

1 Choose File > Open.

2 In the file selector box, go to Music > Logic 8_BTB_Files > Lessons and open **11_MIDI Processing.logic**.

The project opens, displaying Screenset 1, which consists of an Arrange window (with the Library displayed) placed above an Environment window.

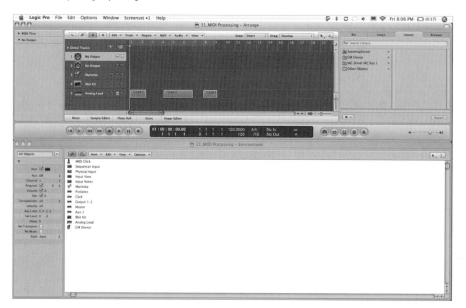

The Environment is divided into layers, displaying objects of like type or function. You are currently looking at the All Objects layer, which provides an easy way to look at all objects currently within the project's Environment. Here, you can see the three software instruments (Marimba, 8bit Kit, and Analog Lead) assigned to the Arrange track list, as well as other objects being used "behind the scenes" for MIDI input.

NOTE ▶ The top two tracks in the track list are placeholders currently assigned to a special No Output destination. Tracks assigned to No Output will not send any data.

3   In the Arrange track list, click the Marimba, 8bit Kit, and Analog Lead tracks (tracks 3–5) one at a time, playing your MIDI keyboard to familiarize yourself with the sound of the software instruments.

When you select a track in the track list, MIDI input from your controller is routed to the track's assigned channel. Notice that when you select tracks in the track list, the corresponding Environment object is also selected.

4   Click the Marimba track (track 3) in the track list, selecting it for MIDI input.

Navigating layers is done by clicking the arrow button next to the Layer menu, located in the upper-left corner of the Environment window.

5   Choose Click & Ports from the Layer menu.

The layer switches, displaying the contents of the Click & Ports layer.

The Click & Ports layer contains objects specific to the routing of MIDI signals from their initial input till they reach Logic's sequencer. The Physical Input object at the far left represents your MIDI interface or MIDI controller (with direct MIDI-to-USB or FireWire connection). All available ports from your MIDI input devices will be listed in the Physical Input object (including the Caps Lock Keyboard and virtual ones like the IAC Bus). Their corresponding cable outputs are depicted by the small triangles running along the right side.

NOTE ▶ The SUM output at the top carries a combination of all MIDI input ports displayed in the Physical Input object that do not have their own output cables. When a cable is connected from one of the remaining MIDI ports, its signal will not be passed through the SUM output.

MIDI signals are passed from object to object in the Environment by cabling them together. The left side of an object represents the input, while the right side represents the output. As you can see in this layer, the Physical Input is cabled to a keyboard object, labeled Input Notes.

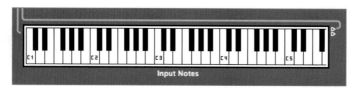

6   Play a few notes on your MIDI controller, observing the keyboard object.

NOTE ▶ If you don't have a MIDI controller handy, the Caps Lock Keyboard will work equally well for the exercises in this lesson.

As you play the keys on your MIDI controller, the software instrument you selected in the track list (Marimba) is triggered, while the corresponding pitches are displayed in the keyboard object.

7   Click some of the keys on the keyboard object.

The Marimba is triggered each time you click the keyboard object.

You have probably noticed that when you play a note on your MIDI controller or click the keyboard object, MIDI events are displayed in the Input View object cabled to the output of the keyboard object. This is a monitor object, which displays all MIDI data passing through it in list form.

The signal chain finally ends with a Sequencer Input object. This represents the connection to Logic's sequencer and routes to the selected track in the Arrange track list.

By having the Physical Input cabled to the Sequencer Input (passing through the keyboard and monitor objects), MIDI signal flows from the MIDI interface or controller providing input, ultimately arriving at the selected Arrange track via the Sequencer Input object.

NOTE ▶ If the connection between the Physical Input and the Sequencer Input is severed, MIDI input signals will not be recorded in the Arrange tracks. This connection is a good place to check when you are having problems receiving MIDI input.

Creating Environment Objects

Now that you've had a chance to observe signal flow within the Click & Ports layer, you can try creating Environment objects to process incoming MIDI signals. Although new objects can be inserted in any layer, in this case it makes sense to create an Environment layer to house the new objects you will be exploring in this exercise.

1 Choose Create Layer from the Layer menu.

An empty layer is created.

2 Select "(unnamed)" in the Layer menu text field, and enter *MIDI Process*. Press Return.

You now have a new layer to house your MIDI processing experiments, ready for new objects to be added.

Using Monitor Objects

As you noticed previously in the Click & Ports layer, monitor objects are used to display MIDI signals passing through them. New ones can be created by choosing them from the Environment window's New menu.

1   In the Environment's local menu bar, choose New > Monitor.

A new monitor object appears.

By itself, a monitor object does nothing. In this exercise, you will be using it to both monitor MIDI signals passing through it and to connect to the Marimba software instrument channel selected in the Arrange area. In order to pass the signal, you need to cable the output of the monitor object to the Marimba software instrument channel, which is housed in a different layer (the Mixer layer). Even though these objects exist in different layers, you can still cable them together by first holding down the Option key, and then clicking the cable output of the monitor object.

2   While holding down the Option key, click the cable output (the small triangle in the upper-right corner) of the monitor object.

A menu appears, allowing you to set the destination for the cable.

3 Choose Mixer > Software Instrument > Marimba.

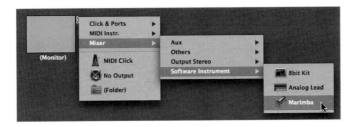

A cable appears, connecting the objects between the layers of the Environment.

NOTE ▸ Once an output from an object is used (cabled to another object), another output triangle automatically appears.

In order to keep things straight, it's a good idea to label objects as you create them.

4 Using the Text tool, click the monitor object to rename it.

5 Enter *To Marimba*. Press Return.

6 Switch back to the Pointer tool and drag the monitor object to the right side of the Environment window, to make room for other objects.

TIP ▸ When creating, moving, and naming objects in the Environment, it helps to alternate between the Pointer tool and the Text tool. These are the default (left-click) and alternate (Command-click) tools in the Environment by default, so you can toggle between them by pressing the Command key.

Using Arpeggiator Objects

Arpeggiator objects receive harmonic input (simultaneous notes), outputting each note individually in a variety of selectable patterns, speeds, and lengths. Logic's arpeggiator objects are extremely flexible and can be configured to create complex rhythmic patterns out of static chords.

1   From the Environment's local menu bar, choose New > Arpeggiator.

A new arpeggiator object appears.

In this exercise you will not only be creating new Environment objects, but also be cabling them in a variety of ways to process MIDI data. To aid in visualizing the signal routing from one object to the next, you can color the objects and their respective cables.

2   Choose View > Colored Cables.

3   Chose View > Colors.

The color palette appears, allowing you to assign colors to selected objects.

4   With the arpeggiator object still selected, click a shade of green in the color palette.

The arpeggiator object becomes green.

5   Click and hold down the cable output of the arpeggiator object, dragging the new cable to the monitor object.

You now have a connection between the arpeggiator and the Marimba software instrument channel (passing through the monitor).

In order for the arpeggiator to receive input from your MIDI keyboard, you need to bring it up on a track in the Arrange area. Rather than go back to the Arrange area to do this, you can use the MIDI Thru tool in the Environment. Any object you click in the Environment using this tool will be configured for the currently selected Arrange track.

6   In the Arrange area, select the top No Output track (track 1) in the track list.

7 Using the MIDI Thru tool, click the arpeggiator object.

The selected Arrange track (track 1) changes to the arpeggiator object.

You can test to see if the arpeggiator is receiving input by playing your MIDI controller.

8 Play a few notes on your MIDI controller, observing the monitor within the Environment window.

You should hear the Marimba software instrument as well as see MIDI data displayed in the monitor object.

The arpeggiator object works with tempo-related material, so in order to have it process the incoming MIDI, the project has to be playing.

9 Play the project.

10 While the project is playing, hold down a chord (any combination of notes) on your MIDI controller.

You should now hear the chord arpeggiated as well as see the resultant MIDI data displayed in the monitor object.

11 Try adding or subtracting notes to your held chord, observing how they change the arpeggio.

NOTE ► It is important for the project to remain playing in order for many of the Environment objects to process incoming MIDI notes. Throughout the lesson, if you reach the end of the project, return to the beginning and start playback again.

In the Object Parameter box, you will find many useful settings for the arpeggiator object. Here, you can select from various patterns as well as adjust the velocity, speed, length, and octave of the arpeggiated notes.

NOTE ► If it is difficult to both reach your MIDI controller with one hand and adjust the Object Parameter box with the other hand, feel free to replay the chords after you make the adjustment so you can hear the result.

12 In the Object Parameter box, click the Direction pop-up menu and choose Up/Down.

The pattern direction changes, arpeggiating up and then down the notes of the chord.

13 In the Object Parameter box, click the Direction menu again, this time choosing Random.

The pattern changes, randomly arpeggiating selected notes from the chord.

The Velocity parameter allows you to adjust the velocities of the arpeggiated notes of the original chord. You can set a positive or negative offset, or even randomize the velocities.

14 In the Object Parameter box, drag the Velocity parameter (it currently displays "Original") down to choose Random.

The velocities of the arpeggiated notes are randomized.

The speed of the arpeggio is governed by the Resolution parameter, which is defined by note divisions (half note, quarter note, and so on).

15 Click the Resolution menu and choose 1/16.

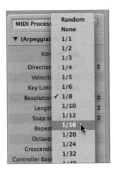

The arpeggiated notes change to a sixteenth-note resolution, playing twice as fast as before.

To enable synchronization with other MIDI data, the arpeggiator can be set to wait for a specific note division before starting. This is done with the "Snap to" parameter.

16 Click the "Snap to" menu and choose 1/8.

This quantizes the start of arpeggiated playback to the following eighth note, keeping it in sync with the project's time grid (bars/beats).

NOTE ▶ The length of each arpeggiated note can be set independently from the speed. You can change note lengths by choosing note durations from the Length parameter's menu. However, this won't have an effect on the Marimba software instrument, as the percussive sound does not sustain very long.

17 Stop playback.

Using Chord Memorizer Objects

Chord memorizer objects map a single note to a set of up to 12 user-selected notes. This allows you to trigger complex chords by pressing a single key on your MIDI controller.

1 Choose New > Chord Memorizer.

A chord memorizer object appears in the Environment window.

NOTE ▶ You might need to move objects around to get them out of the way of one another throughout this lesson. Generally, signal flow in the Environment should flow from left to right, as cable outputs are on the right side of objects.

2   With the chord memorizer object selected, click a shade of dark blue in the color palette.

The chord memorizer object becomes blue.

3   Cable the output of the chord memorizer object to the monitor object.

4   Double-click the chord memorizer object.

The Chord Memorizer window opens.

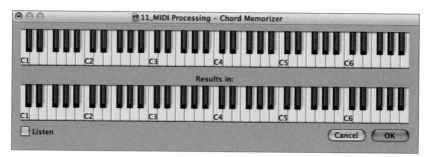

The Chord Memorizer window contains two keyboards. The top keyboard corresponds to the incoming note, and the lower keyboard corresponds to the notes or chords assigned to the incoming note.

5   Click the C4 note on the top keyboard.

C4 is automatically selected in the lower keyboard.

6   In the lower keyboard, click C4 to deselect it.

7 In the lower keyboard, click C3, D3, E♭3, F3, D4, and F4 to select them.

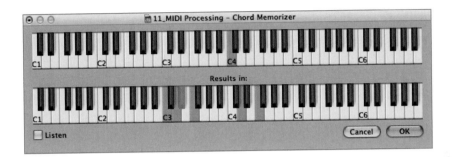

8 Click OK.

In order for the chord memorizer to process the input from your MIDI controller, you need to bring it up in the Arrange track list. Instead of doing this by using the MIDI Thru tool as you did before, you can quickly assign objects in the Environment to the selected track using the Library.

9 In the Library, choose Other Objects > (Chord Memorizer).

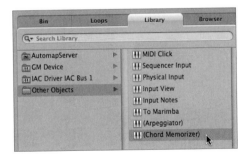

The selected Arrange track (track 1) changes from the arpeggiator object to the chord memorizer object.

Because the chord memorizer is not time based, you don't need to have the project playing in order for it to process MIDI input.

10 Press C4 on your MIDI controller.

A full chord is sounded, outputting the notes you specified within the lower keyboard of the Chord Memorizer window (C3, D3, E♭3, F3, D4, and F4).

Using Delay Line Objects

Delay line objects repeat the MIDI events passing through them, achieving a result similar to that of a delay processor creating echoes from audio signals. The most important difference between the two is that the delay line object creates these echoes with additional generated MIDI notes that mirror the incoming MIDI event, instead of sampling and playing back bits of audio.

1   Choose New > Delay Line.

A delay line object appears in the Environment window.

2   With the delay line object selected, click a shade of yellow in the color palette.

The delay line object becomes yellow.

3   Cable the output of the delay line object to the monitor object.

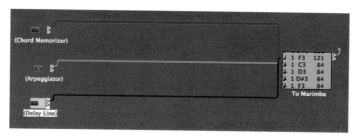

Like the other objects, the delay line needs to be placed in the Arrange track list so it can process the input from your MIDI controller.

4   In the Library, choose Other Objects > (Delay Line).

The selected Arrange track (track 1) changes from the chord memorizer object to the delay line object.

As with the arpeggiator object, the project needs to be playing for you to hear the results of the delay line object's processing.

5   Play the project.

6   While the project is playing, play any note on your MIDI controller, listening to the signal through the delay line object.

The incoming note is echoed by a single repeat.

You can adjust the repeat amount, timing, velocity, and transposition within the Object Parameter box.

7   In the Object Parameter box, double-click the number next to the Repeats parameter, and enter *4*. Press Return.

8   While the project is playing, play any note on your MIDI controller, listening to the signal through the delay line object.

The incoming note is repeated four times. This doesn't sound much like natural echoes, where the repetitions trail off in volume. You can simulate this effect by adjusting the Velocity parameter to a negative value. By doing this, each successive repeat will lower in velocity by the selected amount.

9   Double-click the number to the right of the Velocity parameter, and enter *−19*. Press Return.

10 While the project is playing, play any note on your MIDI controller, listening to the signal through the delay line object.

The incoming note is echoed four times, each echo quieter than the previous one.

The speed of the repeats can be set by the Delay parameter. The left value represents divisions, while the right value represents ticks. This allows you to make musical repeats that sync with the tempo of the project.

11 In the Delay parameter fields, double-click either number and enter *240*. Press Return.

NOTE ▶ You need to use tick values when inputting numbers via the computer keyboard for the Delay parameter. A sixteenth note equals 240 ticks.

12 While the project is playing, play any note on your MIDI controller, listening to the signal through the delay line object.

The delay time between the repeats is cut in half.

So far you have emulated the results you'd get from a typical audio delay processor. The delay line also allows you to do something unusual: transpose the pitch of each repetition.

13 Double-click the Transpose parameter and enter *–7*. Press Return.

14 While the project is playing, play any note on your MIDI controller, listening to the signal through the delay line object.

Each successive repetition drops seven semitones (a perfect fifth).

15 Stop playback.

Creating Signal Chains

So far, you've only applied single processors (arpeggiator, chord memorizer, and delay line) to incoming MIDI signals. The Environment starts to show its potential, however, when you cable processors to each other for complex serial and parallel processing.

In this exercise, you will not only learn how to chain processors together in a series but also how to split signals for parallel processing.

1   Click and hold down the topmost cable output from the chord memorizer object and drag the cable to the arpeggiator object.

2   In the Library, choose Other Objects > (Chord Memorizer).

The selected Arrange track changes to the chord memorizer object.

The incoming MIDI signal now passes from the chord memorizer object to the arpeggiator object, finally ending up at the Marimba software instrument channel (passing through the monitor object). With these two in series, you can trigger complex arpeggiated chords by pressing a single note on your MIDI controller.

3   Start playback.

4   While the project is playing, play C4 on your MIDI controller (which you earlier set to play back a chord).

The chord generated by the chord memorizer object is arpeggiated.

Let's add to this creation by inserting the delay line object into the signal path.

5   Click and hold down the cable output from the arpeggiator object and drag the cable to the delay line object.

With this arrangement, each note from the arpeggiated chord generated by the chord memorizer and arpeggiator objects will repeat four times, dropping seven semitones each time. All of this is triggered by a single note from a MIDI controller.

6   While the project is playing, play C4 on your MIDI controller.

A whole slew of notes is created, with various pitches and rhythmic durations.

7   Stop playback.

Using Transformer Objects

Now that you've investigated chaining MIDI processors in a series, let's create a parallel processing arrangement in which specified notes will be sent down two different signal paths. You can do this by using the transformer object.

The transformer object is an extremely powerful processor whose main function is to change one type of MIDI data to another. However, that would be barely scratching the surface of its capabilities. It also works equally well as a MIDI filter, track automation splitter, SysEx mapper, condition splitter, and much more. For this exercise you will be using the Transformer as a condition splitter, sending data down one of two cable outputs depending on criteria you set.

1   Choose New > Transformer.

A transformer object appears within the Environment window.

2   With the transformer object selected, click a shade of red in the color palette.

The transformer object becomes red.

3   Double-click the transformer object.

The Transformer window opens.

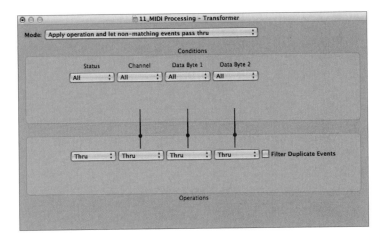

This window is almost identical to the Transform window explored in Lesson 7, "Advanced MIDI Editing," in the section "Using Transform Functions." Like the Transform window you used within the MIDI editors to select and edit MIDI data, the Transformer window has places to specify criteria for selection and transformation. Like the Transform window, the Transformer window also has many modes available.

4   Click the Mode menu at the top of the window and choose Condition splitter (true -> top cable).

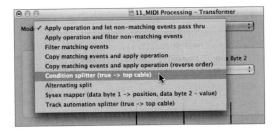

The condition splitter mode sends MIDI data that meets the conditions specified within the top area (Conditions) out the topmost cable output and sends all other MIDI data that does not fit the criteria out the other. In this exercise, you will be using the condition splitter to divide specific notes generated by the chord memorizer object out one of the two cable outlets for separate processing chains.

5 From the Status menu, choose =.

Another pop-up menu displaying Note appears below the Status menu.

6 From the Pitch menu, choose <=.

A value field appears just below the pop-up menu.

7 Double-click in the value field and enter *C4*. Press Return.

With this setup, incoming note values equal to and below C4 will be sent out of the top cable output, while all others will be sent out of the bottom output.

8 Close the Transformer window.

9 Click and hold down the topmost cable output from the chord memorizer object and drag the cable to the transformer object.

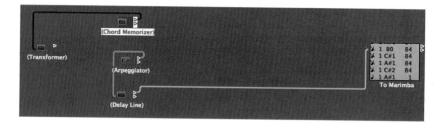

The chord memorizer object will provide the input to the transformer object.

10 Click and hold down the cable output from the transformer object and drag the cable to the arpeggiator object.

You've now set up one of your signal chains distributed by the transformer object. Now all you need to complete the arrangement is to set up another signal path to process data that does not meet the conditions specified in the transformer object. Begin by creating another monitor object cabled to a different software instrument channel.

11 Choose New > Monitor.

A new monitor object appears.

12 Drag the new monitor object down and to the right, moving it out of the way of the first signal chain.

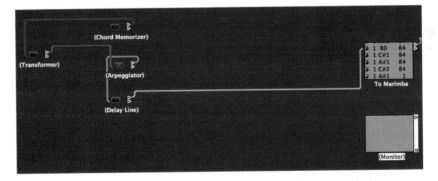

13 Using the Text tool, click the new monitor object and enter *To 8bit Kit*.

14 Option-click the cable output on the monitor object and choose Mixer > Software Instrument > 8bit Kit.

A cable appears, connecting the objects between the layers of the Environment.

15 Choose New > Arpeggiator.

A new arpeggiator object appears.

16 With the new arpeggiator object selected, click a shade of yellow in the color palette.

The arpeggiator object becomes yellow.

17 Drag the new arpeggiator object down, moving it out of the way of the first signal chain.

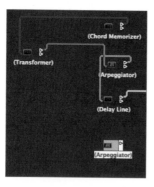

18 In the Object Parameter box, choose Random for the Direction and Velocity parameters, and 1/16 for the Resolution and "Snap to" parameters.

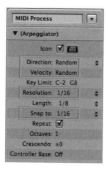

19 Cable the output of the new arpeggiator object to the monitor object labeled To 8bit Kit.

20 Cable the bottommost cable of the transformer object to the new arpeggiator object.

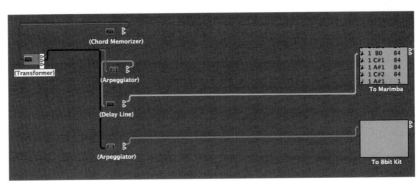

You've now set up two complete signal chains with separate processing. The source events are generated by the chord memorizer object, with the transformer object splitting the data by note range (those equal to or below C4, and those above C4). Now all that's left is to try it out.

21 Start playback.

22 While the project is playing, hold down C4 on your MIDI controller.

What results are pulsating, surging polyrhythms that never repeat twice, activated by a single key on your MIDI controller.

23 Stop playback after you've listened to your creation.

Using Cable Switcher Objects

Like a transformer object, a cable switcher object is used to help direct signal flow. Basically, the cable switcher object is a switch that can be triggered manually to direct the signal flow out of its outputs. The switch can take on different forms, such as a fader button or pop-up menu, allowing you to interact with it in different ways.

In this exercise, you will insert a cable switcher into the signal path, enabling you to switch between two routes at any given time.

1 Choose New > Fader > Specials > Cable Switcher.

A cable switcher object appears.

2 With the cable switcher object selected, click a shade of light blue in the color palette.

The cable switcher object becomes blue.

3 Close the Color window (you won't need it for the rest of the lesson).

4 Drag the cable switcher to the right of the topmost arpeggiator object (the green one connected to the Marimba software instrument channel).

5 Click and hold down the topmost cable output of the green arpeggiator and drag the cable to the cable switcher.

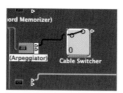

6 Click and hold down the cable output of the cable switcher object, and drag the cable to the monitor object labeled To Marimba.

This will form one signal path, directly feeding the Marimba software instrument channel.

7 Click and hold down the bottommost cable output of the cable switcher object, and drag the cable to the delay line object.

To make signal flow easier to view, it helps to move the delay line object to the right of the cable switcher object.

8 Drag the delay line object to the right, placing it below and to the right of the cable switcher object.

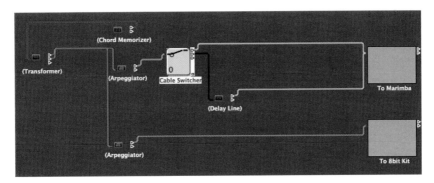

This will form the other signal path, passing through the delay line object and eventually reaching the Marimba software instrument channel.

9 Try clicking a few times on the cable switcher object itself.

The cable switcher changes configuration, routing the input to a different cable output each time you click.

Notice that there are three output destinations to select, and only two are cabled to signal paths. Like any other Environment object, the cable switcher adds an additional cable output (up to 128) when a new output cable is connected.

In order to have the cable switcher route only to the used outputs, you need to alter its range in the Object Parameter box. The Range parameter is expressed by two numbers, forming the bottom (left number) and top (right number) of a specified range.

10 In the Object Parameter box, drag the rightmost Range parameter (127) down until it reaches a value of 1.

This sets the Range from 0 to 1 (two outputs), and allows the cable switcher object to toggle between the two signal paths connected to its cable outputs.

As mentioned earlier, the cable switcher object's interface can be changed to reflect different types of switches. This is done by choosing an option from the Style menu in the Object Parameter box.

11 Click the Style menu and choose As Text.

The cable switcher object changes, displaying text. By default, the displayed text corresponds to the numbered cable output (0 or 1), and the number can be toggled by clicking the cable switcher itself. This is not a particularly elegant solution for labeling and accessing the signal paths cabled to the cable switcher's outputs. However, you can enter your own text instead of the default Range numbers, allowing clearer labels of the signal paths.

12 Double-click the cable switcher object.

The Cable Switcher window opens.

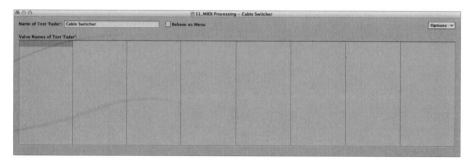

13 Double-click the topmost field of the Value Names of Text 'Fader' column and enter *Bypass*. Press Return.

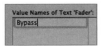

14 Within the second field, enter *Delay*. Press Return.

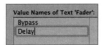

NOTE ▶ There are 128 fields in the Cable Switcher window that can hold text. When using cable switcher objects with large ranges displayed as text, select the Behave as Menu checkbox at the top of the Cable Switcher window. This lets you access the entire range via a pop-up menu, instead of clicking the cable switcher itself.

15 Close the Cable Switcher window.

The cable switcher object now displays the text you entered in the Cable Switcher window.

NOTE ▶ You can resize any Environment object by dragging its lower-right corner, similar to how you adjust window size. This enables the cable switcher object to display longer text.

Now it's time to try out the cable switcher object while the project is playing. In order to have your hands free to interact with the cable switcher object, you can create a MIDI region with a C4 note held to trigger the rhythmic patterns played on the Marimba and 8bit Kit software instrument channels.

16 In the Arrange area, use the Pencil tool to create a one-measure MIDI region in the Chord Memorizer track (track 1), starting at 1 1 1 1.

17 With the region you just created still selected, choose Window > Piano Roll.

The Piano Roll Editor opens in a separate window.

18 In the Piano Roll Editor, use the Pencil tool to create a C4 note with a velocity of 80 that lasts the entire length of measure 1.

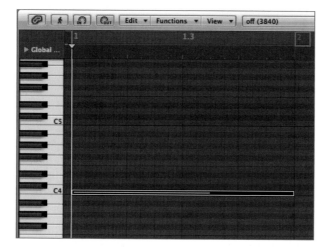

19 Close the Piano Roll Editor.

20 In the Arrange window's Region Parameter box, click the checkbox next to Loop to select it.

The region is now looped and will continually supply a C4 to drive the rhythmic patterns played by the Marimba and 8bit Kit software instruments.

21 Play the project.

22 While the project is playing, click the cable switcher object, switching back and forth between the signal paths (with the delay line object and without).

23 Stop playback.

Using Touch Tracks Objects

Touch tracks objects allow you to trigger MIDI regions or folders by playing single notes. This works especially well in a live performance setting, because you can trigger anything from short passages or phrases to entire songs with a single key from your MIDI controller.

When triggered within a touch tracks object, these MIDI regions or folders play back through the instruments assigned to their tracks, sharing the same track-channel relationship they have in the Arrange window. This means that you can have a single touch tracks object that plays back MIDI regions from different tracks, all through their respective channels (and sound sources).

In this exercise you will be using a touch tracks object to play back the MIDI regions present in the Arrange tracks. Notice that these regions are muted (the track Mute button is active) and have not been sounding when the project is played. However, muted regions will sound when triggered via a touch tracks object. This allows you to create MIDI recordings via normal methods in the Arrange window for import to a touch tracks object, then muting the regions so they don't sound when the project is played.

1   Choose New > Touch Tracks.

A touch tracks object appears in the Environment, and its corresponding Touch Tracks window opens.

In this window you can assign different MIDI regions (or folders) to each key, represented on the far left of the window. Assignment is done by dragging from the Arrange area to the target row in the Region/Folder column.

2   Scroll down in the Touch Tracks window until you can see a range of roughly C2 to E3.

3   Drag the first region (Lead 1) on the Analog Lead track to the Touch Tracks window and drop it on the C3 row in the Region/Folder column (the cursor will change to the Pencil tool).

> **NOTE ▶** You might need to reposition the Touch Tracks window in order to see both it and the Arrange tracks.

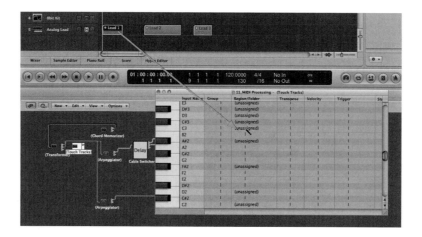

The name of the region now appears in the Regions/Folder column for C3.

4   Drag the second region (Lead 2) on the Analog Lead track to the Touch Tracks window and drop it on the D3 row in the Region/Folder column.

The name of the region now appears in the Regions/Folder column for D3.

5   Drag the third region (Lead 3) on the Analog Lead track to the Touch Tracks window and drop it on the E3 row in the Region/Folder column.

The name of the region now appears in the Regions/Folder column for E3.

Input Name	Group	Region/Folder	Transpose	Velocity		Trigger		Sta
E3	I	Lead 3	I	100%	⌄	Gate	⌄	
D#3	I	I	I	Off	⬍	Multi	⬍	
D3	I	Lead 2	I	100%	⬍	Gate	⬍	
C#3	I	I	I	Off	⬍	Multi	⬍	
C3	I	Lead 1	I	100%	⬍	Gate	⬍	

Now that you've specified the regions to be played back and assigned them to MIDI notes, you need to place the touch tracks object on a track in order for it to receive MIDI input.

6   In the Arrange track list, select the No Output track (track 2).

7   In the Library, choose Other Objects > (Touch Tracks).

> **NOTE ▶** In order to work, the touch tracks object must receive MIDI note input. However, it will not pass MIDI events through to its output, so generally it should not be inserted in the signal chain unless it appears at the end.

In order for the touch tracks object to play back the MIDI regions, the project has to be playing.

8   Play the project.

9   With the project playing, try playing the C3, D3, and E3 keys one at a time on your MIDI controller, holding them down for various lengths of time.

The triggered Lead 1, Lead 2, and Lead 3 regions play whenever you press a key, for as long as the key is held or until the regions end. This playback behavior is referred to as the *gate* trigger mode, and is the default mode for any region imported into the Touch Tracks window.

You can change the triggering behavior for any region by changing the setting within the Trigger column in the Touch Tracks window.

10   In the Touch Tracks window, click the Gate setting in the Trigger column for the C3 note (Lead 1), and choose GateLoop.

This setting acts similarly to Gate, except that it will continue to repeat the region for as long as the key is depressed.

11 Change the Trigger setting for D3 (Lead 2) and E3 (Lead 3) to GateLoop.

12 With the project playing, try playing the C3, D3, and E3 key one at a time on your MIDI controller, holding them down for various lengths of time.

The region playback is looped for as long as you hold down a key.

Using Apple Loops with Touch Tracks

Any type of MIDI region is fair game for use with touch tracks. This means that you can also use imported MIDI regions like Standard MIDI files and software instrument Apple Loops (green Apple Loops). In particular, software instrument Apple Loops consist of MIDI regions paired with a sound source (software instrument and effects settings are instantiated when you drag them to your project) and can be easily dropped into the Touch Tracks window for triggering. In effect, you can use touch tracks to trigger these loops similar to the way a sampler would trigger audio files, mapping individual loops to the keyboard.

In this exercise, you will import a few software instrument Apple Loops for use in the touch tracks object that you created earlier.

1 Click the Loops tab in the Media area.

2 In the search field, enter *disco pickbass*.

The Loop Browser displays a variety of software instrument Apple Loops with the words *disco pickbass* in their names.

3 Click the Disco Pickbass 03 loop in the Loop Browser, playing it in order to familiarize yourself with the material.

4 Drag the Disco Pickbass 03 loop to the blank area below the existing tracks.

A new track is created with the Disco Pickbass channel strip, and the Apple Loops region (Disco Pickbass 03) appears on the track.

5   Click the Disco Pickbass 06 loop in the Loop Browser (you will need to scroll down the list), playing it in order to familiarize yourself with the material.

6   Drag the Disco Pickbass 06 loop to 6 1 1 1 on the Disco Pickbass track (track 6).

7   The Apple Loops region (Disco Pickbass 06) appears on the track.

8   Click the track Mute button for the Disco Pickbass track, muting the regions you just imported.

9   Drag the Disco Pickbass 03 region to the Touch Tracks window and drop it in the Regions/Folder column for C2.

> **NOTE ▸** You might need to scroll down in the Touch Tracks window. The window will automatically scroll when you drag regions to its upper and lower edges.

10   Drag the Disco Pickbass 06 region to the Touch Tracks window and drop it in the Regions/Folder column for D2.

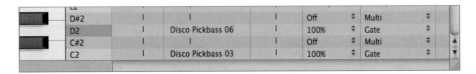

Previously, you set up the Lead regions to be triggered when a key was depressed and to repeat until the key was released (GateLoop). This time, you are going to set up the triggering a little bit differently, allowing the region to continue looping even after the key is released, not stopping until a subsequent key is depressed. You can accomplish this with another Trigger setting, ToggleLoop.

11 In the Touch Tracks window, click the Gate setting in the Trigger column for both the C2 and D2 notes (Disco Pickbass 03 and Disco Pickbass 06) and choose ToggleLoop.

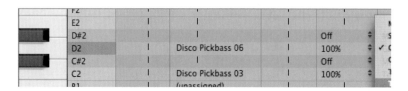

The way things are set up so far, the regions could be triggered at any part of the measure, on or off the beat. While this is fine for the rubato Lead regions, the Disco Pickbass regions could play out of sync with the rhythmic patterns being generated by the arpeggiator and delay line objects.

For just this sort of situation, the Touch Tracks window provides a way to quantize the playback start by changing settings in the Start column.

12 Expand the Touch Tracks window in order to view the Start column.

13 Click the vertical black line in the Start column for the C2 note (Disco Pickbass 03), and choose Next 1/1.

The 1/1 setting quantizes playback to the next whole note, starting the region playback at the beginning of the bar.

14 Click the vertical black line in the Start column for the D2 note (Disco Pickbass 06) and choose 1/1.

In addition to the settings discussed earlier in the lesson, the Touch Tracks window also allows you to transpose individual regions by entering an offset in the Transpose column.

15 Double-click to the left of the vertical black line in the Transpose column for the D2 note (Disco Pickbass 06), and enter 5. Press Return.

This setting will transpose the Disco Pickbass 06 region up five semitones (a perfect fourth) upon playback.

NOTE ▶ This is different from the typical transposition behavior of samplers, as the length and speed of the region will not be altered, keeping it in perfect time with the project.

Now you are ready to test your creation.

16 Play the project.

17 While the project is playing, play the C2 keys and D2 keys one at a time on your MIDI controller.

The Disco Pickbass regions play back in time with the project and are toggled on or off when subsequent keys are depressed. In addition, the Disco Pickbass 06 region plays back a perfect quarter higher, changing the harmonic underpinning of the composition.

18 While the project is still playing, try triggering one of the Disco Pickbass regions (C2 and D2), letting it loop while triggering the Lead regions (C3, D3, and E3) on top.

19 Stop the project.

20 Choose File > Save As.

21 Name the project *11_MIDI Processing_Finished* and save to Music > Logic 8_BTB_Files > Lessons > Completed.

TIP ▶ You can import Environment layers from one project to another by selecting Options > Import Environment > Layer.

Lesson Review

1. How are layers used within the Environment?

2. What does the Physical Input object represent?

3. What does the keyboard object do?

4. What does the monitor object do?

5. What does the Sequencer Input object represent?

6. How do you cable an object from one layer to another?

7. What does an arpeggiator object do?

8. What does a chord memorizer object do?

9. What does a delay line object do?

10. What does a transformer object do?

11. What does a cable switcher object do?

12. What does a touch tracks object do?

Answers

1. Layers are used to organize objects of like type or function within the Environment.

2. The Physical Input object represents the ports of your MIDI interface or MIDI controller (with direct MIDI-to-USB connection).

3. The keyboard object displays incoming MIDI notes as well as generating new ones from its output.

4. Monitor objects display MIDI events passing from their input to their output in a list form.

5. The Sequencer Input object represents the connection to Logic's sequencer.

6. Cabling across layers is performed by Option-clicking the output of the object and selecting the input object from the menu.

7. An arpeggiator object arpeggiates harmonic input (chords), outputting each note individually in a selectable pattern.

8. Chord memorizer objects map a single note to a set of up to 12 user-selected notes.

9. Delay line objects repeat MIDI events passing through them, achieving a result similar to that of a delay processor creating echoes from audio signals.

10. Transformer objects primarily change one type of MIDI data to another. They can also act as a MIDI filter, track automation splitter, SysEx mapper, and condition splitter.

11. Cable switcher objects are used to manually direct the signal flow out of multiple outputs.

12. Touch tracks objects allow you to trigger MIDI regions or folders by playing single notes.

12

Lesson Files	Logic 8_BTB_Files > Lessons > 12_Sintra_Start.logic
Media	Logic 8_BTB_Files > Media > Sintra
Time	This lesson takes approximately 90 minutes to complete.
Goals	Enter and edit note data in the Score Editor
	Create note data using step input
	Format notation using staff styles
	Insert text and chord symbols into a score
	Transcribe a MIDI performance in score notation
	Create accurately notated percussion parts
	Prepare and print scores and parts

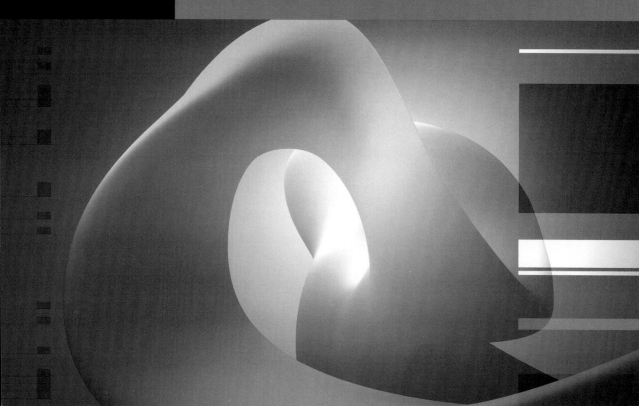

Lesson 12
Working with Notation

Logic was built from the ground up with musical notation as a central part of MIDI sequencing. (In fact, Logic evolved from a 1980s notation application called Notator.) As a result, Logic includes comprehensive notation capabilities for creating and printing parts and scores. You can enter notes directly into the Score Editor or automatically transcribe an existing MIDI recording.

This marriage of notation and MIDI data is integral to Logic. Every note in the score represents a MIDI note event. Logic is often called a notating sequencer because you can access all the powerful arranging and composing functionality of Logic's sequencer within the notation environment of the Score Editor.

In this lesson you will explore Logic's Score Editor, inputting notation and transcribing audio and MIDI regions for the composition "Sintra," which you worked on earlier in this book.

Creating Notation

There are a variety of methods for inputting notation, including graphic input, step input, and real-time transcription. In this exercise you will focus on the first two techniques, entering notes directly into the Score Editor.

Let's start by opening the project file you will be using for this chapter: the composition "Sintra," which you worked on in the Advanced Editing section of this book. This time, you will be notating the rhythm guitar part, transcribing the audio file into notation.

> **NOTE** ▶ You will need to set the Display Middle C As preference to C3 (Yamaha) to accurately follow the directions within this exercise and others throughout the book. This option can be found in Logic Pro > Preferences > Display > General.

1   Choose File > Open.

2   In the file browser, go to Music > Logic 8_BTB_Files > Lessons and open **12_Sintra_Start.logic**.

3   Play the song to familiarize yourself with the material.

As you can see in the Arrange area, the song mainly consists of software instrument tracks outputting to Logic's EXS24 mkII software sampler, mixed with audio recordings of nylon string guitar. Because the Score Editor interprets MIDI data to create notation, you will be working with a transcription of the main nylon string guitar part (track 11), inputting and adjusting notes where needed.

> **NOTE** ▶ Guitar notation sounds an octave lower than written. In order to have the Score Editor display the notation correctly and maintain an accurate playback, all regions within the Guitar Score track have a Transposition value of +12 in the Region Parameter box.

4   If the first region (Guitar Score_Intro) in the Guitar Score track (track 11) is not already selected, click to select it.

5   Open Screenset 3.

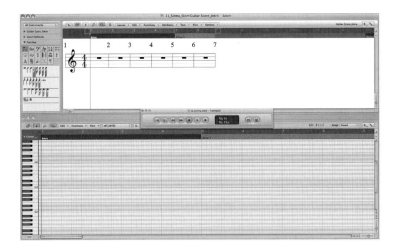

This screenset places the Score Editor in the top half of the screen, Piano Roll Editor in the bottom half, and Transport in the middle. Both editors display the contents of the selected Guitar Score track.

You are viewing a blank region that was created as a place for you to input notational data. Notice that rests are automatically displayed.

NOTE ▶ Like most of Logic's other editors, the Score Editor can be displayed both within the Arrange window and in an independent window. To open the Score Editor in a separate window, choose Window > Score in the main menu bar.

Entering Notes Using Graphic Input

You can graphically input notes and other notational elements in the Score Editor by selecting them from the Part box, a palette of notational symbols in the Inspector (at the far left of the Score Editor).

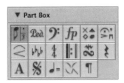

1   In the Part box group menu (the upper section), click each object group button.

The object group is displayed in the panel just below the group menu. The most recently selected object group appears at the top of the panel.

2   In the group menu, click the key signature button.

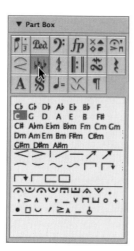

3   Choose the Pencil tool.

4   Since the song is in the key of D major, click D in the key signature object group.

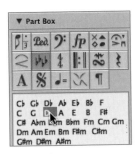

5 Click the staff between the treble clef and the time signature.

A D major key signature is inserted.

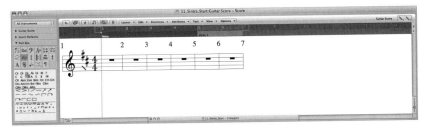

In the Part box, look at the notes group button and you'll see that it contains three areas, represented by an eighth note, a dot, and a triplet symbol. When you click these symbols, you open groups of notes with different rhythmic lengths.

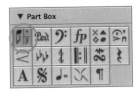

6 Click the triplet, dotted-note, and eighth-note symbols on the notes group button to view those object groups.

Various rhythmic lengths are displayed in each group.

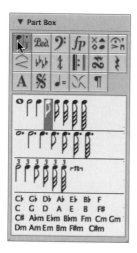

7 If the eighth note is not already selected, select it in the object group.

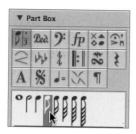

8 Using the Pencil tool in the Score Editor, hold down the B line in the middle of measure 5, using the help tag to position an eighth note at 5 2 3 1. Then release the mouse button.

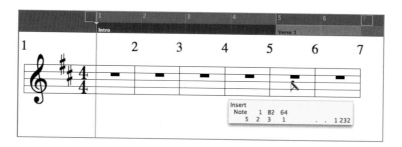

NOTE ▶ When the MIDI Out button is enabled (at the top of the Score Editor), you'll get aural as well as visual feedback as you drag a note around the staff. The note is played by the EXS24 mkII plug-in (using a classical guitar sampler instrument) on the current track.

An eighth note is inserted on the B line at 5 2 3 1.

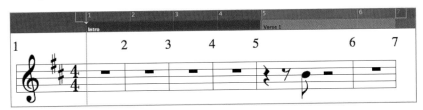

NOTE ▶ The note also appears in the Piano Roll Editor, and it provides a good reference, especially for length.

9 Use the same technique to insert a note on the D line above the first note you created.

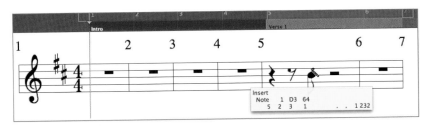

TIP ▶ Setting up the Pencil tool as the alternate Command-click tool works especially well for graphically entering notation. Doing so allows you to switch between selecting the note duration with the Pointer tool and inserting the note into the staff with the Pencil tool.

You might find it a little tricky to land on the correct pitch when graphically inserting a note. If your composition falls into a consistent key, you can make input easier by turning on the Diatonic Insert feature. With this feature activated, you are limited to entering only those notes within the current key signature.

10 Choose Options > Diatonic Insert.

11 Still using the Pencil tool, click anywhere above the D eighth note you created, and drag up and down while looking at the help tag.

The pitch choices are limited to diatonic pitches (so in D major, your pitch choices will not include C natural or F natural).

12 Release the mouse button to place an eighth note at E above the eighth-note D you previously created.

NOTE ▸ The note heads automatically change position, correctly notating adjacent pitches.

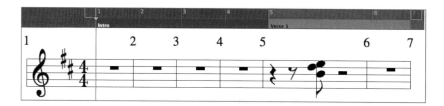

Just as in any of the other MIDI editors in Logic, note data can be copied and pasted.

13 Choose the Pointer tool.

14 In the Score Editor, drag a selection rectangle around the chord you just created.

15 Option-drag the chord to 5 3 1 1.

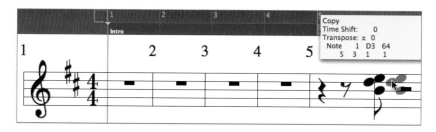

A copy of the chord is created at the new position.

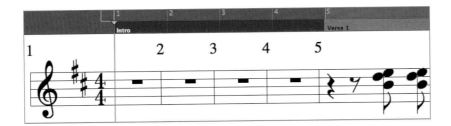

NOTE ▶ When notes are moved and inserted, they automatically snap to the division value set in the Transport bar.

Dragging Notes into the Score

Another way to input notes is by dragging them directly from the Part box.

1 Drag a quarter note from the notes object group to the B line at 5 3 3 1.

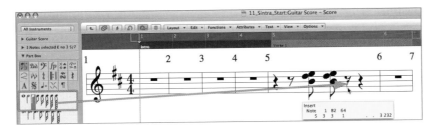

A quarter note is created where you dropped the note.

While this can be a good way to input notes with a variety of durations, journeying back and forth across the screen can get tedious. Fortunately, you can open an object group as a floating palette and position it anywhere on the screen.

2 Double-click the notes button in the group menu.

A floating palette opens with all the objects in the group, including the dotted-note and triplet versions.

3   Drag the palette near the measure you are working on.

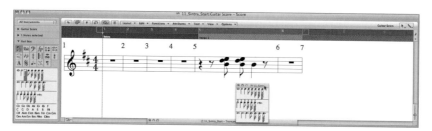

4   Drag two more quarter notes from the floating palette, dropping them on the D and
A above the B you just input, to create a chord.

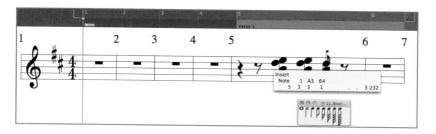

5   Create another chord at 5 4 3 1 by dragging half notes to B (on the same line as the
previous B), and to D and F♯, above the previous B.

A chord lasting two beats is created, tied across the bar line between measures 5 and 6.

NOTE ▶ Ties cannot be inserted graphically in Logic. They are created and displayed
automatically according to the length of the MIDI note.

Adjusting Note Length

Musical notation depicts note length using a specific set of symbols (sixteenth notes,
eighth notes, and so on). Therefore, note length must be edited differently in the Score

Editor than in the Piano Roll Editor (where you can lengthen a note by graphically drag-ging it, for example). To change the length of a note (or a group of notes) in the Score Editor, it is necessary to make an adjustment in the Event Parameter box.

1   Drag a selection rectangle around the final chord, and Option-drag it to 6 2 3 1.

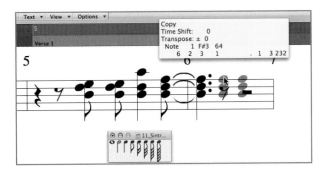

2   In the Inspector, click the disclosure triangle for the selected chord to display the Event Parameter box.

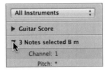

The Event Parameter box displays the parameters for the selected chord, indicated by "3 Notes selected" in the header.

Notice that Logic also supplies a chord analysis of the selected notes (identifying these notes as a B minor chord).

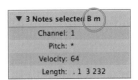

NOTE ▶ When notes are graphically input into the Score Editor, they are given lengths that are slightly less than the full value (hence the high tick numbers), to avoid overlaps in note length.

3 In the Event Parameter box, double-click the numbers next to the Length parameter and enter *0.0.2.0* (signifying an eighth note) in the text field. Press Return.

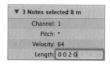

The lengths of the selected notes change from half notes to eighth notes.

NOTE ▸ The division value setting for a project impacts how you interpret the Length parameter. In the project file you are using for this lesson, the division value is set for sixteenth notes (/16), so 0.0.2.0 represents an eighth note value (two sixteenth notes).

4 Option-drag the chord to 6 3 3 1.

A copy of the chord is placed at the new position and is selected, making it ready for editing.

5 In the Event Parameter box, double-click the numbers next to the Length parameter, and enter *0.1.2.0* (a dotted quarter note). Press Return.

NOTE ▸ When entering numbers into the Event Parameter box, you can also use spaces, instead of periods, to separate the digits.

The note lengths of the chord change to dotted quarter notes.

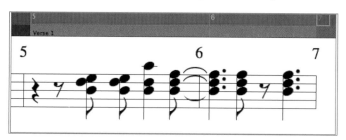

6 Close the floating notes group palette.

Entering Notes Using Step Input

Although graphic input allows the precise entry of notes, it can be slow. A faster technique is step input, which allows you to insert notes at the current playhead position while Logic automatically moves the playhead forward based on the selected rhythmic length. You can set a note's pitch and length by clicking an onscreen piano keyboard, pressing a key on your computer keyboard, or using MIDI input.

To begin step input, you need to place the playhead at the position where you want to begin.

1   Option-click the staff at 5 1 1 1 (use the help tag) to place the playhead at the beginning of measure 5.

> **TIP** ▶ Option-clicking in the staff (not on notes or other symbols) is a quick way to locate the playhead in the Score Editor for playback or editing.

2   In the main menu bar, choose Options > Step Input Keyboard.

The Step Input Keyboard window opens. Buttons in this window can be clicked to set the pitch, length, and dynamics (velocity) of a note.

> **TIP** ▶ The Step Input Keyboard can be used in any Logic editor, and it is especially effective when controlled with an extensive set of key commands (including commands for specific note pitches). This allows you to quickly input notes entirely from your computer keyboard for non-real-time purposes such as creating notation.

3   If necessary, reposition the Step Input Keyboard so it does not cover up the score.

4   Click the whole-note button at the left side of the window.

5   Click the D2 key on the Step Input Keyboard.

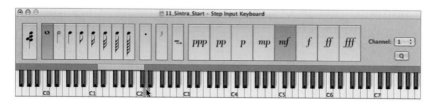

A D note is inserted just below the staff, and the playhead jumps to the end of the inserted whole-note value.

NOTE ► Don't panic! The note you just input is displayed as a dotted quarter note for a reason explained in "Creating a Polyphonic Staff Style" later in this lesson.

Instead of clicking the note on the Step Input Keyboard, you can also use a MIDI controller to insert notes by clicking the MIDI In button in any editor so that MIDI incoming data can be received. When MIDI In is enabled, Logic "listens" for MIDI note input.

6   While looking at the MIDI Activity display within the Transport bar, find the D2 and A1 keys on your MIDI controller.

7   In the Score Editor, click the MIDI In button to turn it on.

8   On the Step Input Keyboard, click the half-note button.

9   On your MIDI controller, press the D2 key, then the A1 key.

A D note is created at 6 1 1 1 and an A note at 6 3 1 1 (spaced by a half-note interval).

As long as the MIDI In button is on, Logic assumes that you are using step input, and it will create notes based on MIDI input. For this reason, it is necessary to turn off the MIDI In button when you are finished using MIDI for note input.

10 Click the MIDI In button to turn MIDI input off.

11 Close the Step Input Keyboard.

Using Staff Styles

Just as text can be formatted depending on the context (such as paragraphs for standard text, stanzas in poetry, and outlines), so music notation can be displayed in a variety of formats, depending on the instrument, transposition, number of voices, and so on.

Logic allows you to format notes using staff styles, which incorporate multiple attributes of the notes in a MIDI region, such as clef, staff size, instrument transposition, and various voice-display parameters.

A staff style acts like a notation-display filter and can be changed at any time. Let's try out a few staff styles to observe their effects on the part you just input.

1 In the Inspector, click the Guitar Score disclosure triangle to show the Display Parameter box.

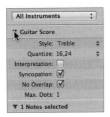

The Display Parameter box contains parameters that affect the display of the selected MIDI region. The Style parameter designates the staff style assigned to the region.

2 Click the Style pop-up menu.

The staff style options are displayed.

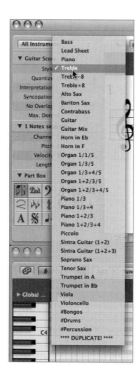

Logic comes with many staff styles that each contain several attributes, such as clef assignment and display transposition.

NOTE ▸ Staff styles are saved in a project file and can be imported from one song to another by choosing File > Project Settings > Import Settings.

3   From the Style menu, choose Alto Sax.

The notation in the Score Editor changes because the Alto Sax is an E♭-transposing instrument. As a result, the part is transposed up nine semitones and notated in the key of B major.

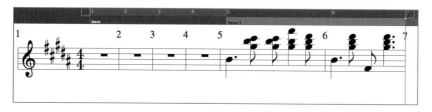

4   From the Style menu, choose Guitar.

The notation in the Score Editor changes to display guitar tablature.

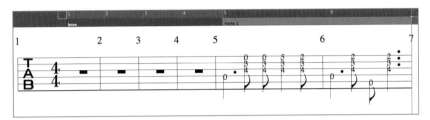

As you can see, staff styles are extremely versatile in their displays of note data.

5   From the Style menu, choose Treble, returning the notation to its default setting.

NOTE ▸ Logic automatically assigns a default staff style (Treble, Bass, or Piano) to a MIDI region based on its octave and range.

Creating a Polyphonic Staff Style

You probably noticed that the three bass notes you created by step input are displayed incorrectly in the Score Editor. The notes do not appear to sustain for the full amount of time and are cut off by the notes that follow. However, if you look at the notes in the Piano Roll Editor (in the bottom half of the screen), you'll notice that the lengths of those notes are displayed correctly.

Our guitar part was input as a single voice, and therefore the note lengths are cut off because there is no voice independence. To solve this problem, you need to create a polyphonic staff style that can display multiple independent voices at once.

1   Shift-click to select the three notes you just created via step input (D2, D2, A1).

The corresponding notes are highlighted in the Piano Roll Editor.

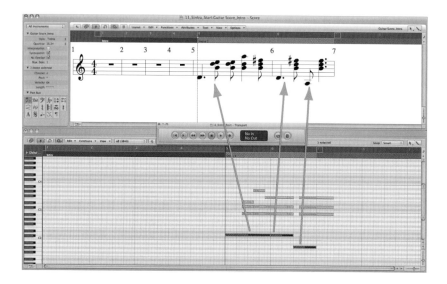

Notice the difference in the representation of the notes in the Piano Roll and Score editors. The reason for this discrepancy lies in the established system for the notation of a polyphonic instrument. A polyphonic instrument notated on a single staff, such as a guitar, needs to have rhythmically different melodic lines displayed in the same staff. These voices, in turn, must be able to display length, stem direction, and rests independent of each other.

2   In the Score Editor's local menu bar, choose Layout > Staff Styles.

The Staff Style window opens, displaying the contents of the default Treble staff style.

3   Expand the window by dragging the lower-right corner to view all of the parameters.

The data displayed in the Treble staff style represents a single-voice staff with various display attributes.

4   Click the arrow button immediately to the right of the name box, and select ****DUPLICATE!**** from the menu.

A new staff style is created with the attributes of the Treble staff style. Let's rename it.

5   In the name field, double-click the staff style name and enter *Guitar (1+2)*, then press Return.

Notice that the new staff style contains a single row of attributes (preceded by the number 1) that represent a single staff. A staff style can have multiple staves with independent settings, each containing as many voices as you need.

In guitar notation, multiple voices are displayed on a single treble staff. Each voice is differentiated by the direction of the stems, ties, and tuplets. Let's continue customizing the staff style to reflect these display parameters by first inserting an additional voice.

6   Click the narrow column to the left of and just below the staff number.

NOTE ▶ Clicking this column enables you to set insertion points for adding new staves and voices. You can also select voices and staves for deletion by clicking within this column, immediately to the left of the number.

The small arrow moves below the staff number, indicating where new staves and voices will be inserted.

7   In the Staff Style window's local menu bar, choose New > Insert Voice.

A new voice is created below the previous staff voice, indicated by the absence of a number at the far left of the line.

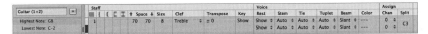

In guitar notation, when more than one voice is displayed at the same time, the stems, ties, and tuplets of the top voice always point upward. You can reflect this in the staff style by modifying the Voice attributes for the top voice.

8   In the top voice, click the Stem parameter menu and choose Up.

9   Do the same for the Tie and Tuplet parameter menus.

10   In the bottom voice, click the Stem, Tie, and Tuplet menus one at a time and choose Down.

By default, each voice in a staff style can display rests. This can create multiple rests in a staff, which are appropriate for divided (divisi) parts but not for a solo part.

11   Click the Rest parameter menu for the bottom voice and choose Hide.

This will hide the rests for the bottom voice.

TIP ▶ Rests can be inserted manually by dragging them into the score from the Part box. These are graphic indicators only and have no effect on the playback of the MIDI region.

The last thing to consider is how to assign individual notes in the region to each voice. By default, a staff style will use a split note to do this. Pitches that fall above the split note are assigned to voice one, and pitches that fall below the split note are assigned to voice two. This split note can be changed in the Assign parameters in the Staff Style window.

However, this technique usually won't work for guitar notation because voices are assigned primarily to represent melody (or bass lines) and the accompaniment, and they can consist of any range of pitches. Instead, voices can be assigned in a staff style using the individual notes' MIDI channel numbers.

NOTE ▶ Each note can have its own MIDI channel in Logic. This setting is applied on input by the MIDI Out channel setting of the MIDI controller, or it can be applied after the fact using Logic's editors.

12 In the Assign columns (far right), click the Chan(nel) menu for the top voice and choose 1.

13 Click the Chan(nel) menu for the bottom voice and choose 2.

With these settings, all notes using MIDI channel 1 will be assigned to the top voice, and all notes using MIDI channel 2 will be assigned to the bottom voice.

Now that you have created the polyphonic Guitar staff style, it's time to apply it to the displayed region.

14 Close the Staff Style window.

15 In the Display Parameter box, click the Style menu and choose Guitar (1+2).

The notation changes slightly, displaying the notes with all stems pointing up. When notes are inserted manually, the same default MIDI channel is assigned to all notes (in this case, channel 1). When you applied the staff style, all the notes in the region were assigned to the top voice.

You don't have to manually change the MIDI channel for each note that you want to assign to the bottom voice. Instead, you can quickly assign notes to adjacent voices by using the Voice Separation tool. This tool works by allowing you to draw a line between voices that need to be separated. Notes below the line are bumped to the adjacent voice below their current assignment, while notes above the line will be bumped up a voice.

16 Choose the Voice Separation tool.

17 Using the Voice Separation tool, draw between the bass notes and the chords in one continuous line.

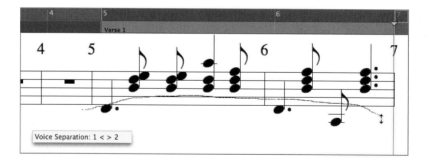

The bass notes are assigned to the bottom voice and are now displayed correctly.

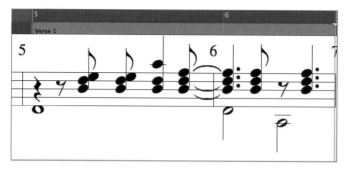

NOTE ▶ You can continually adjust voice assignments with the Voice Separation tool by drawing lines above and below individual notes or entire passages.

Working with Text

Text serves various purposes in musical notation, including supplying performance indications and displaying chord notation. Text can be added by using objects from the Part box, or by using the Text tool.

Entering Text into the Score

Let's create a basic performance indication for the guitar part using an object from the Part box. The easiest way to input text directly into the Score Editor is with the Text tool.

1   Choose the Text tool.

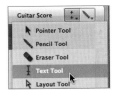

2   Around the first measure, click the area above the staff.

A text insertion point is created.

3   Type *Latin* and press Return.

Inserted text can be formatted in any font or size in the Font window.

4   In the Score Editor's local menu bar, choose Text > Fonts.

The Font window opens.

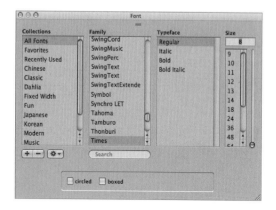

5 In the Size column on the far right, click 12.

The selected text increases in size.

6 Close the Font window.

> **TIP** ▶ If you need to adjust the position of any inserted text, you can drag it from one location to another using the Pointer tool. However, when exact positions are required (as they often are), use the Event Parameter box. When text is selected, you will find parameters there to adjust both the vertical and horizontal positions by single pixels, and to align the text in relation to the page borders.

Creating Chord Symbols

In the Score Editor, chord symbols are a specialized form of text object and carry their own display attributes. Chord symbols can also be created by dragging symbols from the Part box.

Let's create some chord symbols in the Guitar score to indicate the accompaniment chords for the guitar solo. Instead of using the Score Editor/Piano Roll Editor screenset, you'll work with the Score Editor in the Arrange window. So far you've been accessing the editors within the Arrange area by clicking the tabs at the bottom of the window. You can speed up workflow considerably by using the various toggle key commands available, which both open *and* close an editor within the Arrange area with a single keystroke.

1 Press the number 1 to open Screenset 1.

2 In the Guitar Score track, select the last region (Guitar Score_Chords).

3 Press the N key (Toggle Score Editor) to open the Score Editor within the Arrange area.

The Guitar Score_Chords region is displayed in the Score Editor.

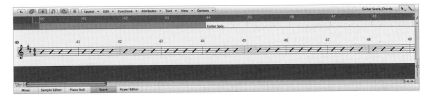

NOTE ▶ The Guitar Score_Chords region doesn't contain any MIDI events or added notational symbols. The chord slashes you see displayed are actually part of the Lead Sheet staff style. You can display chord slashes for any staff style instead of rests by choosing them in the Staff Style window's Rest parameter menu.

4 In the Part box group menu, choose the text group to view its contents.

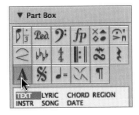

5 Drag the CHORD object to just above the staff at 40 1 1 1.

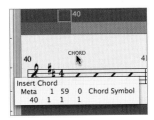

A text insertion point is created at the location.

6 Type *D* (uppercase) and press Return.

A D major chord symbol is entered at 40 1 1 1.

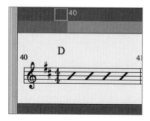

7   Drag the CHORD object from the group to just above the staff at 44 1 1 1.

8   Type *C* (uppercase) and press Return to enter another chord symbol.

This time, you are going to modify the chord by opening the Chord Symbol dialog.

9   Double-click the chord symbol you just created.

The Chord Symbol dialog opens.

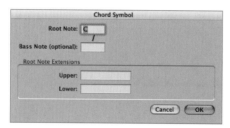

This dialog allows you to add extensions and chord inversions.

10   Click the Bass Note field, and type *D*.

11   Click OK.

The chord is displayed as a C major chord with a D in the bass.

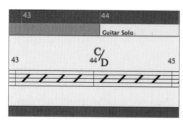

NOTE ▶ You might need to adjust the chord symbol's position by dragging it with the Pointer tool so that it does not overlap the top of the staff.

12 Using the same technique, create a D major chord symbol at 46 1 1 1.

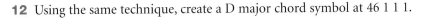
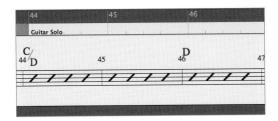

Using Text Styles

Just as you can format notes using staff styles, so you can create text styles to format text elements in the Score Editor. Each text style contains attributes, like font and size, that can be applied to specific types of text objects. You will use the Text Style window to modify the attributes of the chord text objects in the current score.

1 In the Score Editor's local menu bar, choose Text > Text Styles.

The Text Style window opens.

NOTE ▶ You may need to resize the window to view its entire contents.

Name	Example
Plain Text	Times
Page Numbers	Times
Bar Numbers	Times
Instrument Names	Times
Tuplets	*Times*
Repeat Endings	Times
Chord Root	Times
Chord Ext.	Times
Mult. Rests	Times
Tablature	Times
Tempo Symbols	Times
Octave Symbols	*Times*

2 Position the Text Style window so that you can see the chords you recently created.

3 In the Chord Root row, click the Font column.

The Font window opens.

4   In the Family column of the Font window, choose Arial.

The font changes for all chords. This is because they are assigned to the Chord Root text style by default.

5   In the Typeface column, click Bold.

All chords are displayed in bold type.

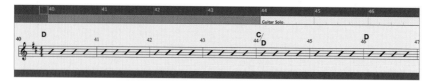

NOTE ▶ Any text style can be assigned to a text element in the Display Parameter box.

6   Close the Font window.

7   Close the Text Style window.

TIP ▶ Text styles are useful for creating specialized text formats commonly used in musical notation, such as rehearsal markings. A new text style is created by choosing New > New Text Style, then selecting its attributes using the technique described previously. The Font window also includes checkboxes for circling or boxing the text (useful for rehearsal markings). After setting up your text style, you can assign it to any input text by choosing it in the Style menu in the Event Parameter box.

Transcribing a Performance

Logic's notation engine is designed to preserve the subtleties of an actual performance while organizing the data into cleanly notated scores. With a little finessing, you can create accurate parts and scores based on existing MIDI tracks without sacrificing any of the original "feel" of the sequenced material.

Logic accomplishes this demanding task by using a separate notation display system that allows you to adjust the look of the notation without changing the original MIDI region data.

In this exercise you'll prepare MIDI regions in the Arrange area to aid in the transcription process, and adjust parameters in the Score Editor to correctly notate the parts without modifying the performance data.

Preparing MIDI Regions for Notation

During sequencing, it is commonplace to have tracks made up of noncontiguous regions (that is, regions that have space between them). However, the Score Editor needs regions to display notation and will display nothing (not even a staff) if no region is present.

For the purpose of notation, it is therefore advisable to fill up MIDI tracks with regions by inserting blank regions, or by merging multiple regions into a single composite region. This has no effect on the playback of a part but allows the Score Editor to create staves and fill them with rests.

1   In the Arrange area, scroll up and select the Bongos track (track 9).

The Bongos track consists of two separate regions.

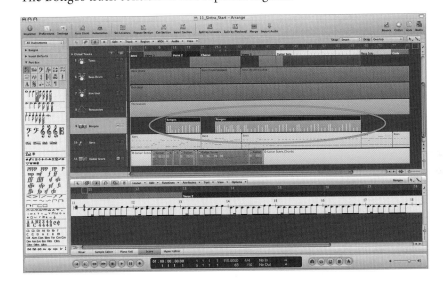

As you can see in the Score Editor, the display starts at measure 11, which corresponds to the start of the first region in the track.

2   Close the Score Editor by using the Toggle Score Editor key command (N).

3   In the Arrange area, choose the Pencil tool, and click the beginning of the Bongos track (at 1 1 1 1) to create a blank region.

4   Create another blank region at 81 1 1 1 in the Bongos track.

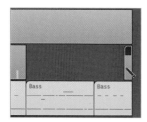

5   In the track list, click the Bongos track to select all of its regions, including the new ones.

6   In the Arrange area's local menu bar, choose Region > Merge > Regions.

One contiguous region is formed for the Bongos track.

7   Press the N key to view the merged Bongos region in the Score Editor.

8   Scroll through the Score Editor to view the part. Rests are now displayed for areas with no activity.

Viewing the Data Accurately

The settings in the Display Parameter box (with the exception of Style) form the basis for the rhythmic interpretation and display of MIDI data. These settings apply only to the score display and do not change the playback of the MIDI regions in any way.

Let's look at how these parameters affect the notation of a selected region.

1   Click the Solo button in the Bongos track to solo the track.

2   Press the "Go to Position" key command (/) to locate to 11 1 1 1.

3   Play the song, listening to the bongos part while watching the notation.

4   When you're familiar with the material, stop the song.

5   Make sure that the Score Editor has key focus by clicking the top part of the area or by pressing the Tab key.

6   In the upper-left corner, open the Display Parameter box (disclosure triangle next to Bongos), if it's not already opened.

You can use the Quantize setting (located below the Style parameter) to apply visual quantization to the notes, dictating the shortest value that can be displayed in the selected MIDI region.

7   Click the Quantize menu and choose 8.

The notation changes to display eighth notes as the shortest value.

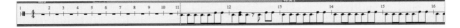

8   Play the song again, listening to the bongos part while watching the notation.

Notice that what you are hearing is not rhythmically the same as what is displayed. This illustrates the independence of display quantization from the actual MIDI performance data.

9   Use the "Go to Position" key command (/) to locate to 11 1 1 1.

10   Click the Quantize menu and choose 16,24.

This default setting works well for the part. It permits sixteenth notes as well as sixteenth-note triplets (indicated by *24*) to appear as the shortest note lengths in the Score Editor.

Let's move on to the Interpretation parameter, which is specifically used to create an easy-to-read score from real-time MIDI recordings. When notes are performed, they generally aren't held for the full length of a given note, but are shortened depending on the articulation and the time needed to move to another note on the instrument. With Interpretation turned on, Logic fills in those performance gaps between notes and makes a guess as to the appropriate notation for each note.

11 Deselect the Interpretation checkbox in the Display Parameter box.

The notes are now displayed as isolated sixteenth notes with rests.

This might be more technically accurate (displaying the actual length of the notes as they are played), but the notation is much harder to read! Considering that the part is a percussive one, it makes sense to have Interpretation turned on (the default setting).

12 Select the Interpretation checkbox to turn Interpretation on.

TIP ▶ Interpretation should be turned off when using graphic or step input, because you want the full value of the selected notes to be displayed.

Each note in Logic can have unique display attributes, independent of the region settings in the Display Parameter box. These are set in the Note Attributes dialog.

13 Double-click the first note of measure 11.

The Note Attributes dialog opens.

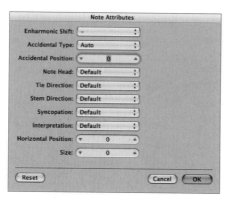

Here you can make adjustments to individual notes via various menus, including one for Interpretation.

14 Click Cancel to close the Note Attributes dialog.

15 Press the N key to close the Score Editor.

16 Click the Solo button on the Bongos track to turn off soloing.

Working with Drum Notation

Logic has a unique and powerful way of notating drum parts using *mapped instruments*. Traditionally, mapped instruments are created in Logic to represent a drum machine or drum channel in a multi-timbral synthesizer, but they also enable you to assign specific notes to voice groups in the Staff Style window and thereby create drum notation.

In this exercise, you will create a mapped instrument to generate a score from the drum tracks used in the song.

Consolidating the Tracks

To create a single drum staff, you first need to consolidate the multiple drum part tracks into a single contiguous region.

1 Shift-click tracks 3 through 7 (Cymbals, Hi Hat, Toms, Bass Drum, and Rim Shot), selecting the regions in each track.

2 In the Arrange area's local menu bar, choose Region > Loops > Convert to Real Copies.

3 In the Arrange area's local menu bar, choose Region > Merge > Regions.

The drum tracks combine into a single region on track 3.

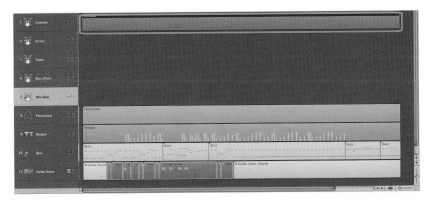

4   In the Arrange area's local menu bar, choose Track > Delete Unused.

The tracks left empty by the merge are deleted.

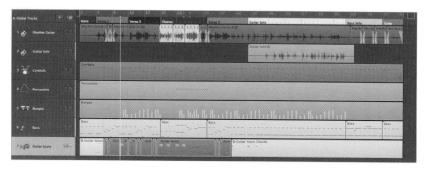

5   Select track 3 (now displays Cymbals as the name).

Creating a Mapped Instrument

Now that everything is consolidated into a single region, you can create the mapped instrument object in the Environment.

1   Choose Window > Environment.

The Environment window opens, displaying the Instruments layer, which has nothing in it yet.

2   In the Environment window's local menu bar, choose New > Mapped Instrument.

A mapped instrument object is created in the Environment layer, and the Mapped Instrument window appears.

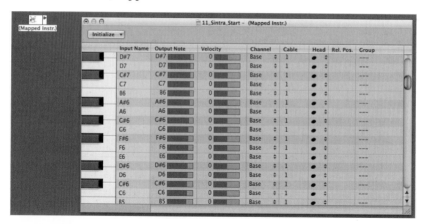

The Mapped Instrument window is used to edit individual notes in a mapped instrument, and it automatically opens when creating a new mapped instrument object.

NOTE ▶ A Mapped Instrument window can also be displayed by double-clicking the mapped instrument object.

3   In the Mapped Instrument window, scroll down until you can see the drum names displayed in the Input Name column (so that B0 is at the bottom of the list).

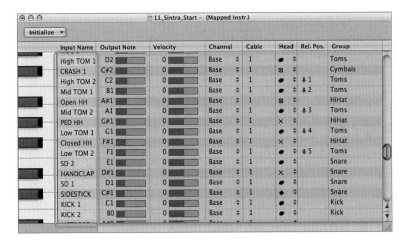

4   Look at the three columns to the right in the Mapped Instrument window: Head, Rel. Pos. (for Relative Position), and Group.

The information in these columns has a direct impact on the drum notation. In these columns you assign note heads and adjust the relative position of the clef for each note. In addition, each note can be assigned to drum groups, which carry common attributes that are interpreted by the staff style in the Score Editor.

NOTE ▶ The default settings in the Mapped Instrument window correspond to the standardized General MIDI (GM) Drum Kit note assignments. This makes it a snap to create drum notation from an EXS24 mkII sampler instrument that also reflects the General MIDI note assignments. If you aren't using a GM-mapped drum sampler instrument to output the part, then adjustments can be made in the Output Note column to trigger the appropriate sound.

5   Close the Mapped Instrument window.

6   In the Object Parameter box (for Mapped Instr.), click the object's name, enter *Drums*, and press Return.

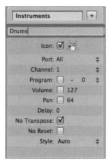

The mapped instrument object's name changes to Drums.

If the track in the Arrange area is to display the drum notation, you need to assign it to the mapped instrument you created. To ensure that it still outputs to the EXS24 mkII plug-in inserted on the software instrument channel, you need to cable the objects together in the Environment.

7   Option-click the cable output from the Drums object, and choose Audio > Software instrument > Inst 1 (the software instrument with the EXS24 mkII sampled drum kit).

NOTE ▶ Option-clicking a cable output allows you to connect objects in different layers of the Environment.

An alert message appears, asking if you want to remove the port setting for the object.

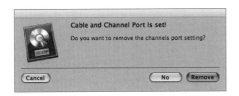

8   Click Remove.

NOTE ▶ By removing the port and channel settings for the object, you are setting the Drums object to output only to the software instrument object.

A cable appears, connecting the objects between the layers of the Environment.

You're now ready to assign the new mapped instrument to the consolidated drums track (Cymbals) in the Arrange area. Instead of Control-clicking the track in the track list and choosing an object from the shortcut menu, you can quickly assign the selected track to any object in the Environment by using the MIDI Thru tool.

9   Choose the MIDI Thru tool.

10   Move the Environment window to the right, so you can see the Arrange window's Inspector and track list.

11   In the Environment window, click the Drums object while observing the Inspector within the Arrange area (Cymbals).

12   Close the Environment window.

In the Arrange area, the selected drums track (track 3) is now assigned to the Drums mapped instrument. (You can verify the assignment by looking at the Arrange channel strip, which now displays a MIDI fader.)

Now all that's left for you to do is assign the staff style in the Score Editor.

13 Press the N key to open the Score Editor.

The Score Editor displays the contents of the drums track but uses the default Bass staff style. In order for the settings in the Mapped Instrument window to be translated into notation, it is necessary to assign a mapped staff style to the region. Mapped staff styles are designated in the staff style list by a # symbol preceding the name.

14 Within the Display Parameter box, click the Style menu and choose #Drums.

The region is now displayed in correct notation.

NOTE ▶ If the display is cut off, you can move the staff by dragging down the clef.

Display the #Drums staff style to see how it affects the settings.

15 In the Score Editor's local menu bar, choose Layout > Staff Styles.

The #Drums staff style is displayed in the Staff Style window.

As you can see, this is a polyphonic staff style of sorts, consisting of multiple voices that are assigned to drum groups instead of a split point or MIDI channel. These drum groups correspond to the Group column entries in the Mapped Instrument window.

NOTE ▶ You might need to resize the Staff Style window to see its entire contents.

16 Close the Staff Style window.

Creating Scores and Parts

Logic's Score Editor allows you to use *score sets* to control which instruments will be displayed (and printed) in a score. A score set can include as many (or as few) of the existing track instruments as you want, and instruments can be arranged independently of their order in the Arrange area. In a score set you can also assign instrument names and determine if the group shares bar lines, brackets, or braces.

Multiple user-defined score sets can be created to display everything from a full score to individual parts. In this exercise, you will use score sets to lay out the full score as well as quickly generate individual instrument parts.

Creating a Score Set

1   Click Stop to return the project to 1 1 1 1.

2   Open Screenset 4.

The screenset contains a full-screen Score Editor in page view.

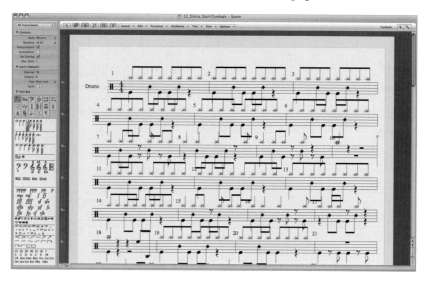

NOTE ▶ Page view can be displayed in any Score Editor window: choose View > Page View from the Score Editor's local menu bar, or click the turquoise Page View button next to the menu bar.

Prior to the creation of any score sets, Logic displays selected instruments using a default score set named All Instruments, which appears at the top of the Inspector.

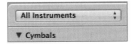

However, you aren't seeing all the instruments at the moment, because you recently selected the Drums region. To display all the instruments, you need to move up a level (reflecting the Arrange area).

3   Click the Hierarchy button, located in the upper-left corner of the window.

All Arrange area instruments are displayed in the Score Editor.

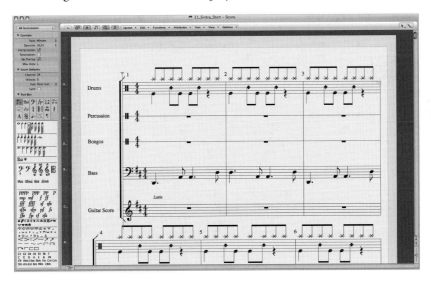

Although the default All Instruments score set works for the basic display of the instruments, you can refine the score display by creating your own score set.

4   In the Score Editor's local menu bar, choose Layout > Score Sets.

The Score Set window opens.

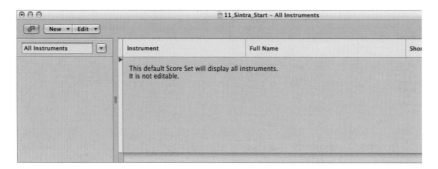

5   In the Score Set window's local menu bar, choose New > New Complete Set.

A new score set, made up of all the instruments used in the Arrange area, is created.

6   Double-click the score set name, and enter *Ensemble* in the text field. Press Return.

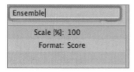

The instrument names that appear in the score relate directly to the contents of the Full Name column. By default, these contents include the names of the objects within the Environment that are assigned to the tracks (channels, mapped instruments, and so on). You can, however, enter whatever you like in the Full Name and Short Name columns.

A score set also allows you to scale the size of the displayed staves, enabling you to fit more systems on a page. This is especially useful when creating full conductor scores.

7   Double-click the number next to the Scale parameter (below the score set name) and enter 65, then press Return.

To apply the score set you created, you need to assign it in the Inspector.

8   At the very top of the Inspector area, click the Score Set menu and choose Ensemble.

The score displays at a smaller scale and shows the instrument names you assigned in the score set.

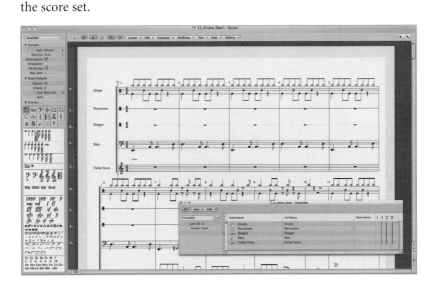

The full score can now be printed.

Creating Parts for Printing

It is desirable to create individual score sets for each instrumental part in the score. This allows the most control over naming and other display attributes, and it enables you to print parts by choosing from the Score Set menu.

In this exercise, you will create an individual, printer-ready score set for the guitar part. You will create a new empty score set, then add the Guitar Score instrument to the set.

1 In the Score Set window, select New > New Empty Set.

An empty score set is created.

2 Choose New > Add Instrument Entry.

A single instrument entry is added to the score set. By default, the first instrument in the track list is added, which in this case is the Drums instrument. To add the guitar part, you must change the instrument in the Instrument column.

3 In the Instrument column, click and hold down the Drums menu, and choose Audio > Software Instrument > Guitar Score.

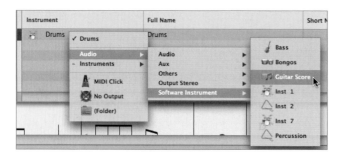

The score set now displays the Guitar Score instrument in the Instrument column.

To complete the part, it is a simple matter to rename the default instrument as Guitar in the Score Set window.

4 Click the Full Name field, and enter *Guitar*. Press Return.

The score now displays *Guitar* at the beginning of the first staff.

Instrumental parts can reflect different layout preferences. To designate a score set as a part, you need to change the Format parameter, which is located below the Scale parameter.

5   Click the setting next to the Format parameter (which currently displays Score). Choose Part from the menu. The Format setting changes to Part.

6   Double-click the score set name in the top-left corner, and enter *Guitar* in the text field. Press Return.

7   Close the Score Set window.

8   In the Inspector, click the Score Set menu and choose Guitar.

The Score Editor displays the guitar part.

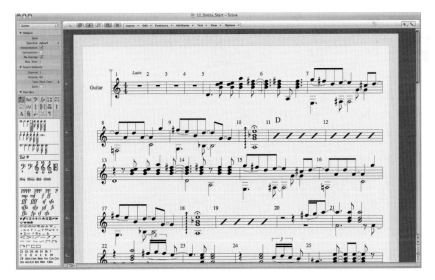

Now that you've designated the Guitar score set as a part, you can change its layout preferences without affecting the Ensemble score set you created earlier. The layout preferences for both scores and parts are located in the Global Score project settings.

9 In the Score Editor's local menu bar, choose Layout > Global Format.

The Project Settings window opens, displaying the Global tab.

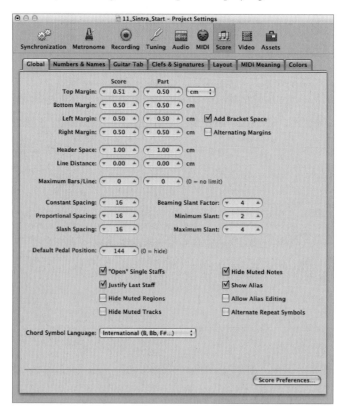

This window includes separate layout settings for scores and parts, designated by the two columns titled (appropriately enough) Score and Part.

The guitar part that you have been formatting needs a bit more space between the staves because the notation is getting crowded. You can create more space between the staves by adjusting the Line Distance setting in the Part column.

10 In the Part column, click the Line Distance field and enter *.25* (with a decimal point), and press Return.

11 Close the Project Settings window.

The staves for the guitar part are more spread out now, making them easier to read.

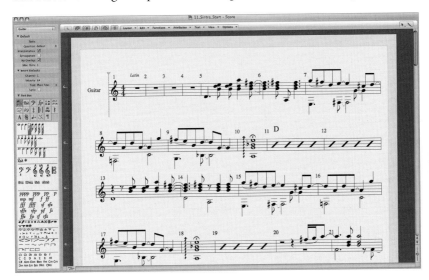

Let's finish by comparing the two score sets you have created. The differences can be seen most easily if you view the pages in their entirety. By zooming out in the Score Editor, you can see entire pages side by side.

12 Press Control–Up Arrow repeatedly to vertically zoom out until you see two pages.

13 From the Score Set menu, choose Ensemble.

The Score Editor displays the full score.

The two score sets display independent scale and line distance settings.

14 Try printing the scores of both the Guitar and Ensemble score sets by selecting them in the Inspector and choosing File > Print.

NOTE ▶ If you don't have a printer connected, you can save the score as a PDF file by first selecting File > Print, then clicking the PDF button and choosing Save as PDF.

Lesson Review

1. In what ways can you enter notation in the Score Editor?

2. Where do you edit note length?

3. What do you use to assign display attributes to notation?

4. How do you assign voices within a score style?

5. What do you use to assign voices in a part in the Score Editor?

6. What do text styles do?

7. Do you need to edit MIDI regions to accurately display notation?

8. Does the Quantization parameter in the Score Editor change both notation and playback?

9. How do you create drum notation?

10. What do you use to display and print only selected parts?

11. Can you retain independent formatting for both parts and scores?

Answers

1. Notation can be entered in the Score Editor using graphic input, step input, and real-time transcription.

2. Note length is edited in the Event Parameter box.

3. Staff styles are used to assign display attributes to notation.

4. Voices are assigned using a MIDI split note or an individual MIDI channel.

5. The Voice Separation tool can be used to quickly assign voices in a polyphonic staff style using MIDI channel assignment.

6. Text styles assign display attributes to text elements in the Score Editor.

7. Yes. MIDI regions must often be edited to display notation accurately.

8. No. Quantization in the Score Editor changes the notation display but does not affect the performance data.

9. Drum parts can be notated by assigning a mapped instrument and a mapped staff style to a track.

10. Score sets are used to display and print individual parts up to full scores.

11. Yes. You can assign separate format settings for parts and scores in the Global Score project settings.

Cusp of Magic— Terry Riley

SINCE THE 1960s, WHEN HIS GROUNDBREAKING

works *In C* and *A Rainbow in Curved Air* helped launch what's come to be known as the minimalist school of composition, Terry Riley has blended advanced technology with improvisation to create music that's both cutting-edge and deeply human. Drawing on such wide-ranging influences as the electronic compositions of Karlheinz Stockhausen and the Indian master vocalist Pandit Pran Nath, Riley has incorporated synthesizers, tape-looping techniques, and non-Western tunings and temperaments into his works. Riley in turn has worked with and/or influenced fellow composers as diverse in style as Steve Reich, John Adams, Philip Glass, and Pete Townshend.

Riley's work remains in high demand, from commissions for the Kronos Quartet to live improvisations with artists and musicians worldwide—and Logic Pro 8 plays an integral role in his work as both composer and performer.

In fact, Riley has used Logic since before it was called Logic: When he discovered it around 1990, the program—known then as Notator—was still in its infancy. "It was somewhat of a miracle," he recalled. "You could play a part on the keyboard and have the notes show up onscreen!"

As Notator migrated to the Mac platform and evolved into Logic Pro, Riley's use of the program naturally expanded as well. "I still use it a lot for notation, and for the kinds of scores I do, Logic covers everything," he said. "Once I got into digital audio, I've been using that feature a lot."

Perhaps surprisingly, given his pioneering use of analog tape loops, Riley doesn't use Logic for digital looping but usually "as a solo instrument."

"I've begun lately to try to use it [Logic Pro 8] for live performance—audio and software instruments."

For instance, when performing his new piece *A Rainbow in Curved Air Revisited*—a return to the influential 1968 composition that gave art rockers Curved Air their name and inspired the synthesizer work (and title) of The Who's "Baba O'Riley"—Riley uses Logic's software instruments for improvisational passages.

Riley has also made considerable use of Logic for sampling, as when he was developing *Cusp of Magic*, commissioned by the Kronos Quartet in celebration of Riley's 70th birthday in 2005. The acclaimed piece includes a vocal section, parts for the pipa (a Chinese lute), and sounds sampled from Kronos leader David Harrington's extensive collection of toys, as well as a number of snippets of spoken word and voice.

"There was notation with audio—it [*Cusp of Magic*] had a lot of audio samples, toy sounds, vocal audio samples," Riley said. Logic was essential to organizing the digital audio elements into a background track that would be played during live performances. "It was so great to lay it out with the notation [in Logic] and get everything precise."

More recently, Riley used Logic to compose *Fairy Tale*, a piece for choir, brass, and percussion. Performances of the work will also feature a storyteller onstage—a wrinkle that once again made Logic indispensable. "It was wonderful," Riley said. "It'll be performed with a live narrator, but I could lay it out in Logic with my own narration as a temp track."

For Riley, a major advantage of composing with Logic is its built-in support for just intonation and other custom tunings, which allow a greater range of compositional freedom than the "standard" equal temperament used in Western music.

"Tuning is one of the most important parameters to work with in composing," he said. "If you use historical temperaments or just intonation, you have a lot more colors available and have to find a way to put them together. They have resonant qualities that aren't possible in equal temperament."

Limiting compositions to Western tuning would be like being "a painter with just three colors," Riley said, adding that he'd encourage anyone who composes with Logic to experiment with alternative tunings. (To do so, choose File > Project Settings > Tuning, and then click the Fixed button. You'll see a menu that allows you to pick from dozens of historical tunings.)

Summing up what he likes best about using Logic Pro, Riley said he appreciates its integration. "The great thing about Logic is that all the different parts of the program are on the same screen," he said. "Using the sequencer or doing a piece using software instruments, I can see and change anything when I want to. You can grab any part at any time. It's a valuable aid to composing."

13

Lesson Files	Logic 8_BTB_Files > Lessons > 13_A Blues for Trane_Start.logic
Media	Logic 8_BTB_Files > Media > A Blues for Trane
Time	This lesson takes approximately 1 hour to complete.
Goals	Configure Logic for surround sound mixing
	Position signals within the surround field
	Apply multi-channel effects
	Check your mix with multi-channel analysis tools
	Encode your surround mix for DVD-Audio and DVD-Video

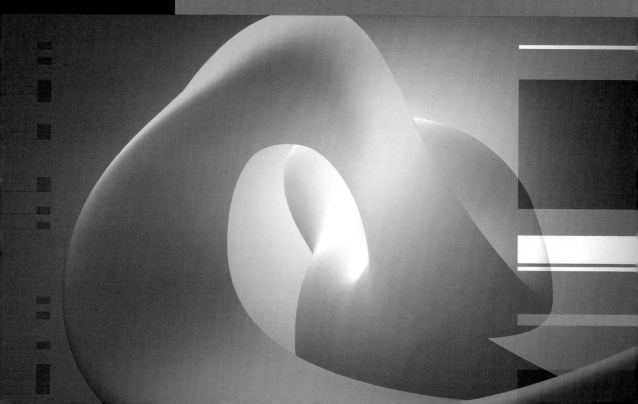

Lesson 13
Working with Surround

Surround sound production has rapidly increased in recent years, due mostly to the proliferation of home theater systems. Not only are surround video (DVD-Video) titles proliferating at a rapid pace, but there is also an increase in the production of surround audio (DVD-Audio, Super Audio CD) titles as well.

Logic provides sophisticated tools to produce a professional surround sound mix, whether you are creating content for visual media (video, film, video games, and so on), or producing surround music.

In this lesson, you will explore the entire workflow of a surround music project, from setup to mixing to encoding.

> **NOTE** ▶ To complete this lesson, you will need an audio interface with at least six outputs wired to a six-channel surround sound playback system. If you do not have such a setup, you can still follow the exercises, but you will hear the results in stereo only.

Configuring Logic for Surround

Working in surround can encompass multiple surround formats, depending on the target playback system (home theater, movie theater, and so on). While Logic can accommodate all popular surround configurations from quadraphonic to 7.1, you will most likely work within the 5.1 (ITU 775) format for your surround productions. This format consists of three speakers across the front (left, center, right) and two speakers in the rear (left surround, right surround). The *.1* in the name represents a sixth channel for low-frequency effects (LFE) sent to a subwoofer.

> **MORE INFO** ▶ The *Logic Pro 8 User Manual* provides excellent explanations and diagrams of the various surround formats. See page 808 for details.

In this lesson, you will mix a jazz quintet session in 5.1 surround format and place the listener in the middle of the performers. Let's start by opening the project file used in this lesson.

1 Choose File > Open.

2 In the Open window's file selector box, go to Music > Logic 8_BTB_Files > Lessons and open **13_A Blues for Trane_Start.logic**.

3 Play the project to familiarize yourself with the material you will be mixing.

Assigning Audio Interface Outputs

To enable Logic to play a project through each speaker in your surround sound setup, the amplifier for each speaker must be connected to a separate output in your audio interface. When all of your hardware connections have been made, before you can begin mixing, you need to configure Logic to specify which output is connected to which speaker. This is done within Logic's preferences.

1 Choose Logic Pro > Preferences > Audio.

   The Audio preferences are displayed.

2 Click the Surround tab.

   The Surround tab contains options for configuring your surround setup.

3   Click the Output tab, if necessary.

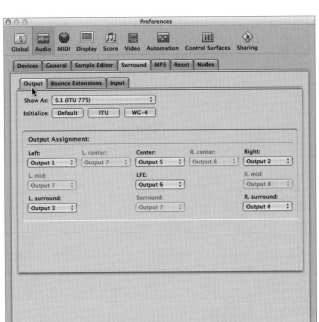

In the Output tab, you can specify which surround channel connects to which output of your audio interface (and, ultimately, to your speakers). While you can match all conceivable setups, the default configuration is highly recommended, and it represents an established standard.

Notice that several channel assignments are dimmed and cannot be set within the Output Assignment area (L. center, R. center, L. mid, R. mid., Surround). These channels are filtered by the Show As menu, which is set to 5.1 (ITU 775) by default. The surround format chosen in the Show As menu makes available only the appropriate output channels.

4   Click the Show As pop-up menu to see the available configurations. When you're done, make sure to leave the setting at its default, 5.1 (ITU 775).

5   Look at each of the channel assignments within the Output Assignments area to verify that your system corresponds to this routing.

6   Close the Preferences window.

Setting the Project Surround Format

While the Surround preferences are global (and remain the same from project to project), each project can be independently configured to any surround format. The surround format is set in the Audio project settings.

1 Choose File > Project Settings > Audio.

The Audio settings for the project are displayed.

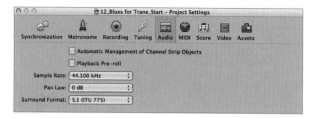

By default, a project's surround format is set to 5.1 (ITU 775), as seen in the Surround Format menu. Alternative formats can be selected in that menu.

2 Click the Surround Format pop-up menu to see the available configurations, making sure to leave the setting at its default, 5.1 (ITU 775).

3 Close the Project Settings window.

Mixing in Surround

In the Mixer, look at the signal routing of the channels. The mix includes mono and stereo channels set to output through a single stereo output channel (Output 1-2). Some channels are also routed via buses to various submixes (Aux 2, 3, and 4), which, in turn, are also set to output through the single stereo output channel. In short, everything is configured to create a stereo mix.

To create a surround mix, you need to change the channel outputs from stereo to surround. You can do this by changing the assignment from a stereo output to surround in the Output slot.

> **NOTE ▶** It is important not to change the output settings for the channels being routed to submixes (trumpet, bass, drums), as that would change the signal flow. Instead, change the output settings for their respective submix channels (Aux 2 through 4) from stereo to surround.

1   Shift-click the Sax M130, Piano LR, Tpt Sub, Bass Sub, and Drums Sub channels to select them.

2   On any of the selected channel strips, click the Output slot and choose Surround in the pop-up menu.

The Pan or Balance control on each selected channel changes to a Surround Panner. To the right of the Mixer, you'll notice that the Output 1-2 channel has been eliminated and that the Master channel now has a multisegment level meter.

3   Click the Mixer background to deselect all channels.

Using the Surround Panner

The Surround Panner is used to position signals within the surround field. Each speaker in the output array is represented by a small blue dot on the circumference of the circle, and the white dot represents the signal position. You can change a channel's position within the surround field by dragging the white dot within the Surround Panner.

1   On the Sax M130 channel, click the Solo button.

2   Press Control–Command–Right Arrow/Left Arrow (the Go to Next/Previous Marker key commands) to locate to the Head marker.

3   Turn on Cycle mode.

4   Start playback, listening to the saxophone.

5   In the Surround Panner, drag the white dot to about the 10 o'clock position, slightly in from the edge.

The saxophone emanates from the front left side of the surround field.

As you most definitely discovered, it is difficult to precisely position a sound using the tiny Surround Panner in the channel. Fortunately, you can open the Surround Panner in a magnified window.

6   Unsolo the Sax M130 channel and solo the Tpt Sub channel.

7   On the Tpt Sub channel, double-click the Surround Panner.

The Surround Panner window opens.

8   Drag the blue puck to the 2 o'clock position, just in from the edge.

9   Stop playback.

In this enlarged view, it is much easier to accurately position a signal within the surround field. In addition, the Surround Panner window also provides precise visual feedback as to the angle (±180°) and diversity (distance from the surround field's center) of the positioning. These values are represented both graphically and numerically.

TIP ▶ Speaker output can be muted by clicking the speaker icons within the Surround Panner.

Adjusting Center and LFE Levels

The Surround Panner window includes sliders to independently adjust the amount of signal sent to the center and LFE channels. By default, the Center Level slider is set to unity (feeding signal to the center channel), while the LFE is muted.

In this exercise, you will adjust the center and LFE levels of various channels. To most effectively do this, start off by improving the Mixer's ergonomics.

1   Drag the Surround Panner window to the Mixer, just to the right of the last mixer channel.

2   At the top left of the Surround Panner window, click the Link button.

When the Link button is on, you can use a single window to display the Surround Panner of any channel strip, without the clutter of multiple windows.

3 Play the project.

4 In the Surround Panner window, drag the Center Level slider all the way to the left, muting the output.

As the amount of signal sent to the center channel is eliminated, the placement of the trumpet should become more focused on the front right side of the surround field.

5 Unsolo the Tpt Sub channel, and solo the Bass Sub channel.

6 On the Bass Sub channel, double-click the Surround Panner.

The Surround Panner window displays the settings for the Bass Sub channel (because linking is turned on).

7 While watching the visual readouts, position the blue puck at an Angle of about 150 (degrees) and a Diversity of about 0.40.

> **TIP** ▶ Double-clicking the numeric displays at the top of the Surround Panner window and entering a number with the computer keyboard will precisely set angle and diversity.

8 Drag the Center Level slider all the way to the left, muting the output.

9 Drag the LFE Level to the right, to a value of –15.5 dB.

As the amount of signal sent to the LFE channel is increased, the bass frequencies should become more pronounced, reinforced by the subwoofer.

10 After you've had a chance to hear the results of your actions, stop playback.

11 Unsolo the Bass Sub channel.

Balancing Stereo to Surround Signals

Depending on the type of input signal (mono, stereo, or surround), Logic uses slightly different types of Surround Panners. So far you've been working with mono source signals. In this exercise, you will use the Surround Panner to accurately position stereo signals in the surround field.

> **NOTE** ▶ A signal's channel input format is indicated by the number of level meters and by the symbol on the button below them. See page 816 of the *Logic Pro 8 User Manual* for detailed descriptions and illustrations of each input format.

1   Solo the Sax M130, Piano LR, Tpt Sub, and Bass Sub channels.

In this exercise, you will adjust the surround placement of the stereo piano channel within the context of other instruments that are already positioned.

2   On the Piano LR channel, double-click the Surround Panner.

The Surround Panner window displays the Piano LR channel, which is a stereo source.

When using a stereo source, the Surround Panner window contains an additional parameter, *Spread*, which indicates the width of the stereo signal in the surround field. This is represented graphically by the L and R pucks (representing the left and right side of the stereo image), and numerically at the top of the window.

3   Play the project, listening to the piano's position in the surround field.

As you can hear, the piano sounds a bit wide, crowding the saxophone and trumpet on either side of it.

The spread of the signal can be adjusted by dragging the L and R pucks in the Surround Panner window.

4   Try dragging the L puck to the left and right, increasing and decreasing the spread while listening to the results.

You have to be careful when dragging the L or R pucks, as you can inadvertently change the angle and diversity. To avoid doing this, Command-drag the L or R puck. This will lock down the diversity and angle, allowing you to adjust only the spread.

5   Position the blue puck to an Angle of 0.0 and Diversity of 0.12.

6   Command-drag the L puck toward the center blue puck until the Spread value is +34.

In effect, you narrowed the stereo signal slightly, causing less overlap with the saxophone and trumpet in the surround field.

7   Stop playback.

8   Option-click an active Solo button on any of the soloed channels.

All the Solo buttons are turned off at once.

Let's now do the same thing with another stereo source, placing the drums submix within the surround field while listening to the entire mix.

9   In the Drums Sub channel, double-click the Surround Panner to display its settings in the Surround Panner window.

10 Play the project.

11 By moving the pucks or changing the numeric values, position the stereo source within the surround field at an Angle of −157.0, Diversity of 0.27, and Spread of +91.

12 Remove any signal fed to the center channel by muting the center level.

This places the drums behind and to the left side in its own space within the surround mix.

13 Stop playback.

14 Close the Surround Panner window.

Using Surround Effects

To preserve imaging, surround mixing often requires the use of specialized surround processors. These are, in essence, effects that independently process the individual channels of the given surround format. There are two types of surround processors available within Logic: multi-channel and multi-mono. With multi-channel effects, the surround channels are tightly integrated, or coupled, processing the entire surround source at once. Multi-mono effects, on the other hand, are essentially multiple mono plug-ins that are individually applied to each surround channel in the signal path.

In this exercise, you will assign both types of surround format plug-ins to channels, creating surround send and insert effects to aid in producing a professional-sounding mix.

> **NOTE** ▶ Logic's surround plug-ins work in all surround formats available to the application (Quadraphonic, LCRS, 5.1, 6.1, 7.1, and so on). The surround format chosen for the project determines the surround format of the plug-ins.

Using Multi-channel Effects

Immersing the listener within an artificially created ambience is the primary goal of surround production. To aid in this task, multi-channel reverb is used to simulate acoustic environments within the surround field. What differentiates the surround reverb processor from its mono and stereo cousins is its ability to simultaneously receive input from and send output to more than two channels.

For this exercise, you will use a multi-channel version of Logic's convolution reverb, Space Designer, as a send effect. This plug-in not only sends and receives over multiple channels; it also utilizes specialized surround recordings of real acoustic spaces for impulse responses.

1   Solo the Sax M130 channel.

2   Click the first Send slot on the Sax M130 channel and choose Bus > Bus 1 (Aux 1).

   A new aux channel is created, receiving input from Bus 1.

3   Below the meters on the Aux 1 channel, click the channel Format button and select Surround from the pop-up menu.

The channel switches from a mono channel to a surround channel. The level meters now display six segments instead of one or two (mono or stereo, respectively). These represent each of the six channels used in a 5.1 configuration.

4 On the Aux 1 channel, click the first Insert slot and choose Reverb > Space Designer > 5.1.

The Space Designer interface opens.

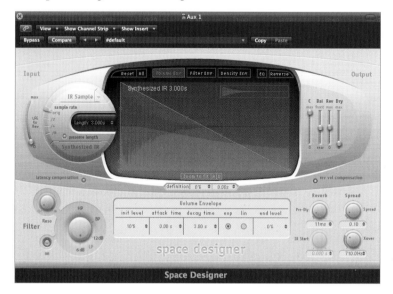

5   Click the Settings menu and choose 04 Surround Spaces > 01 Surround Rooms > 02.9 Hansa Studio +.

Space Designer loads the surround impulse response recording and any control configurations saved to the preset.

NOTE ▶ The new surround impulse responses included with Logic Pro 8 have been recorded with a variety of surround recording techniques, such as circle B-format, omni B-format, and discrete omni. You will even find different format recordings of the same acoustic space.

At first glance, the Space Designer interface looks identical to the stereo version that you explored in Lesson 8, "Working with Mixer Channels." However, closer inspection reveals that the wet-dry controls are replaced by four sliders. Using these you can adjust the amount of wet and dry signal, and you can control the balance between the front and rear speakers. An additional slider is provided to adjust the amount of signal sent to the center channel.

6   Drag the center channel output slider (labeled C) down to a value of –4.0 dB.

This reduces the amount of reverb signal sent to the center channel, creating a more or less equal dispersion of reverb across the surround field.

7   Close the Space Designer window.

As it is now, the Sax M130 channel is set to send to the surround reverb post fader, but pre Surround Panner. In order to have the surround reverb preserve positional information when generating reflections, you need to assign the send post pan.

8   Click-hold the Send slot on the Sax M130 channel and select Post Pan.

9   Play the project.

10   On the Sax M130 channel, increase the send amount to Bus 1 (Aux 1) to –14.0 dB.

You should not only hear the saxophone localized off to the left front of the surround field but also hear the processed signal in all five speakers. This creates a convincing ambient effect of the saxophone in a three-dimensional space.

NOTE ▶ The color of the Send level knob ring denotes pre- or post-pan routing. A green ring denotes pre-pan, a blue ring post-pan routing.

11   Unsolo the Sax M130 channel.

12   Assign the sends on the Piano LR, Tpt Sub, Bass Sub, and Drums Sub channels to Bus 1 (Aux 1), and set each to Post Pan.

13   Adjust the send amount of each of the above channels to the surround reverb, listening to how they sit within the ambient surround field.

14   Stop playback.

Using Multi-mono Insert Effects

In addition to the surround version of Space Designer, Logic offers multi-mono versions of many types of insert effects, including EQ, compression, and modulation types. These are applied specifically to surround input signals and can be thought of as multiple instantiations of the same effect, one for each surround channel. What makes these multi-mono effects especially powerful is the ability to independently process the LFE channel, which is often called for when you're creating a surround mix.

The surround professional generally can't predict how a carefully crafted mix will translate to consumer setups because the subwoofer is often the most inaccurately configured component in a typical home theater system. In addition, the bass-management systems used in consumer receivers vary widely from manufacturer to manufacturer. For this reason, it is recommended that you apply a low-pass filter to the output of the LFE channel while mixing and mastering to catch any stray high frequencies that might otherwise get through.

You can accomplish this by inserting a multi-channel version of the Channel EQ on the Master channel, processing only the LFE channel while leaving the others untouched.

1   On the Master channel, click the first Insert slot and choose EQ > Channel EQ > Multi Mono.

The Channel EQ interface appears.

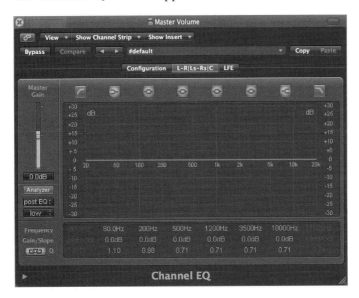

Multi-channel surround versions of plug-ins display an additional set of buttons in the plug-in header compared with their mono or stereo versions. These buttons provide access to surround routing and configuration options.

2   At the top of the interface, click the Configuration tab.

The plug-in interface changes to display the configuration of the multiple channels.

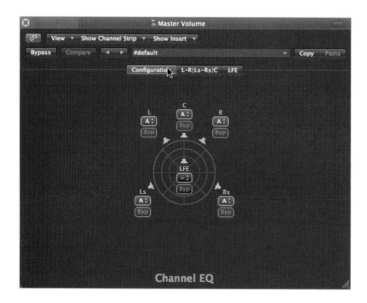

Within the Configuration tab, you can bypass the effect on a channel-by-channel basis. The small pop-up menu located under each channel represents a form of grouping, not unlike the channel groups you created in an earlier mixing lesson (Lesson 9, "Controlling Signal Flow"). Assigning multiple channels to a group (A, B, C, or none) in this window allows you to simultaneously bypass all the channels in the same group.

3   Click the Bypass button on any channel except the LFE channel.

All the channels assigned to group A (L, C, R, Ls, Rs) are bypassed, leaving the LFE channel active.

4   At the top of the interface, click the LFE tab.

The plug-in interface changes to display the EQ settings for the LFE channel.

Click the Low-Pass Filter button (at the far right), enabling the filter band.

5   Double-click the Frequency setting for the Low-Pass Filter band, and enter *120*.

6 Drag the Gain/Slope setting for the Low-Pass Filter band down to 48 dB/Oct.

By using a low-pass filter on the LFE channel, you will remove all frequencies that might cause undue muddiness in the subwoofer channel.

NOTE ▶ There is no hard and fast rule for selecting the frequency for the low-pass filter used on the LFE channel. Usually it is set between 80 Hz and 120 Hz, and it can be different for each monitoring system. To make matters more confusing, some consumer surround systems utilize their own low-pass filters for removing unwanted high frequencies sent to the subwoofer.

Checking the Surround Mix

Logic also offers specialized surround plug-ins that enable you to check your mix. These help identify problem spots by isolating individual channels as well as visually displaying the content within the surround field.

1 On the Master channel, click the second Insert slot and choose Utility > Multichannel Gain > 5.1.

The Multichannel Gain plug-in appears.

The Multichannel Gain plug-in allows you control the gain and phase of each channel of a surround track or bus independently. You can also use the plug-in to individually mute each of the surround channels, allowing you to isolate the speaker output.

2   Play the project.

3   Try muting channels individually or in combination to isolate speaker output.

> **NOTE** ▶ The order of channels as displayed in the channel level meters is determined by the Channel Order setting in the Display preferences (Logic Pro > Preferences > Display). Logic's default Internal setting (L, R, Ls, Rs, C, LFE) can be somewhat confusing if you're using the Multichannel Gain plug-in because the two interfaces display the channels in a different order. However, this can be remedied by choosing the Centered setting (Ls, L, C, R, Rs, LFE) in Logic's preferences, which reflects the Multichannel Gain order.

4   After you have a chance to experiment, stop the playback.

5   Make sure that all channels are unmuted within the Multichannel Gain plug-in.

6   On the Master channel, click the third Insert slot and choose Metering > MultiMeter > 5.1.

The surround MultiMeter plug-in appears.

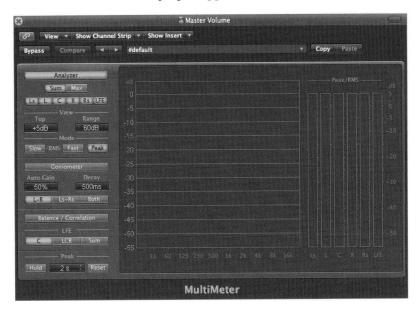

7   Play the project, observing the MultiMeter's frequency analyzer and level meters.

The surround version of the MultiMeter plug-in provides a suite of helpful analysis tools for examining the channels of your surround mix. In addition to a multi-channel frequency spectrum analyzer, level meters, and goniometer, the MultiMeter includes an excellent surround balance analyzer.

8   At the bottom left of the plug-in interface, click the Balance/Correlation button.

The main window displays sound position within the surround field, which responds dynamically to the signal.

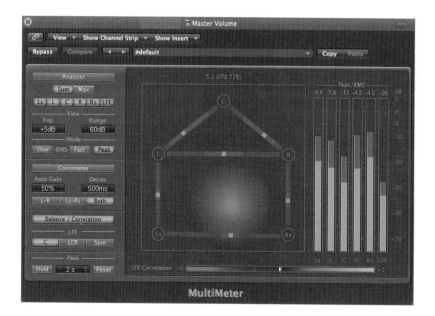

9   Turn off Cycle mode.

10   As the project is playing, listen to your surround mix while watching the balance display.

     Now that you've checked sound placement for your surround mix, you can check the LFE Correlation meter to see if the LFE is causing any phase cancellation. This meter can be displayed in a variety of ways, comparing the phase of the LFE channel to the center, the front (left, center, and right), or the sum of all channels.

11   In the LFE section just below the Balance/Correlation button, click the Sum button.

12   If necessary, rewind to the beginning of the project and start playback, watching the LFE Correlation meter at the bottom of the MultiMeter interface.

     The correlation meter moves to the left of the middle point toward –1, indicating that the LFE channel is out of phase with the other channels. This can be remedied in the Multichannel Gain plug-in by reversing the phase of the LFE channel.

13   In the Master channel, double-click the Multichannel Gain plug-in to display it in the linked window.

14 Click the Phase Invert button for the LFE channel.

15 In the Master channel, double-click the MultiMeter plug-in to display it in the linked window.

The Correlation meter now moves to the right of the middle, toward +1, indicating that the LFE channel is in phase with the rest of the surround channels.

16 Stop the playback after you've checked your mix.

Down Mixing

The act of reducing a surround mix to a four-channel (quadraphonic, LCRS) or two-channel (stereo) version is called down mixing. To aid in this, Logic Pro includes a specialized Down Mixer plug-in that can be applied to the Master channel, automatically folding down the surround mix to a specified format. As most consumer DVD-Video players incorporate a built-in down mixing process, this enables you to check your mix's compatibility with these down mixing systems, as well as quickly create new format mixes for delivery.

1 On the Master channel, click the fourth Insert slot and choose Utility > Down Mixer > 5.1→Stereo.

The Master channel changes to display stereo level meters, and the Down Mixer plug-in appears in the linked window.

2 Play the project, listening to the stereo down mix, which should now be emanating only from the left and right speakers.

> **NOTE** ▸ If necessary, you can adjust the levels of the input surround channels using the level sliders.

3   Stop the playback.

4   In the Master channel, click the Down Mixer plug-in and choose No Plug-in from the pop-up menu, thereby removing it from the channel strip.

> **NOTE** ▸ In addition to its suite of surround effect plug-ins, Logic Pro 8 includes surround versions of the ES2 and Sculpture software instruments.

Encoding Surround Projects

Depending upon the delivery format, different techniques exist for encoding a surround project for distribution. In this exercise, you will create a DVD-Audio disc, as well as encode a surround mix in the Dolby Digital (AC3) format, ready for inclusion in a DVD-Video disc.

Creating DVD-Audio Discs

New to Logic Pro 8 is the ability to create DVD-Audio discs without the need for an external encoding application. This is accomplished within the Bounce window.

1   At the bottom of the Master channel, click the Bnce (Bounce) button.

The Bounce window opens.

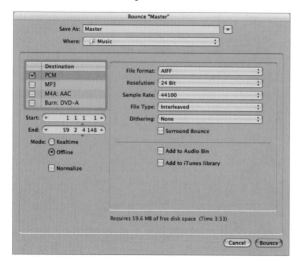

2   In the Destination area on the left, deselect any active checkboxes (PCM, MP3, M4A: AAC).

3   Select the Burn: DVD-A checkbox.

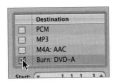

The DVD-A options appear to the right of the Destination box.

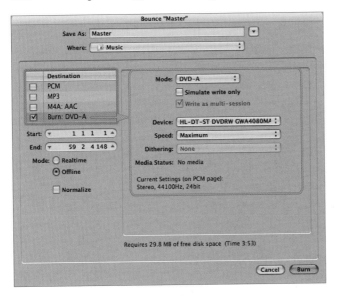

NOTE ▶ If you've never burned a DVD-A before, you might see Burn: CDDA (CD audio) in the menu instead of Burn: DVD-A. If this is the case, select DVD-A from the Mode menu to burn a DVD-A instead of a regular CD.

4   In the Save As field, enter *Working with Surround*.

5   Insert a blank DVD into your DVD burner.

6   Click the Burn button.

After the burn process is completed, you will have a DVD-Audio disc that can be played in the majority of commercial DVD players (make sure your DVD player supports the DVD-A format before playing your disc).

NOTE ▸ You cannot use the Bounce command to create compressed surround files (AAC, ALAC, MP3).

Encoding Dolby Digital Files (AC3) Using Compressor

Encoding surround sound for DVD-Video entails a two-step process:

▸ Creating a master multi-channel file

▸ Encoding a composite surround format file from the master multi-channel file using compression/encoding software or hardware.

A master multi-channel file is also created in the Bounce window.

1 At the bottom of the Master channel, click the Bnce button.

The Bounce window opens.

2 Deselect the Burn: DVD-A checkbox.

3 Select the PCM checkbox.

4 In the options to the right of the Destination box, select the Surround Bounce checkbox.

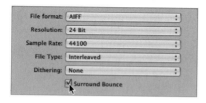

5 At the lower right of the window, click the Bounce button.

NOTE ▸ Logic automatically sets the file path for bounces to a Bounces folder created within the project folder.

A bounce is performed, creating an interleaved multi-channel file named **Working with Surround.aif**.

Now that the master multi-channel file has been created, you can import it into an application such as Apple's Compressor (included with Logic Studio) for encoding as a Dolby Digital (AC3) file.

NOTE ▶ In order to create encoded Dolby Digital (AC3) surround files, some encoder applications need to import multiple "stems," or submix files, corresponding to each surround output channel instead of a single interleaved multi-channel file. You can create these stems when bouncing by selecting Split from the File Type menu within the Bounce window. The resulting files will have extensions added to their names, corresponding to their derived channels (L, R, C, Ls, Rs, LFE).

6   Open the Compressor application.

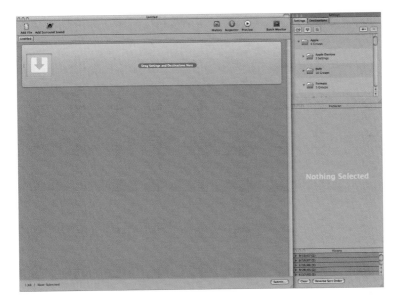

NOTE ▶ Due to the configurability of Compressor, your window arrangement might appear differently than the picture above.

7   Click the Add File button at the top left.

8   Within the file browser, go to Logic 8_BTB_Files > Media > A Blues for Trane > Bounces and select **Working with Surround.aif**.

9 Click the Open button.

The **Working with Surround.aif** file is added to the Batch.

10 Within the Settings window, choose Apple > Formats > Audio > Dolby Digital Professional 5.1.

> **NOTE** ▶ The actual data settings are displayed for each of the presets in the Inspector window to the right of the Settings window.

11 Drag the Dolby Digital Professional 5.1 setting and drop it on the **Working with Surround.aif** icon in the Batch window.

12 Click the Submit button at the lower-right corner of the Batch window.

The submit dialog appears prompting you to name the submitted batch.

13 Click the Submit.

Compressor encodes the interleaved multi-channel **Working with Surround.aif** file as a Dolby Digital AC3 file, ready for inclusion into a DVD-Video project. The new file will be located within the same folder location as the **Working with Surround.aif** file (Music > Logic 8_BTB_Files > Media > A Blues for Trane > Bounces).

As surround sound becomes more and more prevalent in the audio world, it becomes increasingly important to acquire at least a working knowledge of surround mixing. The techniques learned in this lesson will help form the foundation for improving your skills in this growing domain.

> **MORE INFO** ▶ For additional information on Compressor, see Brian Gary's *Apple Pro Training Series: Compressor 3 Quick-Reference Guide* from Peachpit Press.

Lesson Review

1. Where do you assign the outputs of your audio interface to corresponding surround channels?

2. Where do you set the surround format for an individual project?

3. How does the stereo input Surround Panner differ from that of other input formats (mono and surround)?

4. How does the surround version of the Space Designer plug-in differ from the mono and stereo versions when used as a send effect?

5. How do multi-channel insert plug-ins differ from the mono and stereo versions?

6. How can you quickly create a four- or two-channel version of your surround mix?

7. What two steps are involved in creating a Dolby Digital (AC3) file ready for DVD-Video?

Answers

1. Assigning the outputs of your audio interface to corresponding surround channels is done by choosing Preferences > Audio > Surround and clicking the Output tab.

2. The surround format for a project is set in the Audio tab of the Project Settings window.

3. The stereo input to the Surround Panner offers an additional Spread control.

4. The surround version of the Space Designer plug-in loads surround format impulse responses, and it has additional controls to adjust the center level as well as the balance between the front and rear speakers.

5. Multi-channel insert plug-ins have additional configuration settings allowing you to bypass any surround channel. In addition, the LFE channel can be processed independently from the rest of the surround channels.

6. You can quickly create a four- or two-channel version of your surround mix by applying the Down Mixer plug-in to the Master channel.

7. To create a Dolby Digital (AC3) file ready for DVD-Video, you must bounce an interleaved multi-channel surround file from within Logic, then encode the file using a compression/encoder application such as Compressor.

14

Lesson Files Logic 8_BTB_Files > Lessons > 14_Monterey_Start.logic

Media Logic 8_BTB_Files > Media > Monterey Sanctuary

Time This lesson takes approximately 90 minutes to complete.

Goals Set up synchronization for time-locked playback of audio and video

Import media in several formats into a project file while retaining time code data

Modify tempos with beat mapping to sync project events to the picture

Sync audio events to specific SMPTE positions

Scoring to Picture

Composing music for film and video has been greatly facilitated by the advent of computer-based music production. Methods for calculating tempo and ensuring synchronization between music and picture have been made simpler by computers powerful enough to stream digital video and audio in the same application.

Scoring to picture is a collaborative effort integrating a variety of media (including digital video and audio) that are often produced by more than one person or facility. As a result, a key skill is the ability to import and work with many media elements in a variety of formats while maintaining the same timing references, especially when the music needs to synchronize with critical moments in the film or video footage.

In this lesson you will work with a synchronized digital video clip in a Logic project, adjusting its tempo to coordinate with significant events in the movie. You'll also align musical events with SMPTE time to accentuate visual cues.

Setting Up Synchronization

While it is still entirely appropriate to work with an external video deck synchronized to audio using SMPTE time code (converted to MIDI Time Code), the norm for today's media composers is to work with digital video clips in a Logic project.

Using digital video clips simplifies video-to-music synchronization. You no longer have to add significant pre-roll time at the beginning of a project to provide time for the hardware deck to lock in to sync, and you can instantly locate to any point within the project and the video. What's more, the digital video (along with all the synchronization settings) can be saved in the project folder for easy archiving and retrieval.

Logic leverages the Apple QuickTime engine for video playback and, therefore, can open a digital video clip (commonly referred to by the single term *movie*) in any format supported by the QuickTime standard.

In this exercise, you will open a digital video clip in a new Logic project, adjusting the synchronization settings to allow for time-locked playback and reference of audio and video.

Let's start by creating a project file around a useful stock project template created for working with video.

1   Choose File > New.

    The Templates dialog opens.

2   In the Collection column, click the Produce folder.

3   In the Template column, click the Music For Picture button.

    The project template Music For Picture is opened, and a Save As dialog appears.

4   Select the Include Assets checkbox, if necessary.

5   Select the "Copy external audio files to project folder" and "Copy movie files to project folder" checkboxes.

    When "Copy movie files to project folder" is selected, a message appears alerting you that copying a movie file could take up valuable disk space.

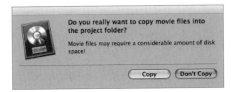

NOTE ▶ The file you will be working with for this exercise is fairly small (19.4 MB), so it should have minimal impact on your disk space.

6   Click Copy.

7   Type *Score to Picture* in the Save As field.

8   Set the save location to Music > Logic 8_BTB_Files > Lessons > Completed.

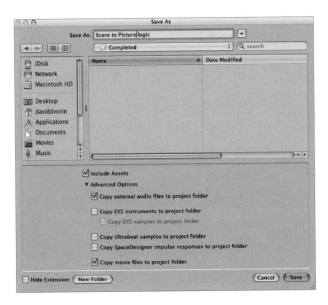

9   Click Save.

Before you begin the lesson, take a minute to explore what the Music For Picture template offers. The Bar ruler is set to display SMPTE time position as well as bars and beats, and a giant SMPTE display is floating within the Arrange area. Both provide easy visual reference to valuable timing information that you will use when scoring to picture.

NOTE ▸ You can display SMPTE time in the Bar ruler of any project by clicking the small down arrow located to the right of the Bar ruler and choosing one of the three settings with *Time* in its name. Displaying the SMPTE ruler also affects what is displayed in the help tags when you're editing regions and events. You can configure the Transport bar to display a large dedicated floating SMPTE time display, which provides easy readability at long distances (especially useful when you're working across the room from your display). Do this by Control-clicking the SMPTE time display within the Transport bar and choosing Open Giant SMPTE Display.

10 Close the Media area by clicking the button in the Toolbar.

Opening the Movie

You can see that Screenset 1 has been configured to display the global Marker, Signature, Tempo, and Video tracks, as these tracks are commonly used when working with video. The Video track provides many useful functions for importing and working with video.

1   In the Video track, click the Open Movie button.

The Open window appears.

NOTE ▸ You can also open a movie by choosing Options > Movies > Open Movie.

2   Go to Music > Logic 8_BTB_Files > Lessons > 14_Movie Files and open **Monterey.mp4**.

The **Monterey.mp4** video opens in a floating window, and a video thumbnail of the movie is created in the Video track.

NOTE ▸ When working with digital video clips in Logic, it is best to use proxy movies. A proxy movie is a low-resolution, highly compressed version of the full-resolution movie that places less processing and disk access strain on your computer. Usually the video editor will provide the compressed clips, but they can also be created in applications like QuickTime Pro. If you are preparing the clips yourself, it is advisable to use high-compression formats such as MPEG-4 or H.264.

3 Play the project to view the video content with which you will be working.

Playback of the movie is controlled by Logic's Transport bar, and it plays in sync with the project.

NOTE ▶ You won't hear audio when playing the video clip because there is no audio recorded in the file.

4 While it's playing, click anywhere in the Bar ruler to locate to another position.

The movie relocates in sync with the project.

5 Drag the playhead in QuickTime Player to the right.

The project relocates in sync with the movie.

6 Stop playback.

NOTE ▶ You can output video via FireWire to an NTSC display (which requires a DV-to-video converter box) as well as to Apple Cinema Display via Digital Cinema Desktop. Choose File > Project Settings > Video and choose a setting from the Video Output pop-up menu. For FireWire video streaming, it is necessary to compensate for the latency in the FireWire setup. This will be a constant amount that you can adjust by choosing Logic Pro > Preferences > Video and dragging the External Video to Project slider until the image and sound synchronize.

Working with SMPTE Time Code

You can establish synchronization between the video and Logic just by opening a QuickTime movie in a project, but a few settings should be set so that the time code will display properly. These settings are found in the Synchronization project settings.

1 Choose File > Project Settings > Synchronization.

The Project Settings window opens, displaying the Synchronization tab.

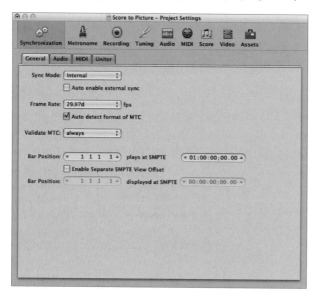

To ensure that the time code display is accurate, the project should reflect the movie's frame rate. This is set in the Frame Rate pop-up menu.

2 Click the Frame Rate menu and choose 24. (This is the frame rate of the digital video clip.)

> **NOTE** ▶ The original footage was shot at 24 fps to high-definition video.

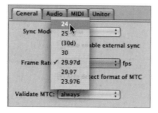

The SMPTE start time can be set individually for each project to synchronize with the video. You will be using a start time of 1:00:00:00.00 for this project, so it is not necessary to change the project template's default setting.

The next thing you need to do is set the Movie Start time. Usually you would set this to match the SMPTE burn-in time code in the video, ensuring that Logic's time code display will match the time code on the video. However, the clip you are using has no burn-in. The video editor did supply the SMPTE offset information so that the audio can be synchronized with the video, indicating an offset of 1 second and 9 frames. Once the Movie Start time is set, the movie will start just shortly after the project starts. This information is also entered in the Video project settings.

3   Click the Video button at the top of the Project Settings window to display the Video settings.

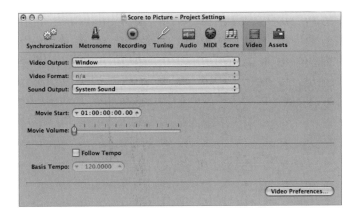

4   In the Movie Start field, single-click the number and enter *01:00:01:09.00*. Press Return.

The video will now start 1 second, 9 frames into the project.

5   Close the Project Settings window.

6   Play the project from the beginning, observing the SMPTE display in relation to the video.

7 Stop playback after the first 10 or 15 seconds.

8 Drag both the movie and the SMPTE Transport display to the lower-right side of the Arrange area to make space for track content.

9 Press Control–Left Arrow as needed to zoom out horizontally, displaying about 1 minute and 10 seconds (37 bars) in the Bar ruler.

Now that you've taken some time to configure the screen arrangement, let's lock the screenset.

10 Lock the screenset by choosing Screenset1 > Lock.

Importing Media

Integration between the editing suites used by video editors, sound designers, engineers, and composers has traditionally proved to be a hurdle when these groups collaborate on media projects. However, integration has been improved with the development of formats that allow you to exchange media with colleagues while maintaining time code and even automation information.

In the following exercises you will import media in different formats into the project file while retaining the time code information.

Importing XML from Final Cut Pro

Logic supports Extensible Markup Language (XML) files as an interchange format. XML is used by some of Apple's Pro applications, such as the video production application Final Cut Pro, to store relevant information. This information can be exchanged between the supporting applications. For example, XML exchange allows you to import audio files used in a Final Cut Pro project, including their timing and automation information, into Logic's Arrange area.

For this exercise, an XML file has been created from a Final Cut Pro project. This file contains information about the file locations, timing, and volume keyframes (automation) for three sound effects that the video editor has placed in a Final Cut Pro sequence.

1   In the track list, select the Audio 1 track.

2   Choose File > Import.

3   Go to Music > Logic 8_BTB_Files > Lessons > 14_XML Exports and open
    Monterey XML.

    A dialog opens, displaying the sequence information from the original Final Cut Pro project file.

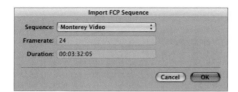

4   Click OK.

    A prompt appears asking you to relink the XML file's associated audio files by choosing the correct file path.

5   Click OK.

6 In the file selector, select the desired file from Music > Logic 8_BTB_Files > Lessons > 14_FX from FCP.

Repeat this process for each file requested by Logic, if necessary. All the files are located in the same folder.

Another prompt appears, asking if you'd like to convert the sample rate.

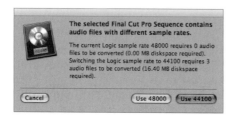

7 Click Use 48000.

NOTE ▶ The Music For Picture template has a default project sample rate setting of 48 kHz, the standard for working in digital video formats. If you wish to change the sample rate when working with this template, choose File > Project Settings > Audio, then choose the desired option in the Sample Rate menu.

The audio files associated with the XML file are imported into four new tracks in the Arrange area.

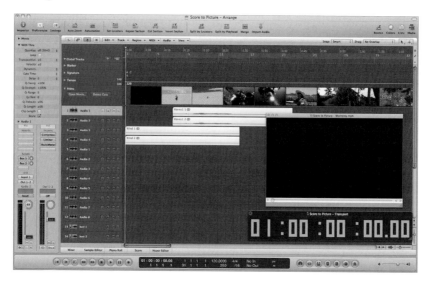

NOTE ► Logic creates pairs of mono tracks panned left and right when importing XML to reflect Final Cut Pro's use of split stereo files (separate mono left and right files) in a project.

8   Press Control–Left Arrow a few times, zooming out horizontally to enable you to see all the imported regions around the video window.

9   In the Arrange area's local menu bar, choose View > Track Automation.

The volume automation information associated with the imported audio regions is displayed.

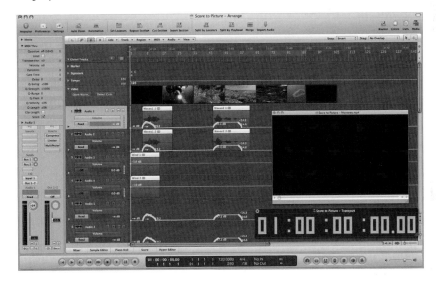

This information was created as volume keyframes in Final Cut Pro and converted to track automation with the Read buttons already turned on for each track.

When importing associated audio from an XML file, Logic will automatically create tracks assigned to the first group of audio channels. The project file you are using in this exercise already has tracks assigned to these channels. As a result, tracks 1 through 4 are duplicated. (You can see the automation duplicated in tracks 5 through 8.) These duplicate tracks aren't needed.

10 Delete tracks 5–8 (the duplicates of audio tracks 1–4 that don't contain audio regions) by individually selecting them and pressing the Delete key.

The duplicates to audio track 1–4 are deleted.

11 Play the project, observing the automation of the channel strip volume fader for track 1.

12 Stop playback.

Importing Broadcast WAVE Files

Broadcast WAVE files are similar to files in other PCM audio file formats (such as AIFF), but they also contain time code information in the header of each file. That information allows you to import and export these audio files between applications while retaining their absolute position in time.

You can test this by importing a sound effect in the Broadcast WAVE format.

1 In the Arrange area's local menu bar, choose View > Track Automation to turn off track automation.

2 Select the Audio 5 track (now track 5), if it is not already selected.

3 Click the Go to Beginning button in the Transport bar to return to 1 1 1 1.

4 Choose File > Import Audio File.

The Open File dialog appears.

5 Go to Music > Logic 8_BTB_Files > Lessons > 14_FX and open **Sub FX.wav**.

The audio file is added to the Audio 5 track at measure 1 1 1 1.

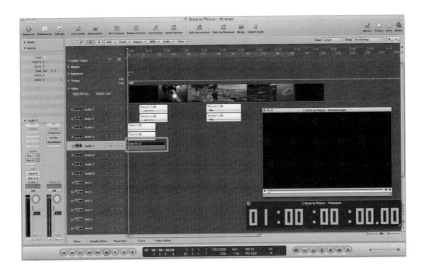

6   With the region highlighted, in the Arrange area's local menu bar, choose Audio >
Move Region to Original Record Position.

The Sub FX Region locates to the time code position contained in the audio file
(01:01:50:10.31).

7   Play the project, observing how the Sub FX audio works with the movie.

> **NOTE ▶** You can save newly recorded audio files in the Broadcast WAVE format by choosing Logic Pro > Preferences > Audio > General and choosing the format in the Recording File Type menu. When this feature is chosen, all saved audio files will include the region's original record position.

Locking SMPTE Position

Now that you've imported the sound effects, it is a good idea to lock their positions to the SMPTE position so that they cannot be moved by mistake. If you time-lock the effects, you can adjust the music tempo freely without changing the effects' placement in relationship to the movie.

1   Choose Edit > Select All.

2   In the Arrange area's local menu bar, choose Region > Lock SMPTE Position.

All regions now display a lock icon in front of their names and cannot be moved.

Now that the regions have been locked, let's see how tempos can be changed without affecting the locked regions' SMPTE positions.

3   Click the background of the Arrange area to deselect all regions.

4   Click the Sub FX region and hold down the mouse button, observing the SMPTE and bar positions displayed in the help tag.

```
Move Regions/Events
5   Sub FX
      56   1   4 112       20   0   3   48
01 : 01 : 50 : 10.31   00 : 00 : 40 : 09.48
```

Note that the SMPTE position is 01:01:50:10.31, which corresponds to the bars and beats position of 56 1 4 112.

5   In the Transport bar, double-click the Tempo display and enter *90*. Press Return.

The project tempo changes to 90 bpm.

6   Click the Sub FX region and hold down the mouse button, again observing the
SMPTE and bar positions displayed in the movie window.

The region's SMPTE position remains the same as before, but the corresponding bars
and beats position is now 42 2 3 144.

When an event is SMPTE locked, it always maintains its time code position, regardless
of the tempo.

Spotting the Movie

When you're choosing the places where music will enhance your project, you can use Logic
during or after the "spotting session" with the director to mark those specific time code
locations for the musical cues. Creating markers for this task enables you to place text
notes at specific SMPTE positions to use as timing references.

Detecting Cuts

Often a director will want musical cues to begin near scene cuts to accentuate the transition from one scene to the next. You can use Logic to identify relevant visual cues in a
video with a unique function called Detect Cuts. When this function is activated, Logic
analyzes the video information and creates a special marker, called a *scene marker*, at
locations where the image changes drastically (such as at scene cuts).

1   In the global Video track, click the Detect Cuts button.

A status bar displays the progress for cut detection.

After the process is completed, scene markers (designated by the movie frame symbol)
are created in the Marker track.

NOTE ▶ Scene markers are automatically locked to SMPTE positions.

2 Press Control–Command–Right Arrow/Left Arrow (Go to Next /Previous Marker) to locate along the scene markers.

The movie locates to scene cuts and other points where the video image changes drastically.

3 Press Stop to return to the beginning of the project.

TIP ▶ The Marker track can contain multiple alternative tracks, similar to those you looked at earlier in the Tempo track (Lesson 3, "Matching Tempo and Pitch"). By choosing options in the Alternative pop-up menu, you can create separate markers for marking musical sections and for spotting sound effects or musical cues.

Using Markers for Beat Mapping

In addition to locating visual points, you can use markers as the basis for beat mapping, which enables you to create tempo adjustments by tying markers to specific bars and beats.

In this exercise, you will use beat mapping to adjust the project tempo and align the downbeat of a measure to punctuate an exact moment in the movie.

1 Click the background of the Arrange area to deselect all currently selected regions.

2 Press the Go to Position key command (/), and, in the As SMPTE field of the Go To Position dialog, enter *1.2.12.3.0*. Press Return.

NOTE ▶ When entering SMPTE time code, you can use colons, periods, or spaces to delineate hours, minutes, frames, and subframes.

The project locates to 01:02:12:03.00 (as seen in the giant SMPTE display).

In the movie, a bird snaps at the camera in a sudden, vicious movement. This would make an excellent place for a musical hit point. To place that hit point, you must first create a marker.

3   From the main menu bar, choose Options > Marker > Create Without Rounding.

NOTE ▶ The Create Without Rounding command creates a marker exactly at the playhead's current position on the SMPTE ruler.

A new marker is created at the current playhead position.

At the current zoom resolution, the marker is difficult to see, but you can zoom in to magnify the current location.

4   Press Control–Right Arrow enough times to view the new marker.

5   Control-click the new marker (Marker 3) and choose Quick Edit Marker from the shortcut menu. Enter *Bird snap* for the marker name, and press Return.

Now that a marker has been created at the visual cue, you can use it as a timing reference for beat mapping. To do this, you must display the Beat Mapping track in the global tracks area.

6   In the track list, Control-click the global tracks area and choose Configure Global Tracks from the shortcut menu.

7   In the Configure Global Tracks window, select the Beat Mapping checkbox.

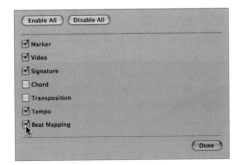

8   Click Done.

The Beat Mapping track is displayed in the global tracks area.

9   Click the disclosure triangle on the Beat Mapping track to expand the track.

Beat mapping lines for selected markers are automatically created in the Beat Mapping tracks. However, to see the line for the "Bird snap" marker, you need to move the playhead slightly (the marker was created at the playhead position).

10 If necessary, scroll the arrange window to the right, so that the video doesn't cover the playhead.

11 Drag in the bottom part of the Bar ruler to move the playhead a little to the left, revealing the beat mapping line.

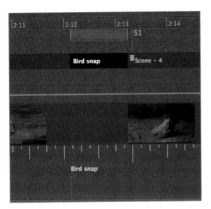

12 In the Beat Mapping track, drag the bar line at measure 50 to the "Bird snap" beat mapping line, connecting the two.

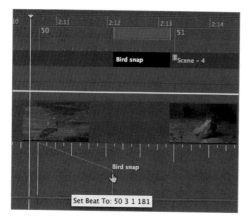

The tempo changes to 89.0066, aligning the "Bird snap" marker with the downbeat of measure 50.

13 Click the Metronome button.

> **NOTE ▶** To hear the click, you should have "Click while playing" selected in File > Project Settings > Metronome.

14 Play the project starting just before measure 50, listening to the click punctuating the movement of the bird snapping.

The click on the downbeat of measure 50 lines up perfectly with the bird snap.

15 Stop playback.

16 Save the project.

> **NOTE ▶** When you save the project, a copy of the video file is saved to a newly created Movies folder within the project folder. You set this up earlier in the lesson by selecting "Copy movie files to project folder" in the Include Assets area when you created a new project from the template.

17 Close the project.

Positioning Events on the Timeline

A common task when working with picture is syncing events to specific SMPTE positions. These events could be sound effects referenced from an Edit Decision List (EDL), or musical hits in the arrangement that punctuate visual cues. Being able to quickly and accurately place events on the timeline is a necessity when you're arranging material in a session that has been locked to an SMPTE position.

For this exercise, you will be using a nearly finished version of the musical cue for the video with which you have been working.

1 Choose File > Open.

2 Go to Music > Logic 8_BTB_Files > Lessons and open **14_Monterey_Start.logic**.

The project is displayed.

3 Play the project to familiarize yourself with the score.

4 Press Stop twice to return to 1 1 1 1.

5 Select the Cymbal Roll track (track 29), if it is not already selected.

As you probably noticed, the movie is viewable in its own area at the top of the Inspector. This provides a space-saving alternative to a floating window, which could obscure track material. However, the display might prove too tiny to work with in some cases, and it can be displayed in the larger, floating window by double-clicking the movie within the Inspector.

6   Double-click the Movie area within the Inspector.

The movie opens in a floating window.

Positioning an Event by Spotting the Video

Let's examine some of the techniques available for positioning events on SMPTE time by using several audio files of cymbal rolls to accentuate visual cues.

1   In the Toolbar, click the Media button to open the Media area.

2   If needed, reposition the floating movie window so it doesn't block the Media area.

3   In the Audio Bin, select the **Cymbal Roll A.aif** audio file.

4   At the bottom of the Audio Bin, click the Play button to listen to the **Cymbal Roll A.aif** audio file.

Notice that the cymbal roll builds to a climax about one-third of the way into the file. The climax should be used when syncing to SMPTE time. You can do this directly in the Sample Editor by setting the anchor point.

5   Double-click the green bar to the right of the Cymbal Roll A region name.

▼ Cymbal Roll A.aif	48000 16 Bit ⊕ 797.2 KB	
Cymbal Roll A		
▶ Cymbal Roll B.aif	48000 16 Bit ⊕ 945.7 KB	
▶ Cymbal Roll C.aif	48000 16 Bit ⊕ 2.1 MB	

The Sample Editor opens, displaying the Cymbal Roll A region.

6   Drag the anchor (the small orange triangle underneath the Cymbal Roll A region) to the right, positioning it at the transient about one-third of the way into the file.

NOTE ▶ Depending on your screen resolution, you may need to resize the Sample Editor in order to view the anchor.

6   Close the Sample Editor by clicking the button at the bottom of the Arrange window.

Let's bring this region into the arrangement, manually spotting the point in the timeline.

7   Drag the Cymbal Roll A region from the Audio Bin tab to the Cymbal Roll track at around measure 45, holding down the mouse button and moving the file back and forth along the timeline while watching the movie. (Continue to hold down the mouse button for step 8.)

Notice how the movie syncs with the position of the dragged audio file. You can use this visual reference to place cues at specific locations.

8   Still holding down the mouse button, position the Cymbal Roll A region to sync with the bird snapping at measure 50. (You aligned this earlier using beat mapping.) Release the mouse button.

9   Use the Play from Selection key command (Shift-Enter) to play the project starting at the selected Cymbal Roll A region.

The cymbal roll effectively punctuates the bird snap in the video.

10   Click the Stop button in the Transport bar to stop the project.

Using Pickup Clock

Let's continue importing audio files into the arrangement, this time aligning the event precisely to the playhead's SMPTE position by using the Pickup Clock command.

> **NOTE** ▸ This function is accessible only via key command or a button added to the Toolbar.

1   Use the Go to Position key command, the / (slash) key (in the main keyboard, not the numeric keypad), to locate the playhead to SMPTE position 01:02:16:21.00.

2   In the Audio Bin tab, click the disclosure triangle for **Cymbal Roll B.aif** and drag the Cymbal Roll B region to the Cymbal Roll track at 53 1 1 1.

3 Press the Pickup Clock key command (semicolon).

The selected region snaps to the playhead position.

NOTE ▶ Depending on your automation preferences, you may see a message asking whether you want to move the automation data with the region. If this is the case, click the Don't Move button.

4 Use the Play from Selection key command (Shift-Enter) to play the project from the newly positioned region, viewing its placement in relation to the movie image.

The cymbal roll accentuates the opening of the sea anemone.

5 Stop the project.

Using the Event Float to Position an Event

The third technique for positioning events involves using the Event Float window to precisely place an event at a SMPTE position.

1 In the Transport bar, click the Go to Beginning button.

2 In the Audio Bin tab, click the disclosure triangle for **Cymbal Roll C.aif** and drag the Cymbal Roll C region to the Cymbal Roll track at 3 1 1 1.

3 Choose Options > Event Float.

The Event Float window appears.

This window functions like a mini Event List, displaying the position and length of the selected event. By default, it displays position and length as bars and beats, but it can be switched to SMPTE time by clicking the music note button at the far right side of the window.

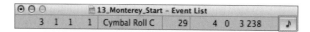

The position display switches to SMPTE time.

4 Double-click the SMPTE display at the left side of the window, and enter *01:00:22:19.09*. Press Return.

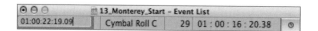

The region locates to the new position in the track.

5 Press Shift-Enter to play the project starting at the newly positioned region, viewing its placement in relation to the movie image.

The cymbal roll accentuates the transition from the man walking on the beach to the undersea divers.

6 Click the Stop button in the Transport bar to stop the project.

7 Close the Media area by clicking the Media button in the Toolbar.

Wrapping the Project

The project used in the last part of this lesson exemplifies the breadth and power of Logic, as well as most of the techniques and concepts you've explored throughout this book. The project file has a large number of tracks (consisting of both audio and software instruments), markers (using alternative marker tracks 1 and 2), and groups; extensive automation; synchronized video; *and* notation.

As this book draws to a close, take this opportunity to explore the project file, viewing the movie in relation to the project, changing screensets (Screensets 3 and 4 show some of the notated score), playing the software instruments, exploring the mixer routings, and listening to the composition in its entirety.

1   In the Transport bar, click the Go to Beginning button to return to the beginning of the project.

2   Play the project in its entirety to observe how the sound and musical events work in the context of the movie.

3   Stop the project.

4   Save the project as 14_Monterey_Finished. (Choose Music > Logic 8_BTB_Files > Lessons > Completed or any other location you wish.)

Lesson Review

1.   What settings govern how a digital video clip is synchronized within Logic?

2.   Where can SMPTE time code be displayed in Logic?

3.   What type of Final Cut Pro exported file format can be imported into Logic?

4.   What audio file format contains timing information and can be imported into Logic?

5.   How can you change the project tempo without changing a region's position?

6.   What kinds of markers are created with the Detect Cuts function?

7.   Besides MIDI events and audio files, what else can be beat mapped as references for tempo changes?

8.   In what ways can regions be positioned on the timeline?

Answers

1. Digital video clips in a Logic project can be synchronized by setting the SMPTE start times, frame rates, and Movie Start times.

2. Logic can display SMPTE time code in the SMPTE ruler, Event Float window, and giant SMPTE display.

3. Final Cut Pro XML files, including automation information, can be imported directly into a Logic timeline.

4. Broadcast WAVE files can be imported directly to a Logic timeline and retain their original recorded positions.

5. SMPTE positions of regions and events can be locked, enabling you to change tempos without changing the SMPTE timing.

6. Detect Cuts creates scene markers that can flag scene cuts and other major visual changes.

7. Markers can be used as beat mapping references for tempo changes.

8. Regions can be positioned on the timeline by placing them manually, by using the Pickup Clock command to align them with the current playhead position, and by entering new SMPTE positions in the Event Float window.

Cameo

Scoring with Logic— Jeff Rona

FILM-SCORE COMPOSER JEFF RONA HAS BEEN using MIDI and digital audio to construct musical soundscapes for years. His credits include compositions for films and television projects directed by Robert Altman, Frank Darabont, Jonathan Demme, Stephen Hopkins, Mark Pellington, Ridley Scott, Steven Soderbergh, Steven Spielberg, Wong Kar-wai, and many others. His projects have received Oscar, Peabody, and Emmy awards as well as countless film festival awards around the world. He is a recipient of an ASCAP film and television music award.

He also produces albums, continuing a career that included a stint in trumpeter Jon Hassell's pioneering world-music group, which often shared the stage with ambient/avant-garde rocker Brian Eno. (Rona co-composed and produced the group's 1990 opus *City: Works of Fiction.*) His most recent album appearance is on Persian singer Azam Ali's latest record, *Elysium for the Brave.*

At the heart of Rona's musical efforts, for film and otherwise, is Logic Pro. "Everything happens in Logic," he said.

Like any other film composer, Rona visualizes his project before he begins work, so he starts with a "spotting session," often building a massive Logic project file that serves as a template for the entire film or TV episode. Before he composes a note, he roughs out the placement of each musical passage in the score and thinks through the appropriate musical style and approach to each.

As Rona explains in his book *The Reel World: Composing for Film* (based on his long-standing column, "The Reel World," in *Keyboard* magazine), each film or TV project makes its own demands. Different projects, or even different scenes within a project, might call for the use of electronica, orchestral music, world beat, or any other musical genre; the key is to make sure the musical approach serves and supports what's onscreen. "Film music," Rona says, "is a collaboration between a group of artists sharing a single vision to tell a story."

Eschewing paper and pencil to sketch out his ideas, Rona uses Logic's arsenal of tools to generate his soundtracks from beginning to end. However, he still finds the Logic Pro's Score Editor extremely important to his process. "It's really helpful on complex music to look at notation," he said. "As a compositional aid, the Score window is fantastic."

Perhaps his favorite feature of Logic Pro 8 is its support for 5.1-channel surround sound buses, which allows him to work fully in surround sound without having to mock up huge "pseudo-surround" mixes—a process he described as painstaking and hardware intensive in previous versions of Logic Pro. "Now everything in the computer can be in surround, so it's super easy," he said. "Surround was good before, and now it's great."

Rona does most of his composition on three Macs synced via MIDI over his studio network. Each machine has its own audio interface outputting via digital Lightpipe to a Digidesign Pro Tools system, which he uses as the final destination for every track of his music.

One Mac serves as his primary Logic workstation, and another acts as an "EXS24 farm," hosting dozens of EXS24 mkII sampler instruments that serve as his orchestra. "The signal flows digitally from one computer to another, and everything gets mixed and processed inside Logic," Rona said. "I don't use a speck of equipment outside Logic" other than his mic preamps, analogue converters, and a small digital mixer that functions as a volume knob.

Using Logic on tandem Macs has proved invaluable, not just for composition and production methods but also for presenting his work to clients. "When you score for film or TV, you deal with dozens of pieces of music that have to be presented to a director or producer," Rona said. "The flow of those meetings is critical; it must be flawless. The way the music is presented is almost as important as the music itself. Running Logic on two computers, one of which is in essence the orchestra, saves a lot of time."

Rona's number one tip to fellow Logic users? "Make generic sounds feel 'ungeneric.'" Rona almost never uses standard presets in Logic and says he generally avoids "anything that anyone else has created." He tweaks Logic effects settings and applies "lots of freebie plug-ins" until every cue and passage sounds unique—and appropriate for the project at hand. "If you're using so many effects that the computer gets sluggish, just freeze the track" and continue, he advises. "Don't let technology dictate your musical creativity."

On a related note, Rona recommends compiling and cataloging the fruits of your tweaking. "Whenever you create a sound you really like, immediately save it as a channel strip, especially when the sound is a complex combination of synth or sample and multiple effects." A good library of channel strips, even if you change them in the future—as you will (and should), according to Rona—can save lots of time.

Keyboard Shortcuts

Automation

Key Command	Action
Shift-click (with Pointer tool)	Select nodes in automation track
Control-Option-drag (with Pointer tool)	Adjust curves in automation track
Command-drag value fader	Scale automation values
Control-Command-Delete	Delete currently visible automation data of current track
Shift-Control-Command-Delete	Delete all automation data of current track

Editing

Key Command	Action
Shift–Left Arrow/Right Arrow (with marquee selection)	Move left marquee border to nearest transient
Left Arrow/Right Arrow (with marquee selection)	Move right marquee border to nearest transient
Command-R	Repeat regions/events
; (semicolon)	Pick up clock (move event to playhead position)

Environment

Key Command	Action
Option-click cable output of object	Allow selection of cable destination via menu

Instruments

Key Command	Action
Command-Option with Ultrabeat	Temporarily toggle Ultrabeat back to Voice mode while in Step mode

Markers

Key Command	Action
Control-K	Create marker
Shift-Control-K	Create marker without rounding to nearest bar
Command-Return	Name marker

Mixing

Key Command	Action
Option-click Record Enable/Solo button	Turn off record-enabling for all tracks
Option-click fader, knob, parameter	Reset to default, or centered, value

Mixing (continued)

Key Command	Action
Option-click Insert/Instrument/ Send slot	Bypass plug-in or send
Option-click channel strip filter button	Display only selected channel strip type in Mixer
Command-G	Toggle group clutch on and off
Option-drag (with Hand tool)	Copy plug-in at dragged location
Option-click Group slot	Assign the most recently selected group to the channel
Command-drag puck in Surround Panner	Change angle or spread without affecting Diversity
Command-Control-drag puck in Surround Panner	Change diversity without changing angle or spread

Playback and Location

Key Command	Action
Click bottom of Bar ruler	Jump playhead to location
Double-click bottom of Bar ruler	Play project from location
/ (forward slash)	Go to position
Shift-Enter	Play from selection
Control-Enter	Play from left window edge

Playback and Location (continued)

Key Command	Action
Control-= (equal sign)	Set locators by regions/events (standard)
Control-' (apostrophe)	Set locators by regions/events (MacBook)
Shift-Spacebar	Set rounded locators and cycle play
Option-click marker in Bar ruler	Locate to marker start
Option–double-click marker in Bar ruler	Play from marker start
Option-click marker in Marker track	Locate to marker start
Control–Command–Left Arrow	Go to previous marker
Control–Command–Right Arrow	Go to next marker
J	Swap left and right locators

Score Editor

Key Command	Action
N	Show/hide Score Editor
Option-click staff	Place the playhead at clicked position

Screensets

Key Command	Action
Shift-L	Lock/unlock screenset

Tools

Key Command	Action
Esc	Open Tool menu at pointer position
Esc-Esc	Access Pointer tool
Control-Option	Access Zoom tool
Control–any tool	Bring up a shortcut menu with associated functions
Option-drag (with Pointer tool)	Create copy at dragged location
Shift-Option-drag (with Pointer tool)	Create alias at dragged location
Shift-click (with Pencil tool)	Import audio file at clicked location
Control-Shift-drag (with Fade tool)	Adjust the crossfade curve
Option-click (with Fade tool)	Delete crossfade
Option-drag (with Pointer tool	Time stretch/expand region when resizing

Views

Key Command	Action
Option-K	Open Key Commands window

Zooming

Key Command	Action
Control–Down Arrow	Zoom in vertically
Control–Up Arrow	Zoom out vertically

Zooming (continued)

Key Command	Action
Control–Right Arrow	Zoom in horizontally
Control–Left Arrow	Zoom out horizontally
Command-F1	Save setting as Zoom 1
Command-F2	Save setting as Zoom 2
Command-F3	Save setting as Zoom 3
F1	Recall Zoom 1 setting
F2	Recall Zoom 2 setting
F3	Recall Zoom 3 setting
Control-Option-Z	Zoom to fit selection vertically and horizontally, and store navigation snapshot
Shift-Control-Z	Zoom to fit locators, and store navigation snapshot

Index

TOM LANGFORD
PLACES YOU KNOW

Go to **www.tomlangford.com** to listen to the featured
track "I Was Raised" on Tom Langford's latest release.

BELLA VISTA
RECORDS

Your *Logic Pro 8* textbook has a Trane track aboard. "Blues for Trane" is from Grant Levin's CD, *Riego*. It features Grant Levin on piano, Christopher Amberger on bass, Te Kanawa "Rufus" Haereiti on drums, Rocky Winslow on trumpet, and Greg D'Augelli on tenor and soprano sax. The CD was recorded live on March 30 and May 13, 2007 in Harlen Adams Theater, California State University, Chico.

Beezwax Records is pleased to have this track included in your *Logic Pro 8* textbook because, like you, Beezwax is dedicated to the most exacting standards when it comes to recorded music. So much so that we hand assemble and document each copy of our recordings one at a time, making each one of a kind.

If you'd like to sample more of what Beezwax is about, then please visit us on the web at www.beezwaxrecords.com.

All the best as you aim toward the best.

The Apple Pro Training Series

The best way to learn Apple's professional digital video and audio software!

The Apple Pro Training Series is the official training curriculum of the Apple Pro Training and Certification program. Upon completing the course material in these books, you can become an Apple Certified Pro by taking the certification exam at an Apple Authorized Training Center.

To find an Authorized Training Center near you, visit:

www.apple.com/software/pro/training

Final Cut Pro 6
0-321-50265-5 • $54.99

**Final Cut Pro 6:
Beyond the Basics**
0-321-50912-9 • $54.99

**The Craft of Editing
with Final Cut Pro**
0-321-52036-X • $54.99

**Motion Graphics
and Effects in
Final Cut Studio 2**
0-321-50940-4 • $54.99

Motion 3
0-321-50910-2 • $54.99

Soundtrack Pro 2
0-321-50266-3 • $54.99

Color
0-321-50911-0 • $54.99

**DVD Studio Pro 4,
Second Edition**
0-321-50189-6 • $54.99

**Apple Pro Training
Series: Logic 8 Pro
and Logic Express 8**
0-321-50292-2 • $54.99

**Apple Pro Training
Series: Logic Pro 8
Beyond the Basics**
0-321-50288-4 • $54.99

**Encyclopedia of
Visual Effects**
0-321-30334-2 • $54.99

The Apple Training Series

The best way to learn Apple's hardware, Mac OS X, and iLife applications.

iLife '08
0-321-50267-1 • $39.99

iWork '08
0-321-50185-3 • $39.99

**Desktop and Portable
Systems, Third Edition**
0-321-45501-0 • $59.99

**Mac OS X Support
Essentials, Second Edition**
0-321-48981-0 • $54.99

To order books or view the entire Apple Pro Training Series catalog, visit: **www.peachpit.com/appleprotraining**